THE LIFE OF MARY
AS SEEN BY THE MYSTICS

THE LIFE OF MARY
AS SEEN BY THE MYSTICS

From the Revelations of
ST. ELIZABETH OF SCHOENAU, ST. BRIDGET OF SWEDEN,
VEN. MOTHER MARY OF AGREDA
and VEN. ANNE CATHERINE EMMERICH

Compiled by
Raphael Brown

TAN Books
An Imprint of Saint Benedict Press, LLC
Charlotte, North Carolina

Nihil Obstat: John A. Schulien, S.T.D.
                 Censor Librorum

Imprimatur: ✠ Moses E. Kiley
                 Archbishop of Milwaukee
                 June 8, 1951

The Nihil Obstat and Imprimatur are official declarations that a publication contains no doctrinal or moral error. They are not an endorsement of the content or views expressed.

Library of Congress Catalog Card No.: 90-71852

ISBN: 978-0-89555-436-9

Cover Image: *The Madonna*, by Giovanni Battista Salvi da Sassoferrato, Wikimedia Commons.

Cover design by Milo Persic.

TAN Books
An Imprint of Saint Benedict Press, LLC
Charlotte, North Carolina
2012

To Gertrude,
who helped
with prayer and counsel.

DECLARATION OF OBEDIENCE

In conformity with the decrees of Pope Urban VIII concerning the publication of private revelations, I herewith declare that:

1. While the sources from which this book has been compiled have frequently been published with the approval of learned theologians and with the permission of the ordinaries of many dioceses in several countries, I willingly submit all that is contained in this work to the judgment of the Holy See;

2. In applying the terms "saint" and "venerable" to persons who are neither canonized nor beatified, I wish in no way to anticipate the final decision of the Church; and

3. For all the private revelations and seemingly supernatural events herein narrated, insofar as they have not received the attestation of the Church, I claim no more than the assent of a merely human credence, according to the dictates of prudence and the principles of mystical theology.

THE COMPILER

CONTENTS

FOREWORD

MYSTICISM, especially of the visionary type, has always been a subject of discussion in the Church. Among its manifestations, some few have merited the approval of the prudent, others are looked upon as doubtful, while many have been rejected as false. In certain cases the Church has intervened with a condemnation. Only recently (February 3, 1951) an unofficial but authoritative warning has been uttered by a member of the Roman Curia, Monsignor Alfredo Ottaviani, against the flood of allegedly supernatural events in various parts of the world which tend to substitute a frenzied religiosity for obedience to the Church and reception of the Sacraments.

Even in the case of holy people and when the supernatural character of the phenomena seems sufficiently guaranteed, caution is necessary. The person receiving the favor may not distinguish with enough exactness the period of illumination from that which immediately follows, in which the soul remains in dispositions of the greatest fervor. St. Ignatius Loyola teaches that in this second period "it often happens that by its own thoughts, from its own habits, and in consequence of its conceptions and judgments, whether by the suggestion of the good or evil spirit, the soul makes various resolves and plans which are not inspired immediately by God Our Lord." Although the Saint is speaking only of resolves and plans, strong reasons lead us to extend this prudent observation to the content of visions. The imagination working on the memory will inevitably supply details.

Difficulties of terminology, which are common to all technical literature, also play a role in spiritual writings. St. Robert Bellarmine's remark still holds good: "Writers on mystical theology are usually blamed by some and praised by others because what they say is not understood in the same way by all." The visionaries whose writings are used in this volume were women of no special competence in theology, but they were possessed of some gifts as writers and especially of lively imaginations. Trying to express in concrete terms their supernatural experiences, they had to borrow a vocabulary from books and persons or, if they were capable of it, forge one of their own. In either case they ran considerable risk of not reproducing faithfully the content of their visions.

Despite difficulties which are obvious to all who have had some experience in this thorny field, the Church has never been adverse to the prudent exploitation of the mystical writings of her saintly children. Catholic doctrine on revelation is clear enough to supply the required safeguards. The Church teaches as a revealed dogma that public revelation ceased with the death of the last Apostle, over eighteen hundred years ago. The Deposit of Faith is complete. No further revelation binding all will be forthcoming to the end of time. "Even if an angel from heaven were to preach a gospel other than that which we have preached to you, let him be anathema." (*Gal.* 1:18). God's revelation in and through His Son is final. The Church which possesses the fullness of this revelation can alone impose beliefs on the faithful at large, and the Church imposes only such as are contained in the Holy Scripture and in divine and apostolic Tradition.

The first law of new revelations is, therefore, that they cannot be really new. They must agree with Holy Scripture and Tradition, with morality and the decisions of the Church. Again, a private revelation will rightly be looked on with suspicion if the person receiving it is not approved by a good life, manifested by irreproachable conduct, by the practice of all the virtues of his state of life and especially by humility—and this before, during and after the favor. Even when satisfied that there is nothing offensive to reason, faith or morals in a revelation and that the character of the recipient is such as to lend probability to the report, and even if the Church should approve, we accept it with a merely human belief. St. Thomas Aquinas remarks that Catholic faith "rests upon the revelation made to the Apostles and Prophets who wrote the canonical Scriptures but not on a revelation, if any, made to others." The Church, in approving of mystical phenomena, affirms that there is nothing against faith or morals in the content of the revelations, but does not guarantee their truth. The possibility of error in the facts is not excluded.

Because of this reserve the attitude of Catholics could, and has not failed to, manifest remarkable divergencies. "We have Moses and the Prophets," many assert, "and we do not require fresh visions and private revelations." Others, on the contrary, read such writings with avidity once competent ecclesiastical authority has sanctioned the publication. In this class are found numerous devout Christians of saintly life. To name but one—Matt Talbot, the Dublin workingman whose solid virtues have greatly edified the Church in our day, was much given to the perusal of this type of spiritual literature. In addition to these two responses to private revelations, there are others which it will not be necessary to specify here.

Some might think that St. Thérèse of the Infant Jesus, who has taught so many the way of holiness, would be out of sympathy with a point of view which stresses the marvelous in the life of Our Blessed Mother. Her little way of humility and love does require that we rejoice in the night

of faith and suffering and wait until death for the revelation of God's glory and that of the Blessed Virgin and
the Saints. Still, the short life of the Little Flower was not
devoid of the charismatic element. She was, for example,
favored with a vision of the Blessed Virgin. Furthermore,
Our Blessed Lady's life differed, in this respect, from that
of even the greatest Saints.

We have scriptural testimony that Mary and Joseph had
visions. Their many years at Nazareth with Jesus were, in
a sense, a long vision of surpassing grandeur which
included much intimate revelation. If we were to accept
as true all the visions of all the Saints, we should still be
obliged to judge that their favors, taken together, are not
worthy to be compared with those of the Incomparable
Virgin. As St. Bernard of Clairvaux, the Doctor of the
Church who was preeminent in Mariology, declared, "What
wonder is there if God, who is wonderful in His saints,
has shown Himself still more wonderful in His Mother?"
It is true, of course, that Our Blessed Lady, unlike her
divine Son, did not have in this life the beatific vision.
She lived, as we her children live, by faith. Indeed, she is
the model and mistress of faith and of the faithful. We
must, however, admit that her faith was aided in many
marvelous ways. And we can readily believe that our loving Mother in Heaven approves of devout writings long
in use in the Church and rightly considered helpful in
the spiritual struggle in which all are engaged.

While some persons may, doubtless, wish that the readers of this book will remember at every page the prudent
warning sounded in the Introduction that the work is to
be read as a religious novel and not as a fifth Gospel, nevertheless many Catholics and non-Catholics too will be
very thankful for this pleasing compilation of vivid narratives of the Blessed Virgin's life "as seen by" four great
mystics of the Church.

REV. EDWARD A. RYAN, S.J., DR. EN SC. HIST.
Professor of Church History
Woodstock College

THE LIFE OF MARY
AS SEEN BY THE MYSTICS

INTRODUCTION

"*When both are united* [the visions of Mary of Agreda and Anne Catherine Emmerich], *we possess the most magnificent contemplations upon the mysteries of the Incarnation of God.*"
DOM PROSPER GUÉRANGER, O.S.B.
ABBOT OF SOLESMES

1. Private Revelations

DUE to the special nature of its sources, *The Life of Mary as Seen by the Mystics* is not, does not purport to be, and therefore should not be considered a historical biography.

The study of history is based primarily on contemporaneous written documents. This work, however, has been compiled entirely from the visions and private revelations of St. Elizabeth of Schoenau (1127?–1164), St. Bridget of Sweden (1303–1373), Venerable Mother Mary of Jesus of Agreda (1602–1665) and Sister Anne Catherine Emmerich (1774–1824), as recorded in their writings or in those of their secretaries.

1

It is therefore essential, in order properly to evaluate this book, that the reader have a clear understanding of the teachings of the Catholic Church concerning the nature and reliability of private revelations. The following brief outline of the subject is derived from the masterful analysis of the Rev. Auguste Poulain, S.J., in his work entitled *The Graces of Interior Prayer, a Treatise on Mystical Theology* (St. Louis: B. Herder, 1912), Part IV, "Revelations and Visions."

First and most important of all, we must always make a very sharp distinction between: 1) the divinely guaranteed, universal public Revelation which is contained in the Bible and the Apostolic Tradition of the Church, and 2) the numerous private or special revelations of saintly Christian men and women. The first came to an end with the preaching of the Apostles and is a matter of faith for all Catholics, whereas the second have occurred throughout the history of the Church and do not require belief, even when approved. "It matters little whether or not one believes in St. Bridget's revelations or those of other saints; these things have nothing to do with faith."[1] "Even when the Church approves them . . . *they are not to be used as deciding questions of history**. . . philosophy, or theology . . ."[2]

Next we must understand why it is possible that the writings or revelations of some saintly mystics have occasionally contained minor inaccuracies or details which do not agree with similar accounts of other equally holy mystics. This is especially observable when their visions represent historical scenes, such as the life and death of Jesus Christ and His Mother. For instance, St. Bridget and Mary of Agreda differ as to various details of the Nativity. Sister Anne Catherine Emmerich saw the Saviour crucified with three nails, whereas St. Bridget saw four nails. And

---

1. Poulain, *op. cit.*, p. 320. (An enlarged ed. was reprinted in 1978 by Celtic Cross Books, Westminster, Vt., now of Westmoreland, N.H.)
* All italics in this Introduction have been added by the compiler.
2. Poulain, pp. 320–21.

all three disagree concerning the number of years which the Blessed Virgin lived after the Crucifixion.

This does not mean that in each case only one mystic saw correctly and the others must have been mistaken. For, as Father Poulain very wisely explains—and *the importance of this statement for our work cannot be overstressed:* "When visions represent historic scenes . . . they often have an approximate and probable likeness only. . . . It is a mistake to attribute an absolute accuracy to them. . . . Many saints have, in fact, believed that the event took place exactly as they saw it. But God does not deceive us when He modifies certain details. If He tied Himself down to absolute accuracy in these matters, we should soon be seeking to satisfy in visions an idle desire for erudition in history or archaeology. He has a nobler aim, that of the soul's sanctification, and to arouse in her a love of Jesus suffering. He is like a painter who, in order to excite our piety, is content to paint scenes in his own manner, but without departing too far from the truth. (This argument cannot be applied to the historical books of the Bible.) . . . God has another reason for modifying certain details. Sometimes He adds them to a historical scene in order to bring out the secret meaning of the mystery. The actual spectators saw nothing similar. . . . We see, therefore, that it is imprudent to seek to remake history by the help of the saints' revelations." [3]

And in his article on the same subject in *The Catholic Encyclopedia,* Father Poulain adds: "A vision need not guarantee its accuracy in every detail. *One should thus beware of concluding without examination that revelations are to be rejected. . . . Much less should one suspect that the saints have been always or very often deceived in their vision. On the contrary, such deception is rare, and as a rule in unimportant matters only. . . .*" [4]

In his treatise on mystical theology, Father Poulain also lists the following possible causes of errors in private rev-

---

3. Poulain, pp. 327-329.
4. *The Catholic Encyclopedia,* Vol. XIII, p. 5.

elations: the human mind may mingle its own action with
the divine action in a certain measure by injecting some
of its own favorite or preconceived ideas; a true revelation may subsequently be altered when its recipient records
it after an interval of time, or the secretary of the mystic
may not write or edit it with perfect fidelity; and finally
a printed text may be an incomplete version or an inac-
curate translation of the original manuscript.[5]

We may therefore concede with the learned Father Herbert Thurston, S.J., that "it seems impossible to treat the
visions of Anne Catherine [Emmerich]—or, indeed, any
other similar visions—as sources which can contribute reli-
ably to our knowledge of past history." [6]

What then is the value of the best private revelations?

The famous Dom Prosper Guéranger, O.S.B., abbot of
Solesmes and pioneer of the modern liturgical revival,
summed up the age-old wisdom of Holy Mother Church's
reply to that question when he wrote: "*Private revelations .
. . are a powerful means of strengthening and increasing Christian sentiments.*" [7] For, according to his biographer, "in the
thought of Dom Guéranger, private revelations, even
though the human element may enter into their compo-
sition with the revealed element, are *one of the channels by
which edification and the supernatural penetrate among the Christian faithful.*" [8]

The following statements on this subject by Dom
Guéranger are significant and relevant:

"In all periods the Church . . . has had in her bosom
souls to whom it pleases God to communicate extraordinary lights of which He allows some rays to fall onto
the community of the faithful. . . .What counts for the
Christian who wishes to know the things of God in the

5. Poulain, *op. cit.*, pp. 323-340.
6. *The Month*, Dec., 1921, p. 519.
7. *Le Monde*, Apr. 15, 1860, quoted in Emmerich, *Lowly Life*, Vol. I,
   p. 136.
8. *Un Moine Bénédictin*, Dom Guéranger (Paris, 1910), Vol. II, p. 181.

measure which is permitted to us here below, is to know that beyond the teaching generally imparted to all the children of the Church, there are also certain lights which God communicates to souls whom He has chosen, and that those lights pierce through the clouds, when He so determines, in such a way that they spread far and wide for the consolation of simple hearts and also to be a certain trial for those who are wise in their own opinion.
. . . Those to whom the seer communicates what he has thus learned from a divine source, being reduced to a human and fallible intermediary, need give it only that assent which we give to probable matters, an assent which we call 'pious belief.' No doubt this is little if we consider the invincible certitude of Faith; yet it is much if we think of the shadows which surround us."

While granting the possibility of human imperfections in private revelations, Dom Guéranger insists on the spiritual value of the best examples in this masterful psychological analysis:

"But there always remains that superhuman tone, both gentle and strong at the same time, an echo of the divine words which resounded in the soul, that unction which penetrates into the reader's mind and soon obliges him to say: the source of this is not human. As we read, our heart slowly takes fire, our soul feels desires for virtue which it had not hitherto experienced, the mysteries of faith appear more luminous to us, bit by bit the world and its hopes vanish, and the longing for the good things of Heaven, which seemed to have been dozing within us, awakens with new fervor." [9]

That generations of devout Catholics, including many learned theologians and prelates and writers, have in fact derived great spiritual benefit and inspiration from a judicious reading of the private revelations which have been compiled here, will be definitively established in the following critical estimates of the works of the four mystics

---

9. *L'Univers*, Aug. 1, 1858.

that constitute our sources, as found in the most authoritative Catholic encyclopedias and treatises on the subject.

2. St. Elizabeth of Schoenau

This daughter of a humble German family in the Rhineland entered the great Benedictine monastery at Schoenau near Bonn at the age of twelve. She became a remarkably fervent and mortified nun, and from the age of twenty-three until her death in 1164 experienced frequent extraordinary mystical graces. Her writings were edited by her brother Egbert, a Benedictine abbot. Though honored locally and in her Order, St. Elizabeth of Schoenau was never formally beatified. Her revelations, like those of Sts. Hildegard, Gertrude and Mechtilde, exercised a profound influence on medieval spirituality.[10]

3. St. Bridget of Sweden

Bridget *(Birgitta)*—not to be confused with the Irish St. Bridget of Kildare (453–521)—was born about 1303, the daughter of a wealthy provincial governor. At the age of fourteen she married Ulf Gudmarsson, and they became the parents of eight children. In 1343 her devout husband entered the Cistercian monastery of Alvastra, where he died the following year. After spending several years at the court of King Magnus Eriksson, Bridget went to Rome in 1349. Except for a number of pilgrimages to Italian shrines and one to the Holy Land in 1372, she resided in Rome until her death on July 23, 1373. So great was her fame for sanctity that she was canonized by Pope Boniface IX on October 3, 1391.

Before leaving Sweden she began to dictate her revelations, at the urging of Jesus Christ and His Mother, to one of the several learned priests who were at various

---

10. Butler-Thurston, *The Lives of the Saints* (London, 1937), Vol. VI, pp. 233–235.

times her spiritual directors. These "Heavenly Revelations" comprise nine books, amounting to over 1,500 pages. They contain numerous lengthy discourses by Our Lord and the Blessed Virgin on such subjects as the Church, moral advice for clergy and laity, marriage and education, Purgatory, as well as accounts of apparitions of St. Ann, St. John the Baptist, St. Matthew, St. Francis of Assisi and other saints.

According to the *Dictionnaire de Spiritualité Ascétique et Mystique*, "Benedict XIV has pronounced the decisive word concerning the orthodoxy of the Revelations of Bridget in the *De servorum Dei beatificatione. . .Therefore there is no doubt: the Revelations of Bridget are included among those which have the approval of the Church; they are orthodox.*" This formal approval, however, means only that they contain nothing contrary to faith and morals and that there is good evidence for their authenticity. For, in the words of Pope Benedict XIV, "even though . . . these revelations have been approved, we cannot and we ought not to give them the assent of divine faith, but only that of human faith, according to the dictates of prudence, wherever these dictates enable us to decide that they are probable and worthy of pious credence." [11]

The Revelations of St. Bridget of Sweden were among the most popular books in Europe during the late Middle Ages.[12] Their "value . . . resides in the spirituality of the Saint." They contain "an entire mariology which is extremely rich. It is the Blessed Virgin most often who describes the scenes of the childhood and of the Passion of Christ." [13]

4. Venerable Mother Mary of Jesus of Agreda

Born in Agreda, Old Castille, Spain, on April 2, 1602, in a middle-class family, Maria Coronel entered in Janu-

11. *Dictionnaire de Spiritualité Ascétique et Mystique* (Paris), Vol. I, col. 1947.
12. *The Catholic Encyclopedia*, Vol. II, p. 782.
13. *Dictionnaire de Spiritualité . . .* , Vol. I, cols. 1954–1955.

ary, 1619, with her mother and youngest sister, a Conceptionist Poor Clare convent which her devout parents had founded in their home town, while her father and two brothers became Franciscans. From 1627 until her death on May 24, 1665, except for a period of three years, Mother Mary of Jesus was re-elected Abbess no less than eleven times.

Mary of Agreda, as she is usually called, is a figure of special interest to Americans because in the 1630's, in one of the most thoroughly documented cases of bilocation in history, without ever leaving her convent in Spain she appeared innumerable times to the Indians of western Texas, Arizona and New Mexico, instructed them in the Catholic religion, and sent them southward to be baptized by the approaching Franciscan missionaries.[14]

Her famous biography of the Blessed Virgin, *The Mystical City of God*, became the subject of considerable controversy among theologians when it was first published in 1670. On November 9, 1681, at the request of King Charles II of Spain, Pope Innocent XI suspended in Spain a condemnation of the work by the Holy Office of the Inquisition of June 26 of the same year.[15] That this suspension was generally interpreted by theologians and ordinaries as being of universal application is indicated by the publication between 1700 and 1750 of about twenty French, Italian, Latin, German and Polish translations in France, Italy, Germany and Belgium.[16] Although, as Dom Guéranger and the Abbé H. Bremond have shown, a Jansenist and Gallican majority of professors at the Sorbonne University in Paris issued a condemnation of the book in 1696,[17] the Spanish Inquisition and "the universities of Granada, Burgos, Cadiz, Madrid, Canarias, Sala-

---

14. Bibliography in Rev. S. J. Draugelis' *Madonna of Nazareth*, pp. 32–34.
15. *Lexikon fuer Kirche und Theologie*, Vol. I, col. 147.
16. List of editions in Draugelis, *op. cit.*, pp. 41-43.
17. Dom Guéranger, "La Cité Mystique de Dieu," *L'Univers*, 1859; Abbé Henri Brémond, *Histoire du Sentiment Religieux en France* (Paris, 1932), Vol. IX, pp. 273–276.

manca, Alcala, Toulouse, Louvain and seventeen of the greatest colleges in Europe have favored *The Mystical City of God* with their official approbation." [18]

According to the authoritative modern Catholic *Lexikon fuer Kirche und Theologie*, ". . . *it contains several errors in profane matters but nothing which contradicts the teaching of the Church.* The point which was most displeasing to its opponents (particularly Gallicans, Jansenists, and followers of the Enlightenment) was the doctrine of the Immaculate Conception. . . . However, the definition of this doctrine as a dogma [in 1854] proved that the Venerable Servant of God was right and again drew the attention of the Catholic world to her writings. *The Holy See has repeatedly permitted them to be read, but has not made a positive declaration concerning the character of the visions.* . . . *Many bishops and scholars have warmly recommended the work.* Despite all controversies, it has been widely distributed in many editions and translations . . . and *has filled countless souls, including priests also, with new love and reverence for the Mother of Our Lord.*" [19]

This remarkable book has indeed gained an ever-increasing favor during the past hundred years, even though the controversies of the eighteenth century resulted in halting the author's Process of Beatification.[20]

In 1850 the scholarly Jesuit editor of the journal *La Civiltà Cattòlica* wrote: ". . .we must conclude that the book, *The Mystical City of God,* must with prudence be judged praiseworthy. . . . Between a blind belief and a no less blind scorn, the middle ground is a clear-seeing respect." [21] Thirty years later the same journal announced "with great

---

18. *Lexikon . . .* , Vol. I, col. 147; D. Francisco Silvela, *Cartas de Sor Maria de Agreda y Felipe IV* (Madrid, 1885), p. 237.
19. *Lexikon . . .*, *ibid.*
20. J. de Guibert, *Doctrina Ecclesiastica Christianae Perfectionis Studium Spectantia* (Rome, 1931), p. 484; *Acta Ordinis Minorum* (Rome), Vol. IX, 1890, pp. 42–43, and Vol. LX, 1941, p. 173. Cf. *Analecta Juris Pontificii* (Paris, 1886), Table générale des matières des Vols. 1–24.
21. *La Civiltà Cattòlica*, Ser. I, Vol. II, 1850, p. 205.

pleasure the new Italian version of the Life of the Blessed
Virgin originally written in Spanish by Venerable Sister
Mary of Jesus, to whom, as we may piously, though by
merely human faith, believe, it was communicated by the
Blessed Virgin herself. . . . Intrinsic reasons render it probable. . . . And extrinsic reasons likewise render it probable, i.e., the opinions of very learned theologians who
have given the work their approval after a most detailed
examination." [22]

According to Ludwig Clarus (Wilhelm Gustav Volk), the
editor of the German version published in 1853, "*The Mystical City of God* has aided many persons to find the True
Faith and to acquire virtue." [23] This statement is especially
noteworthy in view of the fact that Clarus himself joined
the Catholic Church in 1855.[24]

In 1858–1859, Dom Guéranger devoted a series of twenty-
four articles to a thorough analysis and defense of Mary
of Agreda's book. While granting that it was not lacking
in human flaws, he summed up his considered opinion
thus: "The least that one can say in praise of this work is
that it remains one of the most impressive monuments of
the human spirit." Calling it "a marvelous *Summa* . . . amaz-
ing, if not superhuman," Dom Guéranger declared that
"after a lengthy study of *The Mystical City* and of the volu-
minous writings that have been published for and against
it," in his judgment "the revelations of Mary of Agreda on
the life of the Blessed Virgin have a right to the respect
and the esteem of all those who are capable of undertaking to read them, that they deserve to occupy a distinguished place among writings of that kind, and that the
judicious use that can be made of them can serve as a powerful stimulus to a revival of devotion in souls. . . ." [25]

Father Frederick William Faber (1814-1862), the intimate friend of Cardinal Newman and founder of the Con-

22. *Ibid.*, Ser. II, Vol. VI, 1881, pp. 92–93.
23. Ubaldus de Pandolfi, *Life* . . . , p. 147.
24. *Lexikon* . . . , Vol. X, col. 671.
25. Dom Guéranger in *L'Univers*, Sept. 12, May 23, and Dec. 5, 1858.

gregation of the Oratory, whom Dom Guéranger considered a "saint," [26] and whom *The Catholic Encyclopedia* describes as "a master in mystical theology," [27] wrote that he found a "number of beautiful things" [28] in *The Mystical City of God*, from which he frequently quoted passages in his inspiring devotional works.

Typical of the many official recommendations to be found in the editions of that time is the following statement of Archbishop Descamps of Malines and Primate of Belgium (when Vicar-General of the Diocese of Tournai): "*We exhort the pious faithful and the clergy in particular who desire a deeper insight into the grandeur of the Most Holy Virgin to take advantage of this publication, which they cannot read without edification and profit.*" [29] A German edition published by the Redemptorist Fathers in 1885 was recommended by the Bishop of Ratisbon in these words: it "*will surely edify all readers and be the occasion of great spiritual blessings.*" [30]

The famous French writer J. K. Huysmans disclosed in his autobiographical novel, *En Route*, that the writings of Mary of Agreda and Anne Catherine Emmerich influenced him in his return to the Sacraments. After complaining of the former's verbosity and other faults, he added with profound perspicacity: "I know well that the Abbé [the hero's spiritual director] would say that we need not concern ourselves with those singularities and those errors, but that *the* Cité Mystique *is to be read in relation to the inner life of the Blessed Virgin.*" [31]

On February 15, 1900, in Rome, a French-Canadian lady named Rose de Lima Dumas wrote a letter to His Holiness Pope Leo XIII in which she told him that for several years,

26. *Le Monde*, Jan. 25, 1864, quoted in John E. Bowden, *Life & Letters of Frederick William Faber, D.D.* (Baltimore, 1869), p. 452.
27. *The Catholic Encyclopedia*, Vol. V, p. 741.
28. Faber, *Bethlehem* (Baltimore, 1862), p. 317.
29. Pandolfi, *op. cit.*, p. 148.
30. Blatter-Marison, *Mystical City of God* (South Chicago), Vol. I, p. xxii.
31. J. K. Huysmans, *En Route* (New York, 1918), p. 90.

after reading *The Mystical City of God,* she had adopted as a rule of life the moral instructions of the Blessed Virgin that are found at the end of each of its chapters, and that her feelings of gratitude and a desire "to spread the science of the saints had impelled her to publish" a one-volume compilation of those instructions in French "in order to offer it especially to devout persons living in the world." While giving His Holiness a copy of the book, she begged for his blessing "for herself and for all those who will strive to put into practice the counsels of the Mother of God and who will do all they can to persuade others to do likewise." On February 28, 1900, His Eminence M. Cardinal Rampolla wrote to her in reply that "the devout thoughts which you expressed to the Holy Father . . . were received with pleasure by His Holiness, who, wishing to confirm you in your virtuous projects, gladly gives you the Apostolic Blessing. . . ." Of special significance is the fact that the edition involved, entitled *Sublime Doctrine de la Mère de Dieu sur les Vertus Chrètiennes; Extrait de la Cité Mystique de Dieu . . .* was printed by the presses of the Sacred Congregation of the Propaganda in Rome." [32] Consequently, a few months later a Canadian diocesan journal stated: "The reserve which is ordinarily maintained on the subject of revelations really no longer has any reason to exist in relation to *The Mystical City,* since His Holiness Leo XIII has been so good as gladly to encourage the project of spreading among the faithful the science of the saints which is contained in that heavenly life of the Mother of God." [33] And in 1915, the same lady published, also in Rome, a complete French edition of Mary of Agreda's work bearing the statement of the Rev. Reginaldo Fei, O.P., Doctor in Sacred Theology, "that it contains nothing against faith and morals." [34]

Meanwhile, in 1903, the Rev. Van den Gheyn, S.J., one of the learned and cautious Bollandist experts in hagiog-

---

32. Marie d'Agréda, *Sublime Doctrine . . .* , (Rome, 1900), pp. i–iii.
33. *Revue Ecclesiastique de Valleyfield,* Vol. IX, 1901, p. 160.
34. Marie d'Agréda, *Cité Mystique de Dieu* (Rome, 1915), 3 vols.

raphy, wrote in his article on Mary of Agreda in the authoritative *Dictionnaire de Théologie Catholique:* "[*The Mystical City of God*], says Goerres, '. . . contains a truly grandiose mystical contemplation.' However, we must admit that there are in this work some very extraordinary assertions. On the other hand, it must not be forgotten that the author's only aim was to edify and that she had no intention of engaging in critical history. Mary of Agreda herself said: 'Error on my part is possible, for I am only an ignorant woman. . . . Moreover I submit to my guides and to the correction of the Holy Catholic Church.'

"What credence does the work . . . deserve? . . . In the present case the saintly life of Mary of Agreda creates a prejudice in favor of the complete good faith of the author. There is no serious reason to doubt her sincerity, which is evidenced by an admirable obedience and a profound humility. But on the other hand, the limited spiritual culture of the writer, her ignorance of positive theology and of history, render possible and even probable some error in the description of revelations which may have been supernatural. . . .

"In brief, if we wish to judge the work of Mary of Agreda without the partisan spirit which has unfortunately vitiated a good number of appreciations that have been made of her writings, *it must be recognized that from the point of view of mystical theology and of edification,* The Mystical City of God *deserves the popularity which it has enjoyed.*" [35]

At the same time, Father Poulain was writing in his *Graces of Interior Prayer:* "Whatever opinion we may form as to Mary of Agreda's revelations, taken as a whole, we are obliged to admit that they contain some errors. Thus . . . she says that the earth's radius is 1,251 miles. . . .* *Let us not, however, conclude from this that Mary of Agreda deceived herself also as to her purely intellectual visions of the Divinity. . . . Amort, who criticized her a great deal . . . adds:*

---

35. *Dictionnaire de Théologie Catholique* (Paris, 1903), Vol. I, cols. 627–631.
* Actually it is about 3,960 miles.

'*I unhesitatingly admit that she received wonderful lights from God . . .*'"[36]

In 1911–1912 a new critical Spanish edition of *The Mystical City of God* based on the author's original manuscripts was published with the approval of the Bishop of Tarazona, whose diocese includes Agreda.

In 1910 the Very Rev. Ubaldus de Pandolfi compiled an excellent life of Mary of Agreda in English, which was published by the Poor Clares of Evansville, Indiana. And in 1914 the Rev. George J. Blatter brought out his complete four-volume English translation of *The Mystical City of God*, with the Imprimatur of the Rt. Rev. H. J. Alerding, Bishop of Fort Wayne, Indiana.

It is also a significant fact, especially in view of the early Dominican opposition to this work for its Scotistic leanings, that the foremost modern Spanish Dominican "champion of the true traditional doctrine in mystical theology," the saintly Rev. Juan G. Arintero (1860–1928), who was "an authority in the discernment of spirits," did not hesitate to quote freely from *The Mystical City of God* in his masterpiece, *The Mystical Evolution in the Development and Vitality of the Church*.[37]

The Rev. S. J. Draugelis of New York City has written a series of sacred dramas on the life of the Blessed Virgin which are based entirely on the work of Mary of Agreda. "Madonna of Nazareth," the first of the series to be printed, was published in 1949 by the Marian Fathers in Stockbridge, Massachusetts. A favorable review of this work which appeared in the Sunday edition of the *Osservatore Romano* referred to the "noble task" undertaken by the author and to the "important influence" of Mary of Agreda "not only on the strictly religious but also in the political and moral fields of 17th century Spain."[38] On November 10, 1949,

---

36. Poulain, *op. cit.*, pp. 335–336.
37. Juan G. Arintero, O.P., *The Mystical Evolution in the Development and Vitality of the Church* (St. Louis, 1949), pp. v, xii. Reprinted by TAN, 1978.
38. *Osservatore Romano*, Rome, July 24, 1949.

His Eminence P. Cardinal Fumasoni-Biondi wrote to Father Draugelis: "I hope and pray that Almighty God will bless this undertaking and that He will grant you great success not only in increasing devotion to the Immaculate Virgin, but also in making Her better and more widely known in a world that has so much need of Her." [39]

And last, but not least in importance, is the following impressive statement in the new Italian Catholic encyclopedia, *Enciclopedia Cattòlica*, edited by the foremost ecclesiastical scholars in Italy and published in the Vatican City in 1949: "Considered objectively, although historical, geographical and chronological errors are not lacking in *The Mystical City of God*, from which it follows that the work does not contain only 'revelation,' *its high ascetical and mystical value must be recognized.*" [40]

5. Sister Anne Catherine Emmerich

Born on September 8, 1774, in a family of poor Westphalian peasants, Anne Catherine entered the Augustinian convent in Duelmen in 1802. When the convent was closed in 1812, due to the Napoléonic Wars, she moved to a private home, in which she resided until her death on February 2, 1824.

From childhood she experienced many extraordinary mystical graces. Before becoming a nun she endured the pains of the crown of thorns, and in 1808 those of the other wounds of Christ. In 1812 the stigmata became visible.

When Clemens von Brentano (1778–1842), a prominent German romantic poet, visited her in 1818, soon after his return to the Catholic Church, she recognized him as the secretary who was destined to be the editor of her revelations. He remained with her throughout the last five years of her life, taking extensive notes of her visions

---

39. *Marian Helpers Bulletin* (Stockbridge, Mass.), Jan., 1950, p. 9.
40. *Enciclopedia Cattòlica* (Vatican City, 1949), Vol. I, col. 571.

of the life of Christ, whose public ministry she witnessed day by day in 1821–1824.

"In editing his notes, Brentano did not exercise such fidelity that these visions may simply pass for verbal communications of Emmerich." (Huempfner). As a result, the Emmerich-Brentano writings are not being considered as evidence in her Process for Beatification. They have nevertheless merited the recommendations of numerous learned prelates and theologians like Father Poulain, Dom Guéranger, and Cardinals Gibbons and Ehrle, and they have been a source of profound spiritual benefit to many persons, including such distinguished writers as J. K. Huysmans, Father Gerard Manley Hopkins, S.J., Léon Bloy, Jacques and Raissa Maritain, and Paul Claudel, as the following quotations will demonstrate:

J. J. Goerres: "I know of no revelations richer, more profound, more wonderful, or more thrilling in their nature than those of Sister Emmerich." [41]

The Catholic Encyclopedia: "The rapid and silent spread of her works through Germany, France, Italy and elsewhere speaks well for their merit. Strangely enough they produced no controversy." [42]

Dom Prosper Guéranger, O.S.B.: "In the publication of this work (*The Life of Jesus Christ*) we must recognize a disposition of Divine Providence, who has deigned to console Catholic Germany in the midst of the most dreadful blasphemies that have been and still are uttered against the holy Gospels, by thus placing before our eyes the facts of the Gospel narratives. Indeed Catherine Emmerich has her mission! God does not lavish the extraordinary gifts which have been revealed in her. Not in vain has He placed her in the heart of Germany just before the outbreak of the most frightful infidelity. . . . I shall allow no favorable opportunity to pass without paying Anne Catherine Emmerich the tribute she deserves. Her revelations have

---

41. Emmerich, *Lowly Life*, Vol. I, p. 9.
42. *The Catholic Encyclopedia*, Vol. V, p. 407.

found no reader who has perused them with greater diligence and appreciation than I, and I have ever been most eager to communicate my impressions concerning them to all my acquaintances." [43]

Most Rev. August Maria Toebbe, Bishop of Covington, Ky. (1882): "The writings of the venerable Anne Catherine Emmerich breathe so deeply a spirit of faith and so heartfelt a love for God that the devout perusal of them must afford the faithful a rich treasure of blessings and edification." [44]

Most Rev. Wm. H. Gross, C.Ss.R., Archbishop of Oregon (1888): "It is a masterpiece of its kind . . . .We heartily approve its translation, and sincerely hope that a copy of it will soon be found in every Catholic family." [45]

Most Rev. William H. Elder, Archbishop of Cincinnati (1892): "The Life of Our Lord, according to the revelations of Catherine Emmerich, I have found extremely interesting and edifying. . . . If received according to the explanations given and if read in the spirit of piety, it is wonderfully adapted to increase in our heart the love of Our Lord Jesus Christ, by giving us vivid pictures of what He did and said during His mortal life." [46]

His Eminence J. Cardinal Gibbons, Archbishop of Baltimore: ". . . from our own deep conviction of the great advantage to be derived from the pious perusal of the work . . .we do not hesitate in its approval to add our signature. . . ." [47]

Father Gerard Manley Hopkins, S.J.: "One day in the Long Retreat (which ended on Christmas Day) they were reading in the refectory Sister Emmerich's account of the Agony in the Garden and I suddenly began to cry and sob and could not stop. I put it down for this reason, that if I had been asked a minute beforehand I should

---

43. Emmerich, *op. cit.*, pp. 135–136, 230.
44. *Ibid.*, p. 218.
45. *Ibid.*, p. 219.
46. *Ibid.*, pp. 219–220.
47. *Ibid.*, p. 221.

have said that nothing of the sort was going to happen and even when it did I stood in a manner wondering at myself. . . ." [48]

Léon Bloy and the Maritains: "At the very beginning [of the latter's conversion], Léon Bloy made us read Schmöger's three thick volumes on the life and visions of Anne Catherine Emmerich . . . one of the greatest mystics of the nineteenth century . . . the religious beauty of the visions and spiritual illuminations . . . is so great that there must have been at least one mystic involved—either Catherine or Brentano. No mere poet could have given a picture of such depth, coherence and theological value, of the inner life of a co-sufferer in Christ's Passion . . . .

"The *Revelations* of Anne Catherine Emmerich gave us a picture of Catholicism that was crowded and vivid, moving and yet familiar. They taught us countless things—we, who knew nothing of Catholic history, dogmas, theology, liturgy, mysticism." [49]

Paul Claudel: "The books which proved very helpful during that period [of his conversion] were . . . Pascal . . . Bossuet . . . Dante . . . not to forget the marvelous private revelations of Catherine Emmerich." [50]

J. K. Huysmans: ". . . the tonic, the stimulant in weakness, the strychnine for failure of faith, the goad which drives you in tears to the feet of Christ, the *Dolorous Passion* of Sister Emmerich. . . ." [51]

Émile Baumann: "We find that Catherine Emmerich's originality is most valuable in her visions, thanks to the ability which she had of revealing their essential elements. Theologically hers are inferior to those of St. Teresa and of many others. . . .

---

48. *The Note-Books and Papers of Gerard Manley Hopkins* (London, 1937), p. 128 (see also pp. 339, 348, 372–373).
49. Raissa Maritain, *We Have Been Friends Together* (New York, 1942), p. 151; see also her *Adventures in Grace* (New York, 1945), p. 36.
50. Paul Claudel, "In the Grip of God," in *Through 100 Gates*, edited by Severin Lamping, O.F.M. (Milwaukee, 1939), p. 203.
51. Huysmans, *En Route* (New York, 1918), pp. 138–139.

"The three books of her revelations nevertheless constitute . . . one of the most beautiful supernatural poems that can be described as inspired."[52]

Rev. Paul de Jaegher, S.J.: "But as Brentano himself pointed out in the first edition of *The Dolorous Passion,* Anne never claimed historical accuracy for her visions. They are just powerfully realistic pictures, whose vividness and imaginative force have helped many a soul to appreciate the Passion with more intensity and love."[53]

Georges Goyau: "Henceforth, too, the veneration of the humanity of Christ was to play an increasingly important role in religious fervor. The visions of Catherine Emmerich deserve to be taken as a landmark in the development of this worship.

"All the detail which they add to the dramatic story of Christ is an enrichment, not indeed of the Deposit of Faith itself . . . but of Christian piety. They do not impose themselves on belief, still less on erudition; but the light they cast, the emotions they arouse, bear up the wings of meditation. . . .

"Clement Brentano, by making himself, at the bedside of the stigmatized woman, the assiduous chronicler of all that Catherine saw and said, thereby brought a fresh source of sustenance to the devout curiosity of believing souls. Before the eyes of that Germany in which certain schools were beginning to regard the story of Christ as a kind of myth, he developed scenes of pathos, scenes picturesque in their tragedy, in which the face of Christ became animated by a new life, more troubled, more poignant, one might almost say more in the raw, than the one which the sobriety of the Gospel narrative shows us.

"And thanks to Brentano, she who, through her stigmata, let herself become 'in conformity with Christ,' was

---

52. Émile Baumann, *L'Anneau d'Or des Grands Mystiques* (Paris, 1924), pp. 294, 297.
53. Paul de Jaegher, S.J., ed., *An Anthology of Mysticism* (London, 1935), p. 231.

to lead coming Christian generations, if not to know Christ better, at least to feel for Him better, in a compassion in which faith and love mingle and kneel together . . ." [54]

His Eminence Franz Cardinal Ehrle, S.J. (in 1934): "One cannot deny the Divine touch in them." [55]

The new Italian Catholic encyclopedia: Her revelations "exercised a widespread influence on the piety of the Catholic faithful, particularly in the devotion to the Passion of Jesus, and not only in Germany." [56]

6. Summary

In concluding this study of our sources, we submit the following profoundly wise and enlightening comments of Dom Prosper Guéranger, O.S.B., and the Rev. Auguste Poulain, S.J., on the value of the revelations of both Mary of Agreda and Anne Catherine Emmerich, which, as will be explained in the next section, have the largest share in this compilation.

DOM GUÉRANGER:

"While we acknowledged Mary of Agreda's superiority in point of ideality, we accorded to Sister Emmerich a preeminence with regard to the richness and exactness of facts. *Both bear upon them the marks of supernatural visions, and the contradictions between them that we notice here and there should not prejudice one against the communications as a whole.*" [57]

"If I have drawn a parallel between Mary of Agreda and Catherine Emmerich, it was not done with the intention of undervaluing the German ecstatica. *I look upon both the one and the other as true prophetesses;* and if I think that Catherine Emmerich is to be accused of some errors in

---

54. Jeanne Danemarie (pseud. of Mme. Marthe Ponet), *The Mystery of the Stigmata* (London, 1934), pp. 234–235.
55. *Ibid.*, p. 12.
56. *Enciclopedia Cattòlica* (Vatican City, 1951), Vol. V, col. 314.
57. Emmerich, *Lowly Life*, Vol. I, p. 228.

regard to facts, I find no difficulty in making the same charge against Mary of Agreda. Private revelations like theirs are always mixed with imperfections. God permits this, in order that they may not be confounded with the inspired (canonical) Books. . . . I think the proper rule in judging such private revelations is that we be satisfied here and there to stumble upon certain innocent mistakes. . . . We may say that Catherine Emmerich supplies Mary of Agreda's deficiencies. The former received the aesthetic, the latter the doctrinal mission. *When both are united, we possess the most magnificent contemplations upon the mysteries of the Incarnation of God.*" [58]

FATHER POULAIN:

"It may also be that the revelation can be regarded as Divine in its broad outlines, but doubtful in minor details. Concerning the revelations of Mary of Agreda and Anne Catherine Emmerich, for example, contradictory opinions have been expressed: some believe unhesitatingly everything they contain, and are annoyed when anyone does not share their confidence; others give the revelations no credence whatsoever (generally on a *priori* grounds); finally there are many who are sympathetic, but do not know what to reply when asked what degree of credibility is to be attributed to the writings of these two ecstatics. *The truth seems to be between the two extreme opinions.* . . . In particular instances these visionaries have been mistaken ... *if there be question of the general statement of facts given in these works, we can admit with probability that many of them are true.* For these two visionaries led lives that were regarded as very holy. Competent authorities have judged their ecstasies divine. *It is therefore prudent to admit that they received a special assistance from God, preserving them not absolutely, but in the main, from error.*" [59]

---

58. *Ibid.*, pp. 149-150.
59. *The Catholic Encyclopedia*, Vol. XIII, p. 5.

7. This Compilation

In accordance with the enlightened caution of those distinguished theologians and with the sound principles of mystical theology governing private revelations, the method of selection adopted in compiling this book has been to examine all available critical analyses of the writings which constitute its sources and to exclude any statements which might appear to be either unacceptable or implausible or unsuitable for a narrative designed only for popular edification.

The specific editions used are indicated in the Bibliography, which also includes references to standard works on the lives and writings of the four mystics.

It should be clearly understood that, except for a few scriptural quotations, every statement in THE LIFE OF MARY AS SEEN BY THE MYSTICS has been borrowed directly from one of its four sources. The compiler has merely combined, condensed and adapted into a unified style the materials which he found therein. Occasionally elements from the two or three principal sources have even been brought together in one sentence or phrase, as one or the other supplied a relevant detail.

With regard to the relative contribution of each of the sources, in general Venerable Mother Mary of Agreda and Sister Anne Catherine Emmerich have provided approximately two thirds of the total text. Of those two, the former contributed most of the material concerning the interior life of the Blessed Virgin, while the latter was usually responsible for exterior actions. St. Bridget of Sweden supplied valuable light on the major events, whereas St. Elizabeth of Schoenau's contribution was limited to the years in the Temple and (in part) to the Annunciation.

The compiler wishes to acknowledge his gratitude to the many priests, religious and lay persons who have prayed for the spiritual success of this work, and particularly to the Reverend Oblates of Mary Immaculate, editors of *The Annals of Our Lady of the Cape*, the official magazine of the

National Canadian Shrine of Our Lady of the Rosary at Cap de la Madeleine, P.Q., in which it appeared as a series of articles in 1946–1949.

In conclusion he urges his readers to adopt the prudent and wise counsel of the learned Bollandist Hippolyte Delehaye, S.J., who (referring only to the Emmerich-Brentano writings) advised: *"Let them read [this book] as a religious novel, but not as a fifth Gospel."* [60]

If any of them should be laboring under the dangerous illusion that visions and revelations are to be desired or that they constitute an essential rather than a secondary element in Christian contemplation and perfection, let them study attentively the several treatises on Catholic spirituality which are listed in the general section (I) of the Bibliography. From THE LIFE OF MARY AS SEEN BY THE MYSTICS we may learn to be true Christian mystics, not seekers of "phenomena" but cultivators of the interior life of contemplative union with God through the practice of the virtues and the humble love of Christ and His Cross.

The principal lesson for us in this life of Mary is that she is above all a model of the interior life, and that only insofar as we imitate her recollection and prayer and charity of heart will we be pleasing to God and capable of serving Him, for only thus will we be united to Him and do His Will. Thus too we will become like Mary, and so Christ will be born and grow in our souls. By our progressive self-purification through penitential loving sacrifices, by the grace of God we will be able to give Him to others.

THE LIFE OF MARY AS SEEN BY THE MYSTICS is hereby offered with filial love, as a bouquet of "Little Flowers," to Mary Immaculate, Co-Redemptrix and Mediatrix of All Graces. May she deign to give it her blessing so that it may help its readers to live—as she did—in ever closer union with her divine Son, the Saviour of mankind.

THE COMPILER
Feast of Our Lady of Mount Carmel, 1950

---

60. *Analecta Bollandiana*, Vol. XLIII, 1925, p. 235.

OUR LORD AND SAVIOUR JESUS CHRIST
is reported to have said to

ST. BRIDGET OF SWEDEN:

"Know that it is not for your own sake alone that I speak to you, but also for the salvation of all Christians . . . Know too that when it pleases Me, men shall come who will take up the words of 'The Heavenly Revelations' with joy and consolation."

VEN. MOTHER MARY OF AGREDA:

"Many mysteries pertaining to My Mother . . . are still hidden, especially the interior secrets of her life, and these I wish now to make known. I desire to make known to mortals how much her intercession is worth. If men would now seek to please Me by reverencing, believing, and studying the wonders which are intimately connected with this Mother of Piety, and if they would all begin to solicit her intercession from their whole heart, the world would find some relief."

SISTER ANNE CATHERINE EMMERICH:

"I give you these visions, not for yourself; they are given to you in order that they may be recorded. I give you these visions—and I have ever done so—to prove that I shall be with My Church till the end of days. But visions alone sanctify no one; you must practice charity, patience, and all the other virtues."

CHAPTER ONE

ST. ANN AND ST. JOACHIM

BEFORE TIME BEGAN, the Holy Trinity decreed that one day, after the creation of the world and of man and after man's fall, God the Son was to be born of a Virgin Mother. In order that this Mother should be the purest human being who ever lived, Almighty God decreed that she was to be miraculously exempt from all stain of Original Sin.

And as a fitting preparation for the Incarnation of the God-Man among men, the Blessed Trinity also planned to train a chosen people to serve and to worship the Lord faithfully in the religion which He Himself revealed to them through their patriarchs and prophets. Thus He taught them to purify their hearts by leading a decent and holy daily life, and to pray for the coming of the Messias or Saviour that He promised to send them as their King.

In the course of time, however, most of the Chosen People of Israel were unfaithful to God in many ways. And as they became more and more materialistic, they imagined that the Messias would appear as a great ruler who would free them by political power from their oppressors, the

Romans. But some of the Israelites continued to love and to serve the Lord in humility and detachment from the world, for they knew that the Saviour would come to free men from the oppressor within their own hearts.

It was from these pure families that, by His grace, God developed and guided the ancestors of His future Mother. They were extremely simple and devout persons, very gentle and peace-loving and charitable. Out of love for God, they always lived a very mortified life. Often the married couples practiced continence over long periods of time, particularly during holy seasons, for their highest ideal was to raise saintly children who in turn would contribute toward bringing salvation to the world. They lived in small rural communities, and they did not engage in business. They worked on the land and tended flocks of sheep; they also had gardens and orchards. They were very conscientious in fulfilling their religious duties. Whenever they had to go to Jerusalem to offer their sacrifices in the Temple, they prepared themselves by prayer and fasting and penance. When traveling, they always helped as best they could any sick persons or paupers whom they met. And because they led such an austere and detached life, these good people had to endure the scorn of many of the other Jews.

Thus Mary's grandparents inherited from their ancestors a love of humility, chastity, mortification and the simple life. Her mother, St. Ann, and her father, St. Joachim, were the very finest products of this long line of pure and holy servants of God.

St. Ann was born in Bethlehem of rich parents who owned many flocks of sheep and herds of cattle. But they regularly gave away to the poor a large part of their possessions and kept very little for themselves. After Ann's birth they moved to a beautiful country estate at Sephoris near Nazareth.

From her childhood Ann loved to pray and to think about God, but she also grew to be an industrious helper around the home. In fact, while very modest and retiring, she became such a model daughter that other mothers used to tell their young girls to imitate her. And the more she learned about the awaited coming of the Saviour, the more ardently did she pray that God might hasten that happy event.

Just before her holy mother died, she told Ann that she was a chosen vessel and that she should pray for a worthy husband. Ann was now a comely, sturdy girl in her teens, with all the modest simplicity of a devout peasant maiden. Several young men were hoping to become her husband.

One day Ann happened to be praying fervently to God to give her a husband who would help her to live according to the Divine Law. And at the very same moment on another farm near Nazareth an unusually pious middle-aged bachelor named Joachim was also praying for God's help in choosing a wife. Although he knew and greatly admired Ann, he was so extremely humble that he did not dare think she would become his wife.

When the prayers of St. Ann and St. Joachim were presented by the angels before the throne of the Blessed Trinity, God decreed that this pure couple should unite in marriage and be the parents of the future mother of the Messias. The Archangel Gabriel was sent to announce this decision to them both.

He appeared in visible form to Ann while she was praying. He alone of the angels knew her destiny, but all he was allowed to tell her now was:

"The Lord give thee His blessing, servant of God! Continue to pray for the coming of the Redeemer and rejoice in the Lord. It is His Will that thou accept Joachim as thy husband."

Leaving Ann greatly comforted, the Archangel went to Joachim and said to him while he slept:

"Blessed be thou by the Lord, Joachim! Persevere in the practice of justice and perfection. The Lord wants thee to take Ann as thy wife. Take care of her, esteem her, for she is dear to Him, and give thanks to God."

The very next day, Joachim, who was small, lean, and broad-shouldered, went and asked Ann's father for the hand of his daughter. And soon the couple were solemnly wedded in a simple open-air ceremony. St. Ann was about twenty-four at the time, and St. Joachim was forty-two.

They made their home on the estate of Ann's father. Though they were quite wealthy, they lived very economically and charitably. Each year they divided all their rents and income and sheep into three parts. Then they gave one-third to the Temple for God's service, one-third to the poor, and they kept only what was left. And yet their flocks and herds continued to increase amazingly. Very often they gave food to poor travelers and lambs to their needy relatives.

In their home they frequently talked together about God and the coming of the Redeemer, for which they prayed long and fervently. Both Ann and Joachim had been serious even in their youth. Now as they matured, they made a distinguished and devout couple. Neither told the other about the message of the angel.

In His wisdom Almighty God proceeded to purify them still further by giving them a heavy cross to bear, a cross which only grew heavier as the years passed: they remained childless. Among the Israelites in those times, this was considered not only the greatest misfortune and disgrace socially, but also a clear indication that the Lord thought such a couple unworthy to contribute toward the coming of the Messias. And so Ann and Joachim had to suffer increasing contempt and even insults from their neighbors and acquaintances. But they took these humiliations with patience and continued to pray that God might bless their marriage with children.

Seven years passed without an answer to their prayers. Then they decided to move to a smaller farm near Nazareth and to begin a new life, a much more mortified and holy life, in order thus to earn God's blessing. For in their profound humility they felt that their great affliction was entirely due to their own unworthiness before the Lord.

They also increased their charity and gifts to the poor. And they trained themselves in continence, for they always aspired to greater purity. They even took a solemn vow to dedicate their child, if God gave them one, to His service in the Temple.

Thus they lived through another thirteen long, trying years.

Then one day when Joachim was offering his sacrifices in the Temple, the priest rebuked and insulted him, saying: "Why do you come here, Joachim? Your offerings are not acceptable to the Lord!"

His face burning with shame, the poor man withdrew to a corner of the Temple and prayed:

"O Lord, my sins merit this disgrace. But as I accept it according to Thy will, do not cast me away. . . ."

Then with a sore heart he left the city and went to some of his flocks on the distant slopes of Mount Hermon. He was so troubled that he stayed there in prayer and penance for several months without communicating with Ann.

Through friends she heard about his being reproached by the priest, and this only added to her keen suffering. She often wept, lying flat on the ground in her room.

Once when she refused to allow a lightheaded servant to go out to a party, the girl exclaimed bitterly:

"God has inflicted a double punishment on you because you are so severe: you are sterile—and now your husband has abandoned you!"

With a sad heart Ann sent the girl back to her family.

That evening St. Ann was sitting under a great tree in her garden, reading prayers on a parchment roll and begging God to send Joachim home and to let them have at least one child—she was now forty-four. Then she prayed fervently for the coming of the Messias, and her thoughts turned to the fortunate family, to the holy mother that God would choose. With a sigh she said to herself:

"Oh, who shall be worthy to be the servant of her servants?"

Just then the Archangel Gabriel suddenly appeared

before her in a resplendent human form and declared:

"Ann, servant of God. The Lord has heard thy petitions. If He delays their fulfillment, it is in order to prepare thee and to give thee much more than thou askest. The Most High has resolved to give thee and Joachim holy and wonderful fruit, for those who pray to Him in humble confidence are most agreeable to Him. Now He sends me to give thee joyful news: He chooses thee to be the mother of her who is to give birth to the Redeemer of mankind! Thou shalt bring forth a daughter and she shall be called Mary. She shall be blessed among women and filled with the Holy Ghost. I have announced to Joachim that he shall have a holy daughter, but he does not know that she is to be the Mother of the Messias. Therefore guard this secret. And now go to the Temple to give thanks to the Lord, and thou shalt meet Joachim at the Golden Gate."

Gabriel vanished, and St. Ann's humble heart was so overflowing with amazement, heavenly joy and gratitude that the Holy Spirit sustained her lest she faint. She immediately prostrated herself on the ground and for a long time poured out her thanks to God with tears of happiness.

That night she dreamed that an angel came and wrote the name of Mary in big luminous letters on the wall of her room, and after midnight she awoke and saw the large bright letters. Deeply moved, she kept gazing at them and thinking lovingly of this marvelous daughter Mary until the letters disappeared with the dawn. Then she arose, prepared herself for the trip to Jerusalem, and left with a servant. She was so deeply happy that she looked much younger.

Meanwhile Joachim had been visited by the Archangel Gabriel during the night while he slept among his flocks. Gabriel told him that Ann was going to give birth to a blessed daughter who was to be consecrated to God, and that he should go and give thanks in the Temple, where he would meet Ann at the Golden Gate. Joachim awoke filled with joyful consolation and hastened to Jerusalem.

This time the Holy Spirit moved the priests in the Temple to accept Joachim's offerings courteously, and several of his friends congratulated him. Then two priests led him into the Holy Place and left him there alone, after burning incense on the altar. While Joachim prayed on his knees with his arms extended, a bright angel appeared and told him that his childlessness was not a disgrace but an honor, for the child who was to be born of his wife would be the most perfect flower of the race of Abraham. Next the angel took him into the Holy of Holies, anointed his forehead, and gave him a certain mystic blessing which freed him from all sensuality. Then he led him back to the Holy Place and vanished, as Joachim sank to the floor in an ecstatic trance. Soon the priests found him thus and revived him with marks of respect. When he recovered consciousness, his face was radiant with spiritual joy and he seemed considerably younger. He told the priests that he wanted to meet his wife at the Golden Gate, and they showed him the way, which led through a long, beautifully decorated and well-lighted underground corridor.

St. Ann had just made her offering in another part of the Temple, and she told a priest that an angel had ordered her to find her husband at the Golden Gate. Accompanied by several devout women (among whom was Anna the Prophetess), St. Ann was taken to the same corridor.

Thus it happened that near the Golden Gate St. Joachim suddenly perceived his beloved wife coming toward him, her beautiful face shining with joy. They hastened toward each other and embraced with tender emotion.

Then each told the other what had happened, and together they gave fervent thanks to God for His marvelous answer to all their prayers. As they now renewed their vow to offer their child to His Temple, they seemed to be rapt in a holy ecstasy. A cloud of heavenly light enfolded them, while a great number of angels hovered above them. St. Ann and St. Joachim became luminous. Never had a human couple achieved such supernatural purity of soul. Then suddenly the heavens opened up, and the Blessed Trinity looked down with joy and love on this saintly pair and gave them a special blessing.

Later St. Ann and St. Joachim left Jerusalem and returned to their home near Nazareth, where they gave a great feast for the poor and distributed alms abundantly.

Now they were both transfigured with fervor, happiness, and intense gratitude. And very often as they prayed together they wept tears of joy and love.

Thus did Almighty God prepare and purify Mary's good parents until the great day at last came when the glorious mystery of the Immaculate Conception of the Mother of God took place.

THE BLESSED VIRGIN SAID
TO ST. BRIDGET OF SWEDEN:

"It is a truth that I was conceived without Original Sin and not in sin. A golden hour was my conception. My Son joined my father and my mother in a marriage of such chastity that a purer union has never been seen. Sensuality was extinguished in them. Thus my flesh was formed through divine charity."

CHAPTER TWO

THE NATIVITY OF MARY

AFTER GOD HAD CREATED Mary's immaculate soul, He showed it to the choirs of angels in Heaven, and they felt intense joy upon seeing its unique beauty.

Then, as Mary's soul was infused into her body, her holy mother St. Ann was filled with the Holy Ghost and experienced an extraordinary devotion and happiness. Throughout the rest of her life and especially during the next nine months, she constantly received new graces and enlightenment concerning the great mystery of the Incarnation, and she frequently praised the Lord in canticles of love.

One night she felt for the first time a slight tremor from the presence of her daughter in her womb. With profound joy she arose, dressed, and told St. Joachim the happy news, and then both gave thanks to God together.

However, in order to increase her merit, God allowed St. Ann to undergo grievous trials during her pregnancy. Although Satan did not know that her daughter was to be the Mother of the Saviour, he perceived that a strong spiritual influence proceeded from Ann, and therefore he did his best to tempt and disturb and harm her. But she resisted all his attacks with humble fortitude, patience and prayer. Then the enraged Devil tried to make St. Joachim's house crash to the ground, but Mary's protecting angels prevented such an accident from happening. Next, Satan incited some of St. Ann's women friends to treat her with open scorn and mockery because of her late pregnancy. St. Ann did not permit herself to be upset by this injustice, but in all meekness and humility she bore the insults and acted with still greater kindness toward these women. In the end, as a result of her prayers, they amended their ways.

Early in September, St. Ann was informed interiorly by the Lord that the time of her daughter's birth was near. Filled with holy joy, she humbly prayed for a happy deliverance and sent for three of her closest women relatives. When she told St. Joachim, he rejoiced and went among his flocks in order to choose the finest lambs, goats and bulls, which he sent to the Temple in care of his servants as an offering of gratitude to the Lord.

One evening the three woman arrived and embraced St. Ann, congratulating her warmly. Standing with them, she poured forth her deep joy and thankfulness in a beautiful spontaneous canticle, which surprised and thrilled her friends. Then, still standing, they took a light meal of bread, fruit and water, after which they went to lie down and rest.

St. Ann prayed until nearly midnight, when she woke her relatives and went with them into her oratory and lit the lamps. From a closet she took a small box containing some relics of the Patriarchs of Israel. Then she knelt before her little altar. While she was praying thus, a supernatural light began to fill the room. Noticing it, the three friends threw themselves onto the floor and hid their faces in awe. Soon the dazzling light entirely surrounded St. Ann, making her invisible.

A moment later she was holding in her hands a beautiful, spotless, radiant baby, which she tenderly wrapped in her cloak and pressed to her heart. With tears of fervent love and joy, she gazed at her child and then, raising her eyes to Heaven and holding up the baby, she prayed:

"O Lord and Creator, with eternal thanks I offer Thee this blessed fruit of my womb which I have received from Thy bounty without any merit of mine. But how shall I be able to treat such a child worthily?"

God gave her to understand that she was to bring up her daughter with all motherly love and care but without any outward show of reverence, while retaining inwardly her profound veneration for the future Mother of the Messias.

In this marvelous yet natural childbirth, St. Ann had been free from the usual labor and pains experienced by mothers. Now she herself bathed and wrapped the babe in red and gray swaddling clothes. As the bright mystic light vanished, the three relatives got up and to their keen surprise and joy perceived the lovely child in her mother's arms. Then they sang a hymn of praise and thanks to the Lord while many invisible guardian angels also greeted the tiny Mary with heavenly music.

Later St. Ann retired to her room and lay down on her bed with her baby in a little cradle next to her, and St. Joachim was called in. The holy old man knelt beside the bed, deeply moved at the sight of this lovely daughter for which he and his dear wife had waited and suffered for twenty long years. While warm tears flowed freely down his cheeks, he carefully took the baby in his arms and sang a fervent hymn of praise to God. Then, as he tenderly embraced his daughter and put her back in the cradle, he murmured with touching humility and piety:

"Now I am ready to die . . ."

At the moment of Mary's birth, Almighty God gave to her pure soul a mystical vision of the Blessed Trinity in Heaven, and by a miraculous privilege He endowed her from birth with the full use of her reason and all her senses. Thus, like many of the Saints, though to a far greater degree, even as an infant she knew and loved God with all her heart. And as soon as she opened her eyes on earth, she perceived with keen affection her good parents, St. Ann and St. Joachim, and then she saw the many angels which God had assigned to guard and protect her throughout her life.

The Archangel Gabriel was sent to announce the great news of the birth of Mary to all the Prophets, Patriarchs and souls in Limbo. Upon hearing that at last the Mother of the Redeemer was in the world, they rejoiced and praised God for His mercy toward mankind.

In all Nature there was at this time an extraordinary movement of joy, and many good people felt an unusual spiritual exaltation without knowing its cause. On the other hand, many evil men and possessed persons felt sorely disturbed.

Near the Temple in Jerusalem, old Simeon was awakened by the shouts of a possessed man, who cried:

"I must flee—all of us must flee! A Virgin has been born . . . !"

Simeon prayed fervently, and the devil left the man.

Anna the Prophetess and another holy woman were shown in visions that a child of election had been given to Israel.

The next day many friends and neighbors of St. Ann and St. Joachim came to see the baby and congratulate the happy parents. Everyone was deeply touched upon seeing little Mary lying in her cradle, wrapped in her red and gray swaddling clothes, and there was general rejoicing.

Now in Heaven the Blessed Trinity announced to the choirs of angels:

"Our Chosen One shall be called Mary, and this name is to be powerful in grace."

CHAPTER THREE

INFANCY

EIGHT days after Mary's birth, all the friends and relatives of the family gathered in St. Joachim's house for the ceremony of naming the baby. According to custom, the mother could not attend the celebration, but remained in her room. Several priests came from Nazareth, and St. Joachim placed his daughter in the hands of their richly robed leader, who lifted her up as if offering her to the Lord, and recited some prayers. Then he wrote the name Mary on a parchment and placed it on her chest. After the singing of some psalms, the ceremony was over and Mary was taken back to St. Ann, while all the guests sat around a long low table and were served a banquet meal.

Later, St. Ann and St. Joachim took Mary to the Temple in Jerusalem for the ceremony of the purification of the mother. St. Ann humbly gave her offerings of a lamb and a turtledove, and prayed to the Lord to forgive her all her faults. Then, entering the Temple with her daughter in her arms, she offered up Mary to God with devout and tender tears. In her heart she heard a voice urging her to renew her vow to give Mary to God's service in the

Temple within three years.

At the same time, Mary herself, seeing the grandeur of these buildings dedicated to the worship of the Lord, wished that she could prostrate herself on the floor and kiss it. But as she could not, she prayed:

"O Most High God, I adore Thee in Thy holy Temple. Accept me, O Lord, so that I may serve Thee in this holy house according to Thy blessed Will!"

As a proof that her prayer was granted, a beam of bright light shone down from Heaven onto the mother and child. And while St. Ann renewed her vow, the angels sang hymns of praise to Almighty God.

The holy man Simeon had been deeply moved when he saw St. Ann and Mary, and now as he dimly perceived the mystic light, he asked himself: "Are these women perhaps the parents of the Messias?" And he prayed still more fervently for the coming of the Redeemer.

The devil had also been studying St. Ann, but when he saw that she humbly submitted to all the regulations of the priests and even asked them to intercede for her, he decided that she was just another pious woman.

During the next three years in the home of her loving mother, Mary was treated as other children of her age and passed her infancy subject to the common laws of nature. However, she never cried or caused anyone any trouble. Even as a baby, she maintained a pleasant countenance mixed with gravity and a certain majesty. While she showed a special affection for her mother and father, they were inspired by God to handle and caress her with unusual restraint. She ate less than other children and she slept much less, for whenever she could, she prayed and meditated and performed interior acts of love for God. When she accepted any service or benefits from anyone, she always received it with humble gratitude and begged the Lord to reward that person.

Being in possession of all her faculties even from birth, Mary could have talked quite clearly and intelligently even as a baby, if she had wished to. But out of modesty and submission to the Will of God, she deliberately refrained from speaking at all until she was a year and a half old. However when alone she did often converse with her guardian angels, and in secret she also prayed verbally to the Lord.

Though she was thus filled with the light of God and His mysteries, nevertheless Mary judged herself to be the least of all His creatures, and she always ascribed to herself the last place of all. Whenever, during that first year and a half, St. Ann freed her daughter's little arms and hands, Mary would immediately grasp her dear parents' hands and kiss them with reverent humility. In fact she continued this practice as long as they lived.

When she reached the age of eighteen months, Almighty God urged her to pray many times every day for the coming of the Messias, and He told her that it was now time for her to converse with others. But Mary exclaimed:

"O my Lord, I beseech Thee, consider my frailty. To avoid all risk of losing Thee, I would rather keep silence all my life. . . .

God promised her, however, that He would assist her in directing all her words to His service and glory.

Therefore one day little Mary spoke her first words to her beloved parents, asking their blessing. At the same time she showed them that she could walk by herself.

With intense joy St. Ann took Mary into her arms and said:

"O darling of my heart, this is a blessed hour! Let your words be few and well considered, and may all your footsteps be directed toward the honor of our Creator!"

During the remaining year and a half before she went to the Temple, Mary spoke very little, except to her mother. In order to make her talk, St. Ann used to call her and ask her to speak of God and His mysteries. Mary, however, would humbly beg her mother rather to instruct her. Thus mother and daughter passed many hours in sweet conversation about holy things.

Often when St. Ann watched her dear little girl in their

home, she shed tears of love and gratitude at the thought that this lovely child was actually chosen by God to be the Mother of the Saviour of mankind. Often they spoke together about His coming and about the fortunate maiden of Israel who would give Him to the world, and then Mary would become inflamed with ardent love and would innocently picture this happy creature in the most glowing terms of awe and reverence. But St. Ann never revealed the great secret of her heart.

Being eager to express in her actions her conviction that she was the least of God's creatures, little Mary tried to help in cleaning and scrubbing the house whenever she could. And sometimes, when she was alone, her angels helped her.

While St. Ann naturally wished to dress her daughter as beautifully as she could, Mary, soon after she began to talk, begged her mother to clothe her in plain ash-gray cloth of cheap and coarse material. St. Ann yielded as to the form and color, but not to the material.

Almighty God had already revealed to Mary how grievously the sins of men offended Him. Consequently she would often retire to her room and prostrate herself on the floor and beg for mercy for poor sinners. Even as an infant she practiced penances and mortifications to a point where she taxed her bodily strength.

When Mary reached the age of two, she began to perform works of charity toward the poor. She begged alms for them from her parents, and she set aside parts of her meals for them. Then she would give them what she had, saying in her heart: "This man, my brother, deserves what he needs and what I possess without deserving it." When she gave her alms to the poor, she used to kiss their hands, and if she was alone, their feet. And in each case she prayed fervently to God to give them spiritual graces as well.

THE BLESSED VIRGIN SAID
TO VENERABLE MOTHER MARY OF AGREDA:

"At the first sight of the Highest Good, my heart was wounded with love, and I gave myself entirely to Him.

"I underwent the hardships of infancy like other children. I felt hunger, thirst, sleepiness and other infirmities of the body. In all the difficulties which I endured after I was born into the world, I was resigned and contented, since I had merited none of God's gifts.

"Be very devout toward my most sweet name."

CHAPTER FOUR

PRESENTATION

A S THE time approached when Mary was to be taken to the Temple, St. Ann often gave her lessons, teaching her various prayers and rules of religion. She already knew how to read. Though only three and a half years old and very delicate, Mary seemed like a girl of five or six. Her long, dark hair hung straight down with curls at the end.

One day, three old priests came from Nazareth to give her an examination, in order to determine whether she was worthy of being accepted for service in the Temple. This was a very solemn proceeding. After explaining to her the different duties she would fulfill, they asked her some questions. Her replies were so filled with naive wisdom that the priests could not help smiling their approval, while her parents wept tears of joy. Then during a meal the oldest priest said to her:

"In consecrating you to God, your father and mother promised that you would give up wine, vinegar, grapes and figs. What other sacrifice do you wish freely to add to those? Think it over and tell us later."

Mary was very fond of vinegar. Meanwhile the priests made it clear to her that she was still free to eat whatever she wanted, and all sorts of delicacies were offered to her, but she took very little and from only a few dishes. After the meal, in another room, Mary said that she had decided to give up fish and meat and milk and all fruits except berries. Also she wished to sleep on the floor and to get up and pray three times every night.

Her parents were deeply moved when they heard this. Taking her up in his arms, St. Joachim wept as he said to her: "My dear child, that is far too much! If you lead such a hard life, your father will never see you again. . . ."

The priests then insisted that she should pray only once during the night, like the other girls, that she should allow herself several other relaxations, and that she should eat fish on all the great feast days. They also told her that she would not have to join the poorer girls in washing the bloodstained robes of the sacrificers, but Mary unhesitatingly replied that she would willingly do that work if she were thought worthy. The priests were filled with surprise and admiration, and the oldest gave her a solemn blessing. Then St. Ann, who was deeply moved, pressed Mary to her heart and kissed her with tender love, while St. Joachim caressed her respectfully. Throughout the examinations, under the guidance and inspiration of her angels, Mary had remained perfectly recollected and serious, and at the same time strikingly beautiful and lovable.

A few days later everyone in St. Joachim's home was busy preparing for the trip to Jerusalem. Several fine ceremonial dresses which had been made for Mary were carefully packed up. Finally one morning, at dawn, two donkeys were loaded with baggage, and St. Joachim and St. Ann set out, the latter carrying Mary in her arms. The holy child was very happy to be going to the Temple. During the trip they often had to travel through cold fogs, as it was the rainy season. When they stopped overnight at an inn or some friend's home, Mary often went up to her mother and joyfully put her arms around St. Ann's neck.

Several times St. Joachim repeated sadly: "My dear child, I will never see you again. . . ."

On arriving in the Holy City, they were met by a group of friends and children who led them to the house of Zacharias the priest, the future father of John the Baptist, where they were made welcome and given refreshments. Then everyone attended a great reception and feast in an inn which St. Joachim had rented for the occasion, as he wished to spare no expense for this great event. Among those present was a ten-year-old girl, later to be known as St. Veronica.

Early the next morning, St. Joachim took his animal offerings to the Temple with several men, while St. Ann, accompanied by many women and girls, led Mary to God's House in a beautiful solemn procession through the streets of the Holy City. Little Mary walked behind her mother. She was dressed in a lovely sky-blue robe with garlands of flowers around her arms and neck, and in one hand she carried a candle decorated with flowers. On each side of her were three girls in white with flowers and candles. Then came other girls and women. Everyone who saw them was touched by Mary's extraordinarily holy appearance.

At the outer entrance to the Temple, they were met by St. Joachim, Zacharias and several other priests. As they passed through the gate, Mary's parents inwardly offered their beloved daughter to the Lord with a fervent and devout prayer. And Mary too, in deep humility and adoration, offered herself to God. She alone perceived that the Almighty welcomed her and accepted her, for she heard a voice from Heaven saying:

"Come, My beloved, My spouse, come into My Temple, where I wish thee to offer Me praise and worship."

Then, crossing the Women's Court, they came to the fifteen steps leading up to the great Nicanor Gate. It was here that St. Joachim and St. Ann had to make the formal offering of their child to the Temple. After a priest had placed her on the first step, Mary, with his permission, turned and knelt before her parents. Kissing their hands with keen love and gratitude, she asked for their blessing and their prayers. With tears in their eyes, her father and mother laid their hands on her head and solemnly pronounced the words by which they gave her to the Lord, while a priest clipped a few locks of her hair. During this moving ceremony, the young girls who had come with the party sang these words of Psalm 44:

"Thou art beautiful . . . therefore hath God blessed thee for ever. . . . Hearken, O daughter, and see, and incline thy ear: and forget thy people and thy father's house. And the King shall greatly desire thy beauty; for He is the Lord thy God. . . . Therefore shall people praise thee for ever: yea, for ever and ever!"

Then, after St. Ann and St. Joachim had tenderly blessed her, little Mary, without hesitating and without looking back, began to climb up the fifteen steps. She would not let anyone help her, but with remarkable resolution and dignity she hastened up all by herself, filled with holy fervor and joy. Everyone who saw her was visibly affected.

Two priests then led her up to the gallery, from which the Holy Place could be seen, and read some prayers over her, while incense was burned on an altar. Taking from her the garlands of flowers and the candle, they put a brown veil over her head and conducted her to a hall in which ten girls in the service of the Temple welcomed her by throwing flowers before her. Here she met her teacher, who was the holy prophetess Anna.

As the priests left, Mary's parents and relatives came in to say goodby. St. Joachim was especially moved. He took Mary into his arms and wept as he murmured: "My child, pray to God for my soul!" St. Ann embraced her beloved daughter sadly and tenderly. Then, resigning herself with courage to the Will of God, she turned away. As she walked out, she said to the women accompanying her: "The Ark of the Covenant is now in the Temple." With keen sorrow in their hearts, St. Joachim and St. Ann returned to Nazareth. But in answer to Mary's prayers, God mercifully consoled and comforted them.

Now Mary humbly knelt before her teacher Anna and asked her blessing and forbearance for the trouble she would give her. Next Mary greeted and embraced each of the other girls, offering herself as their servant and urging them to instruct and command her. After taking a meal together, they retired to their little cells.

Mary's room was high up, with a view over the Holy Place and the Inner Temple containing the Holy of Holies. Her cell was very plain, its only furniture being a lamp, a low round table, and a rolled-up carpet which served as her bed. As soon as she found herself alone, Mary prostrated herself on the floor and kissed it, for to her it was holy ground, being part of God's Temple, and she considered herself unworthy of treading upon it. Then she turned to her angels and prayed:

"Messengers of the Almighty, faithful friends, I beseech you to remain with me in this holy Temple of my Lord and to remind me of all that I should do. Please instruct me and direct me so that in all things I may fulfill the Will of God."

Humbling herself before God, she said:

"Infinite and Eternal Lord, if trouble and persecutions suffered in patience are precious in Thy sight, do not consent that I be deprived of so rich a treasure and pledge of Thy love. But give the rewards of these tribulations to those who deserve them better than I."

This prayer of Mary pleased Almighty God, and He gave her to understand that He would allow her to suffer and labor for love of Him during her life, though she would not know in advance how it would happen. Mary thanked Him with all her heart and then asked to be allowed to take in His presence the vows of chastity, poverty, obedience and perpetual enclosure in the Temple. The Lord answered:

"My chosen one, thou dost not yet understand why it is impossible for thee to fulfill all thy desires. The vow of chastity I permit and wish thee to make. And from this moment I want thee to renounce earthly riches. It is My

Will that thou observe whatever pertains to the other vows as if thou hadst made them."

Then the holy child solemnly made the vow of chastity before God, and renounced all affection for created things, while she resolved to obey all creatures for the love of God. Her angels proceeded to adorn her with a gorgeous robe and sparkling jewels of many colors that symbolized her virtues.

Next the Lord told her to ask for whatever she desired, and Mary immediately beseeched Him with burning fervor to send the Redeemer to the world so that all men might know Him, to bless her parents with grace, and to console the poor and the afflicted in their troubles.

THE BLESSED VIRGIN SAID
TO ST. BRIDGET OF SWEDEN:

"From my infancy the Holy Spirit was perfectly with me. And as I grew, It filled me so completely as to leave no room for any sin to enter.

"When I had attained an age to know something of my Creator, I turned to Him with unspeakable love and desired Him with my whole heart.

"I vowed in my heart to observe virginity if it was pleasing to Him, and to possess nothing in the world—but if God willed otherwise, that His Will, not mine, be done, I committed my will absolutely to Him."

CHAPTER FIVE

IN THE TEMPLE

O N HER first day in the Temple, after having taken before God the vows of poverty and chastity, little Mary went to her teacher, the holy prophetess Anna, and asked her to give away to the poor all the clothes, money, and other personal belongings which St. Ann had left there for her, except for a few dresses and prayerbooks. Anna agreed to do so and to take care of Mary as of someone destitute and poor, for the other girls had spending money.

Then Mary asked for a rule of life. Anna consulted the old priest, and summoned Mary, who remained on her knees throughout the interview. The priest said to her:

"Pray always for the Temple of the Lord, for His people, and for the coming of the Messias. Retire to sleep at eight o'clock, and rise at dawn to praise the Lord until nine. During the day, as your teacher directs, engage in manual work and study the Scriptures. Take exercise before meals. In all things be humble, courteous and obedient."

Then Mary asked for his blessing and kissed his hand and Anna's.

During the days that followed, she willingly set about

learning all her new duties. Unlike the other girls, she asked her teacher to be allowed to serve them all and to scrub the rooms and wash the dishes. Often she did her own work so quickly and efficiently that she was able to help the others in theirs. To each of her companions she was always sincerely kind, friendly and humble. With them she spinned and sewed, mended and washed the vestments of the priests, or took lessons in Holy Scripture, in singing, and in the ceremonies of the Temple. Her gratitude toward her teachers was touching.

Thus through the years she grew in wisdom and grace and infused mystical knowledge. Even as a child she had a remarkably advanced understanding of the Scriptures, and she loved to spend hours studying and meditating on them, especially on their inspired prophecies of the coming of the Redeemer of mankind in human form.

Often she asked profound, penetrating questions of her angels, and spoke with loving tenderness about the Messias. And with their help she gradually pieced together many of the significant scriptural references to the Mysteries of Christ's life, such as:* *The Promise of His Incarnation:* "the Desired of all nations shall come. . . rejoice greatly, O daughter of Sion, shout for joy; behold, thy King will come to thee, the just and Saviour." *The Nativity:* "Behold a virgin shall conceive and bear a Son." *His Apostolate:* "He is poor. . . . He will teach us His Way. 'I will open My mouth in parables. Behold I Myself will seek My sheep. I will feed My sheep. I will save My flock.'" *His Passion:* "He hath borne our infirmities and carried our sorrows. He was wounded for our iniquities. . . . 'All My enemies whispered together against Me: Let us condemn Him to a most shameful death. Strike the shepherd, and the sheep of the flock will be scattered.' 'I have given My body to the strikers. . . .' He will crown Thee with a crown of tribulation. Why then is Thy apparel red? From the sole of the foot unto the top of the head, wounds and

---

* Quotations supplied by the compiler.

bruises and swelling sores; they are not bound up. . . .
'They have dug My hands and My feet. And in My thirst
they gave Me vinegar to drink . . . . I am become as a
man without help, free among the dead. They have laid
Me in the lower pit.'" *His Resurrection:* "And His Sepul-
chre shall be glorious!" *His Ascension:* "Be ye lifted up, O
Eternal Gates, and the King of Glory shall enter in. God
is ascended with jubilee!" *His Church:* "And He shall rule
from sea to sea . . . . And all peoples, tribes and tongues
shall serve Him." *His Second Coming:* "God shall come man-
ifestly: our God shall come . . . to judge His people."

Very often during her ten years in the Temple, Mary
would meditate on these and many other prophecies in
the Old Testament, and then she would retire to her little cell at night and pray for many hours. When she thought
of God's love for men and of how He was soon to come
among them and suffer as one of them, in order to save
them, tears flowed from her eyes as she prayed, and a
supernatural light surrounded her.

Six months after Mary entered the service of the Temple, the Lord appeared to her in a vision and said:

"My beloved and chosen one, I love thee with an infinite love, and I desire of thee what is most pleasing in
My eyes. Hence I wish that thou dispose thyself for tribulations and sorrows for love of Me."

Mary replied: "I wish only to choose suffering unto death
for love of Thee."

Then the Lord continued:

"I accept thy desires. And as a beginning of their fulfillment, I announce to thee that thy father Joachim must
pass from this mortal to eternal life. His death will happen shortly, and he will pass away in peace and be placed
among the saints in Limbo, to await the Redemption of
mankind."

Little Mary, who loved St. Joachim with a holy love, felt
a keen sorrow and compassion, and she immediately
offered a fervent prayer for him. The Lord assured her
that He would assist her father.

Eight days before St. Joachim's death, Mary was told the day and hour in which he was to die, and she requested several of her angels to console him in his sickness, which they did. During his last hours, she sent the rest of her angels to help him, and she asked God to let him see them. This favor was granted, and the angels were commanded to say to him:

"Man of God, in order that the pain and sorrow of natural death may be relieved by the joy of thy spirit, the Almighty wishes thee to know now that thy daughter Mary is to be the happy Mother of the Messias! Since thou leavest to the world a daughter through whom God will restore it, do thou part from it in the joy of thy soul, and may the Lord bless thee!"

St. Ann, who was standing at the head of her husband's bed, also heard this message. In the same moment St. Joachim lost the power of speech, and he commenced his agony in conflict between joy at this great news and the pains of death. Making many fervent acts of love, faith, humility and thanksgiving, Mary's holy father died the precious death of the Saints, and his soul was carried to the Limbo of the Patriarchs and the just, where amid intense rejoicing he shared with them the happy tidings that from Mary was to be born the Redeemer of the world.

When the angels returned and told Mary of her father's death, she begged God to console her mother, good St. Ann.

Soon afterward, the Lord in His wisdom decided to train her further in the science of suffering. From birth she had enjoyed the delights of His love in frequent sensible consolations. Now He suspended all visions and similar graces, and ordered all her angels to conceal themselves from her.

Feeling utterly forsaken in this sudden and unexpected "dark night," in her humility Mary began to fear that it was due to her unworthiness and ingratitude for such precious graces. For days she suffered and longed for the sweet presence of her Lord. Often she said to herself sadly:

"I seek Him, and I do not find Him. Alas for me, my striving serves only to increase my sorrow. My Beloved absents Himself. I call Him and He does not answer me. Daughters of Jerusalem, I beseech you, if you find my Beloved, tell Him that I am faint and that I am dying with love. . . . Tell me where is my Beloved. Tell me where He has hidden Himself. Tell me where I can find Him. . . ."

Then, while the Lord continued to hide Himself from Mary, He also allowed Satan to try her, in order to increase her merit and reward. Irritated by her perfect virtue and holiness, the devil vainly attempted to incite her to commit even a slight venial sin of thought, word or deed. During these various tests, Mary never stopped praying to the Lord for help, and though she suffered from the strain and at times she wept, nevertheless without once losing her inner union with God she successfully fought and conquered all these temptations.

Consequently Satan changed his tactics. Since he could not influence her directly, he incited others to persecute her. Without much trouble he made the other girls become inflamed with envy against her. Seeing what a model Temple-servant she was, they began to fear that because of her their virtues would be overlooked and their faults would stand out. Driven on by the devil, soon they let themselves be moved to anger and hatred against her. Finally they plotted together to persecute her until she would be forced to leave the Temple. Now they often spoke to her in a sharp, haughty and cruel way, accusing her of being hypocritical and of seeking the favor of the priests and their teacher. When they did this, Mary answered quietly:

"My friends, you are right in saying that I am the least and most imperfect among you, but then you, my sisters, must pardon me and teach me in my ignorance, for as a servant I love you and reverence you, and I will obey you in all things."

Her sincere humility only made them more furious. For many days they continued to persecute and insult her, at times even hitting her. But little Mary remained humble, patient and charitable, returning good for evil and pray-ing for her enemies.

At last one day the other girls decided to provoke her to do something rash, so that they could accuse her before the priests and have her expelled. Therefore they took her to an isolated room and began to insult and hit her. But when she showed herself immovable and only reacted with kindness and humility, it was they who lost control of themselves and screamed their hatred of her so loudly that some priests came running into the room and asked severely who was to blame for this commotion. While Mary remained meekly silent, the other girls cried out:

"Mary of Nazareth makes us all quarrel—she irritates and provokes us so much that there can be no peace among us unless she leaves the Temple! When we allow her her own way, she becomes overbearing. But if we correct her, she makes fun of us by pretending to be humble—and then starts another quarrel!"

Taking Mary into another room, the priests scolded her very strongly and threatened to send her away if she did not change her conduct. Deeply hurt by this threat, the innocent child answered them in tears:

"My masters, thank you for correcting and teaching me, the most imperfect and despicable of creatures. But I beseech you—forgive me and direct me so that I may reform and henceforth please the Lord and my companions."

After the priests dismissed her, Mary went to the other girls and, prostrating herself at their feet, she asked their pardon. However, they continued to treat her with scorn and hostility, while she kept praying to God for help in overcoming her faults.

Then one night the Lord said to a priest in his sleep: "My servant Mary is pleasing in My eyes. She is entirely innocent of anything of which she is accused."

The same revelation was given to Mary's teacher, Anna. And that morning, after consulting together, she and the priest called in Mary and asked her pardon for having believed the false accusations. But the holy girl simply begged them not to consider her unworthy of being scolded, and kissed their hands as she asked for their blessing.

Thereafter God restrained both the devil and Mary's companions from persecuting her so much. But during all the ten years that she spent in the Temple, the Lord continued to absent Himself from her view, with only a few rare exceptions. This was of course a source of keen and prolonged suffering for Mary, though she felt herself unworthy of His loving visits and continually sought to make amends for her own negligence.

One day, when she had reached the age of twelve, her angels said to her, still without showing themselves:

"Mary, as ordained by the Lord, the life of thy holy mother Ann is now about to come to an end."

This unexpected sad news filled Mary's affectionate heart with sorrow. Prostrating herself before God, she fervently prayed:

"O Eternal Lord, dismiss Thy good servant in peace. Strengthen her, assist her, and let her enter into the peace of Thy friendship and grace, since she has always sought it with an upright heart."

God did not answer in words, but that night He commanded Mary's angels to carry her bodily to St. Ann's bedside. Upon seeing her dear mother again, Mary kissed her tenderly and exclaimed:

"Good mother, may the Lord be your strength, and may He be blessed, since He has permitted me to receive your last blessing!"

With grave affection the dying St. Ann said slowly:

"My beloved daughter, do not forget me in the presence of the Lord, and remind Him of the need I have of His protection in this hour—do not leave me before you close my eyes. You will be an orphan, but you will live under the guardianship of the Lord. Do not leave the Temple before choosing your state of life, with the advice of the priests. Pray that if it be God's Will to give you a husband, he may be of the race of David. Share your inheritance with the poor in loving generosity. Without ceasing ask the Almighty to show His mercy by sending His promised Messias. Beseech Him to be your protection. And may His blessing come over you, together with mine. . . ."

Then, after giving Mary her blessing, good St. Ann reclined in her daughter's arms and died in perfect peace. She was fifty-six years old. As the angels carried Mary back to her cell in the Temple, her loving heart suffered a keen sense of loneliness. However, while praying for St. Ann, she gratefully thanked the Lord for having given her such a perfect mother and for having showered so many graces on her parents in life and death.

One day not long afterward, for the first time in years, Mary's angels again became visible to her, and said:

"Soon thou shalt see Him whom thy soul desires! In order to console His beloved, He afflicts them. In order to be sought after, He withdraws."

Then gradually, by a series of mystical experiences, God endowed Mary's pure soul with new gifts and tranquilized her spirit. At last, having raised her to a still higher spiritual plane, He again revealed Himself to her in an exalted vision which amply rewarded all her suffering and loving anxiety. Once again overwhelmed with joy, Mary prayed:

"O infinite Goodness and Wisdom, purify my heart and renew it, so that it may be humble, penitent and pleasing in Thy sight!"

THE BLESSED VIRGIN SAID TO ST. BRIDGET OF SWEDEN:

"As soon as I understood that there was a God, I was always solicitous and fearful for my salvation. And when I heard more fully that God was also my Creator and Judge of all my actions, I loved Him intensely, and every hour I feared and pondered lest I should offend Him in word or deed. Then when I heard that He had given a Law to His people and wrought so many wonders with them, I firmly resolved in my mind to love naught but Him, and all worldly things became most bitter to me.

"Hearing that this same God was to redeem the world and be born of a virgin, I was filled with such love for her that I thought of naught but God. I withdrew as much as possible from the conversation and presence of others. All that I could have, I gave to the poor, reserving to myself only scanty food and clothing. Nothing pleased me but God. Ever did I long in my heart to live to the time of His birth, if perchance I might be the unworthy handmaid of the Mother of God."

—AND TO VENERABLE
MOTHER MARY OF AGREDA:

"It is true that on account of the blessings of the Lord, sin was impossible in me. But (this) was hidden from me. I saw that as far as it depended on myself alone, I could fall. Thus God left me in holy fear of sinning during my pilgrimage. From the instant of my conception until my death, I never lost this fear, but rather grew in it with time."

—AND TO ST. ELIZABETH OF SCHOENAU:

"I want to teach you the prayers that I said while I was in the Temple. When my father and mother left me in the Temple, I resolved in my heart to have God as my Father, and I frequently and devoutly pondered what I might do to please God so that He would deign to give me His grace. I studied the Law of God. And of all the precepts of the Divine Law I kept three with particular care in my heart, namely 'Thou shalt love the Lord thy God with thy whole heart and with thy whole strength. Thou shalt love thy neighbor as thyself.'

"I kept these precepts in my soul, and I quickly understood all the virtues which they contain. A soul cannot have any virtue if it does not love God with all its heart, for from this love the abundance of grace descends into the soul. But after descending, it does not remain, but flows away like water, if the soul does not hate its enemies, that is, its sins and vices.

"I always used to rise in the middle of the night, and, with as much longing and will and love as I could, I used to beg

Almighty God to give me the grace to observe those three precepts and all the other commandments of His Law. And I used to pray these seven petitions:

"1. I prayed for the grace to fulfill the precept of charity: to love God with all my heart.

"2. I prayed for the grace to love my neighbor according to His Will and pleasure, and that He should make me love all that He Himself loves.

"3. I prayed that He make me hate and flee all that He hates.

"4. I prayed for humility, patience, kindness, gentleness, and all virtues by which I might become pleasing in His sight.

"5. I prayed that He should let me see the time when that most holy virgin would be born who was to give birth to the Son of God, and that He preserve my eyes that I might see her, my ears that I might hear her, my tongue that I might praise her, my hands that I might work for her, my feet that I might walk as her servant, and my knees that I might adore the Son of God in her lap.

"6. I prayed for the grace of obeying the orders and rules of the High Priest of the Temple.

"7. I prayed that God should preserve the Temple and all His people for His service.

"I assure you that as I considered myself a most worthless creature and one unworthy of God's grace, therefore I begged Him to give me grace and virtues.

"The Lord did with me what a musician does with his harp. The musician sets and tunes all the strings so that they give forth a sweet and harmonious melody, and then he sings while playing on it. Thus God brought into harmony with His Will my soul and heart and mind and all the senses and actions of my body. And being trained in this manner by His wisdom, I used to be carried by the angels to the bosom of God the Father, and there I received such consolation and joy, such bliss and well-being, such love and sweetness, that I no longer remembered that I had ever been born in this world. Besides, I was in such close intimacy with God and His angels that it seemed to me as though I had always existed in that true glory. Then, when I had stayed there as long as pleased God the Father, He gave me

back to the angels, and they carried me back to the spot where I had begun to pray. When I found myself on earth again and recalled where I had been, this memory inflamed me with such a love of God that I embraced and kissed the ground and stones, the trees and other created things, out of love for Him who had created them. And it seemed to me that I should be the hand-maid of all the Temple-women, and I wished to be subjected to all creatures, out of love for their supreme Father. And I frequently had this experience.

"Once when I was thinking that I never wanted to be deprived of God's grace, I arose and went to read in the Scriptures, desiring something to console my soul. When I opened the book, the first thing I saw was this passage of Isaias: 'Behold a virgin shall conceive and bear a son.' As I understood from this that the Son of God was going to choose a virgin to be His Mother, I immediately resolved in my heart, out of reverence for that virgin, to remain a virgin myself and to offer myself to her as a handmaid and always to serve her and never to leave her, even if I had to travel all over the world with her.

"I did what a man does when he wants to build a beautiful fountain. He goes to the foot of a hill and carefully investigates where the springs of water are located, and having found their source, he digs with care until he finds them, and then he directs their flow to the spot where he wants to have the fountain. Next he makes the place neat and wide and clean, so that the water will stay clear. Then he puts up a wall around the fountain and erects a column in the middle and makes channels around it so that the water can flow out freely for everyone's convenience. That is what I did: I went to the hill when I applied myself to studying the Law; I found the spring when through prayer and study I realized that the principal source of all good is to love God with all one's heart; then I prepared and cleaned and enlarged the site when I conceived the desire of loving all that He loves. I also wanted the water to be pure and clear— that was when I resolved to flee and hate all stain of sin. Then I built the walls when I inseparably united the virtues of humility, patience, kindness and gentleness by the fire of charity, and kept them thus fused together until the end of my life. I erected

the column and made the channels when I offered myself as an example and helper for all mankind, for I am ever ready to give generous gifts of grace to all who invoke me for themselves or for others. God placed me on earth as a teacher and example for all the elect. And I want you to do as I did.

"My daughter, you think that I had all these graces without trouble, but it is not so. I assure you that I received from God no grace, no gift or virtue, without great labor, continual prayer, ardent desire, profound devotion, many tears and much affliction, and by always saying, thinking and doing what was pleasing to God, as far as I knew how and was able to do—except for the grace of sanctification by which I was sanctified in the womb of my mother.

"I assure you that no grace descends into the soul except through prayer and mortification of the body. And after we have given God all that we can give by our own efforts, however small they may be, He Himself comes into the soul, bearing with Him such exalted gifts that it seems to the soul as though she faints away and loses her memory and forgets that she has ever said or done anything pleasing to God, and then she seems to herself more vile and more despicable than she has ever been.

"And what must the soul do then? She must give fervent praises and thanks to God for these graces, and she must consider herself unworthy of the divine gifts, and she must weep. And then God, seeing the soul humiliate herself still more after receiving His gifts, is moved to give even greater gifts. . . .

"Thus did He do with me. For my mind yearned for the Son of God. My spirit burned with longing to have Him. My whole soul became inflamed with such sweet bliss that it seemed to me as though I already had Him, but as the human tongue does not have the power to express my inner fire of love—I prayed only to keep my external senses, in order to place them at the service of that virgin.

"My dearest daughter, I have revealed to you the prayers that I used to say, in order that by following my example you should confidently ask God in prayer for the graces and virtues which you do not have, and in order that you should humbly persist in asking for them. And I want you to pray with fervor and

devotion for your salvation and for that of others, because God wants those who have to help those who have not."

CHAPTER SIX

THE ESPOUSALS

WHEN MARY reached the age of thirteen and a half, having grown considerably for her age, Almighty God in a vision commanded her to enter the state of matrimony. Because of her intense love of chastity and her early vow of perpetual virginity, which she had often renewed, this divine order meant to her a sacrifice as painful as that of Abraham when God commanded him to offer up his son's life.

When Mary heard this unexpected decree, she was astonished and became greatly afflicted. Nevertheless she prudently suspended her own judgment and preserved her faith and hope more perfectly than Abraham. Still hoping against hope, she meekly replied:

"Eternal God, Thou, O Lord, canst dispose of me, Thy worthless little worm, according to Thy pleasure, without making me fail in what I have promised. And if it be not displeasing to Thee, my good Lord, I renew my desire to remain chaste during all my life."

Thus Mary in her great trial, though she felt some human uneasiness and sadness, obediently resigned herself entirely to the Will of God. And the Lord answered her:

"Mary, let not thy heart be disturbed, for thy resignation is acceptable to Me. And by My disposition, that will happen which is best for thee."

Then, as God intended, while left between uncertainty and hope, Mary gave herself over to fervent prayer and inner acts of love, faith, humility, obedience and chastity.

Meanwhile the Lord spoke in sleep to the High Priest, who happened to be St. Simeon, and commanded him to arrange the marriage of Mary, whom He regarded with special love, to whomever it seemed right to the council of priests. After consulting together, the priests appointed a day on which all the bachelors of the line of David, which was also Mary's, were to assemble in the Temple.

Nine days before that date, Simeon called in Mary and gently explained to her that as she was an orphan and a first-born daughter with an inheritance, now near the age when the young girls had to leave the service of the Temple and marry, the priests were planning to find her a worthy husband. Though deeply moved, Mary replied with great composure and modesty:

"As far as my inclinations are concerned, I desire to preserve chastity during all my life, and I never had the intention to enter the married state. But you, my master, will teach me God's holy Will."

During the nine days that followed, Mary continually prayed to God with many tears and sighs for that which she had so much at heart. And once the Lord appeared to her and said:

"My dove, let not thy heart be sad or disturbed. I will guide the priests by My light, and I will give thee a husband selected by Myself, and one who will not hinder thy holy desires. I will choose a man perfect and according to My heart."

This good man whom God found worthy of becoming Mary's husband and the foster father of the Word Incarnate, and who is now honored and loved throughout the world as St. Joseph, the Protector of the Universal Church, was at this time a humble, unmarried carpenter who worked for a master in a small town in Galilee.

Joseph was born near Bethlehem, the third of six brothers. His parents were well off and lived in a large two-storied country house which had a bubbling fountain in a court and was surrounded by lovely streams. The Saint's marvelous holiness began when he was sanctified in the womb of his mother seven months after his conception. At his birth he was a beautiful baby with a perfectly formed body, and he caused an extraordinary delight to his parents and relatives. From his third year, thanks to unusual graces, he began to know God by faith. With surprising understanding he eagerly learned all that was taught to him about religion and already practiced advanced forms of prayer. At the age of seven he had attained the perfect use of reason and a high degree of holiness. He was a quiet, likable and humble boy.

The parents, who were neither very good nor bad people, did not spend much time with their children, but left them to the care of an elderly tutor, who gave the boys lessons on a porch that went around the upper floor. Joseph's brothers used to tease him and make fun of him and often tried to hurt him. Each boy had a small garden, and his brothers sometimes stole into his and tore up the plants he liked best. When he was praying on the porch with his face to the wall and his eyes closed, they sneaked up behind him and pushed him over. At such moments he seemed to awaken from a trance, but he did not become angry or seek revenge. He merely withdrew somewhere and continued his prayers.

As the boys grew up, the parents complained that Joseph was too serious and solitary, too simple and lacking in ambition. They wanted him to take advantage of his good qualities and prepare himself for a prosperous career, but he had no desire for such a life. All he wanted was to pray and quietly to perform some manual labor. Often during his teens, to escape from the continuous persecution of his brothers, he went to the other side of Bethlehem among some good, devout families, and worked with an old carpenter or prayed in some grottoes, in one of which the Child Jesus was later born.

Finally, one night when he was about twenty, Joseph left home and went off to earn his living in the country north of Jerusalem. For some time he worked as assistant to a poor carpenter in a small town near Mount Gerizim. He was finishing his apprenticeship, and he humbly did all sorts of jobs for his master. Often he had to carry heavy loads of wood on his back.

When, after a long search, his brothers found him, they scolded him bitterly, for they were ashamed of his modest position. But he was too humble to change it. Later he moved to Taanach on the Plain of Esdraelon, and then to Tiberias, where he dwelt alone in a little house by the Lake of Galilee. Wherever he lived, he was always loved by those who knew him. He was a good, kind and devout workingman—lovable, gentle and utterly sincere. He spent much time in prayer, fervently asking God for the coming of the Messias. He led a very retiring life and consistently avoided the society of women. From the age of twelve he had made and perfectly kept a vow of chastity, and his purity of soul, which was known to all, was that of an angel.

One day, when Joseph was adding a little oratory to his house, an angel appeared to him and told him not to go on with the work, because just as formerly God had given to the Patriarch Joseph the superintendence of the grain in Egypt, so now the granary of salvation was going to be confided to him. St. Joseph in his humility was not able to understand this message. Soon afterward he heard that as an unmarried descendant of King David, he was to go to the Temple in Jerusalem with his best clothes. He was at this time thirty-three years old, a handsome, modest and serious man, with pleasing, honest features.

It was on Mary's fourteenth birthday that the young men gathered in the Temple, dressed in their feast-day robes. After the High Priest had presented Mary to them

and explained the purpose of the meeting, she returned
to her cell and wept, while he gave to each youth a dry
branch and announced that they were all to pray that the
Lord might single out the one whom He had chosen as
Mary's spouse. Knowing that she was an unusually beautiful and virtuous maiden with a good inheritance, they
were eager to win her hand.

One pious young man from Bethlehem was particularly
anxious to become her husband, hoping that perhaps the
expected Messias might be born of their union. Although
the humble carpenter Joseph had a deeper veneration for
her than any of the others, he alone considered himself
unworthy of such a blessing, and remembering his vow of
chastity, he inwardly renewed it and resigned himself
entirely to the Will of God.

After a number of prayers had been recited, each suitor
came forward and placed his branch on an altar facing
the Holy of Holies. When Joseph, the last in line, was
about to deposit his branch, all of a sudden it blossomed
into a white lily-like flower, and at the same time a dove
of the purest and most dazzling white was seen to descend
and rest on his head for a moment, during which God
said in his heart:

"Joseph, My servant, Mary shall be thy spouse. Receive
her with all care and respect, for she is pleasing in My
sight. She is just and pure in mind and body. And thou
shalt perform all that she shall ask."

Thereupon the priests announced that Joseph was the
husband selected for Mary by the Lord Himself, and they
sent for her, while the other suitors departed—the young
man from Bethlehem joined the hermits of Elias on Mount
Carmel and continued to pray fervently for the Messias.

When Mary appeared, calm and beautiful and humbly
resigned to God's Will, the priests introduced her to Joseph
and proceeded solemnly to betroth the holy couple. Then,
according to the Jewish custom, the two parted until the
wedding.

This touching ceremony took place later in a rented

house on Mount Sion. Besides Mary's teachers and friends from the Temple, the guests included some relatives of her parents, who had prepared for her a lovely sky-blue wedding gown and cape, though in her humility she hesitated to accept it. St. Joseph wore a plain, long, gray robe.

After the wedding, Mary sadly took leave of the priests and her teachers and companions, thanking them all for their kindness to her during her years among them. And then, offering up her own wish to remain in the Lord's House all her life, with keen grief she left the Temple, and in the company of St. Joseph and some attendants sent by the priests, she set out, with perfect resignation and trust in God, for the new life to which He was leading her in Nazareth.

CHAPTER SEVEN

PREPARATION FOR THE ANNUNCIATION

WHEN Mary and Joseph arrived at the modest house which she had inherited in Nazareth, they were joyfully welcomed by her friends and relatives.

Then they were left alone in their new home. And Joseph said:

"My dear spouse, though I judge myself unworthy even of your company, I give thanks to the Lord for having chosen me as your husband. Please help me to make a proper return in serving Him with upright heart. Therefore consider me your servant, and by the true love which I have for you, I beg you to put up with my deficiencies in the domestic duties which as a worthy husband I should know how to perform. Just tell me what you want, so that I may do it."

Mary replied humbly:

"My master, I am fortunate that the Lord has chosen you for my husband and that He has thus shown me that He wishes me to serve you. But if you allow me, I will tell you my thoughts and intentions which I wish you to know for this purpose."

As God inflamed Joseph's sincere heart with grace and love, he said:

"Speak, dear Lady. Your servant is listening."

Because this all-important interview was the first time that Mary had ever spoken alone to a man, and because with her natural shyness she also felt respect and reverence for her husband, she asked her guardian angels to stand around her, visible only to herself. As they obeyed, she spoke with a serene earnestness:

"My lord and spouse, our Creator has manifested His mercy to us in choosing us to serve Him together. I consider myself more indebted to Him than all other creatures, for while meriting less, I have received from His hand more than they. As a child, therefore, being compelled by the force of this truth, which His divine light made known to me, I consecrated myself to God by a solemn vow of perpetual chastity in body and soul. I am His, and I acknowledge Him as my Spouse and Lord, with the firm resolve of preserving my chastity for Him. So I beseech you, my master, to help me in fulfilling this vow, while in all other things I will be your servant, working willingly for your well-being all my life. My dear spouse, yield to this resolution and make a similar one, in order that, offering ourselves as a sacrifice to God, He may accept us and bestow on us the eternal reward for which we hope."

St. Joseph was overjoyed, and with true supernatural love he replied:

"My heart rejoices in hearing your welcome feelings in this matter. I have not told you my thoughts before knowing your own. But I also consider myself under greater obligation to the Lord than other men, for very early He called me by His enlightenment to love Him with an upright heart. And I want you to know that at the age of twelve I also made a promise to serve Him in perpetual chastity. So now I gladly ratify this vow, and in the presence of God I promise to help you as far as I can in serving Him and loving Him according to your desire. With His grace

I will be your faithful servant and companion, and I beg you to accept my chaste love and to consider me your brother."

Both Mary and Joseph were now filled with heavenly joy and consolation. And God gave to St. Joseph new purity and complete command over his natural inclinations, so that he might lovingly serve his holy wife without any trace of sensual desire.

The happy couple then set about dividing Mary's inheritance: they put aside one third for the Temple; they distributed one third to the poor; and the last third Mary assigned to Joseph to dispose of as he wished. For herself she reserved only the privilege of serving him and of attending to her household duties, for throughout her life she avoided contact with outsiders and the management of property or business.

Joseph now humbly asked her whether it was agreeable to her that he continue to work at his trade as carpenter for their support and to earn something to help the poor. Mary willingly approved, saying that she knew that the Lord did not wish them to be rich but poor and lovers of the poor, desirous of helping them as much as their means allowed.

Then they both courteously and selflessly disputed as to who should obey the other, but Mary won this holy contest in humility by declaring that since the man is the head of the family she would not permit this natural order to be changed, and that all she wanted was to obey Joseph in all things and to have his permission to help the poor, which he gladly gave.

During the days that followed, as St. Joseph observed Mary's rare nobility and purity of soul, his admiration and love for her greatly increased, and he often joyfully thanked the Lord for having given him a companion so far above his merits. God also filled his humble heart with an indescribable reverence for her by means of the heavenly light which shone from her calm, beautiful and majestic features.

At this time Mary had a vision of the Lord in which He said to her:

"My Chosen One, observe all the laws of a spouse in holiness, purity, and all perfection, and let My servant Joseph help thee. Obey him and listen to his advice."

Mary replied in humility and love:

"My Lord and Maker, show me Thy good will and blessing, and with it I will strive to obey and serve Thy servant Joseph."

After settling in her home, Mary was never idle. Apart from her housework, she diligently prepared wool and linen for her husband and for the poor, whom she always helped by the labor of her hands. For without making this personal contribution of her own exertion and labor, she could not have satisfied her compassionate and generous charity toward the poor. Also she had no servants, because her love of obedience and humility made it impossible for her to order anyone but herself to do the servile work of her household. In serving and caring for St. Joseph and later for her Son, she was never guilty of any negligence or forgetfulness. And yet in all her daily work she was never interiorly at leisure, for she spent every moment in profound inner recollection, prayer, and spiritual communion with God in her heart, worshiping and beseeching Him to send the promised Redeemer to suffering mankind.

The few persons who knew her during these hidden years in Nazareth were often filled with a mysterious joy which they knew came from her. Many turned from sin at the mere sight of her. Others amended their lives. All were affected by some divine influence. Realizing this, she prayed to God to permit her to be ignored and despised by all mortals, and by His power He prevented these persons from communicating their admiration and seeking her out.

Now the time which Almighty God had appointed for the Incarnation of His Son was drawing near, although the humble and lovely maiden in Nazareth who was destined to be His Mother never once thought that this great and widely expected event would directly involve her. Therefore, as a necessary and fitting preparation for the glorious Mystery of the Annunciation, during the nine days which immediately preceded that decisive turning point in history, the Lord gave His Chosen Spouse and future Mother a series of marvelous mystical experiences which raised her pure soul to a hitherto unparalleled degree of holiness and fervor, and which also infused into her mind a thorough and profound knowledge of His Creation.

On the first day of this first "novena," when Mary according to her custom rose at midnight and prostrated herself on the floor to praise the Lord, her soul was raised to a closer union with God. He revealed to her how He had created the universe purely out of overflowing Love, and He showed her all that He had made on the first day of creation. When she saw that she too was formed of low earthly matter, she humbled herself profoundly. The Lord urged her to pray constantly for the union of the Divinity with human nature, which He informed her was now due. Whereupon Mary exclaimed:

"O Eternal God, the sins of men are increasing—how shall we merit the blessing of which we become daily more unworthy? If perhaps I am a hindrance to such a limitless benefit, O my Beloved, let me perish rather than impede Thy Will!"

Then with the deepest humility she lay on the ground in the form of a cross, as the Holy Ghost had taught her, and prayed for the Redemption.

On each of the following six days she not only received an infused knowledge of the various works of God on the corresponding day of Creation, but she was also given comprehension and power over the elements of nature, such as the stars, winds, waters, minerals, plants and animals, although she never thereafter used this power for herself, because she was too humble and she knew the value of suffering. Then she was shown the creation and fall of man. And by her participation in God's love and mercy for sinning humanity, she was prepared to become the Mother of Mercy and Advocate of sinners. God revealed to her the new Law of Grace and the healing blessings which He was going to pour on men through the Sacraments of His holy Church, and He also showed her how many souls would ungratefully reject the salvation which the Redeemer was to offer them. After praying fervently for all men, she was given an explicit promise by the Holy Trinity that the Son of God was now to be sent into the world.

On the seventh day Mary heard God say to her:

"Our Chosen Dove, We wish to accept thee anew as Our Bride, and therefore We wish to adorn thee worthily."

As Mary abased herself with charming modesty, two seraphim proceeded to vest her with a beautiful white robe and bejeweled girdle, golden hair clasp, sandals, bracelets, rings, earrings and a necklace—all symbolizing the various virtues that adorned her lovely soul.

At midnight on the eighth day Mary heard in prayer the voice of God saying:

"Come, My Chosen One, come to Me. I am He that raises the humble and fills the poor with riches. Thou hast Me for thy Friend. Since thou has found grace in My eyes, ask of Me what thou desirest, and I shall not reject thy petition, even if it be for a part of My Kingdom."

To which Mary replied with touching humility and love:

"O Lord, I do not ask for a part of Thy Kingdom on my own behalf, but I ask for the whole of it for all the race of men who are my brothers. And therefore I beseech Thee to send us our Redeemer!"

And the Lord answered:

"I desire what thou seekest, My Daughter. It shall be done as thou askest."

All afire with love and gratitude, Mary passed that day in unceasing praise of God.

On the ninth day the Lord, after revealing to her the entire harmonious constitution of the universe, said to her:

"My chosen Dove, I have created all creatures, which

thou beholdest in all their variety and beauty, solely for the love of men, for the elect congregation of the faithful. Thou, My Spouse, hast found grace in My sight, and therefore I make thee Mistress of all these goods, so that if thou art a loyal spouse, thou mayest dispose of them as thou desirest."

Then a symbolic crown was placed on Mary's head which bore the mystic inscription: "Mother of God"; but she did not see these words. And all the heavenly spirits duly revered and honored her. Lastly the Lord renewed and increased the unique beauty of her pure soul, so that her entire being dazzlingly reflected His own divine light.

Yet Mary continued to humble and abase herself in her own estimation. Her eyes and heart were not elated. On the contrary, the higher God raised her, the more lowly were her thoughts concerning herself. She did not once have a suspicion of anything great or admirable in herself. And her humility was so genuine and so deep that even now the mere thought of her being chosen to be the Mother of the Messias simply could not enter her Immaculate Heart.

CHAPTER EIGHT

THE ANNUNCIATION

NOTE: In this as in other great mysteries of the Blessed Virgin's life which she herself described to the mystics, quotations from her own words are printed in *italics*.

MY LOVE for God *burned in my heart even more intensely than before and every day my soul was enkindled with new fervor and longing. So I withdrew from everything even more than formerly. . . .*

On the day before the occurrence of this mystery I thought I would die and my heart would burst with love and longing, if God's Providence had not comforted me. He filled my soul with the firm hope that the Saviour would descend from Heaven without delay. But on the other hand my humility made me fear lest my presence in the world might perhaps delay His coming

I was afraid that my lips might say or my ears might hear something against God, or my eyes see something evil. Even in my silence I was timid and very anxious that I might be silent when I should rather speak. When I was thus troubled in heart, I committed all my hopes to God. . . .

On the eve of the Annunciation, at the bidding of the

divine will the Archangel Gabriel presented himself before the throne of God, and the Blessed Trinity instructed him in the exact words with which he was to greet and speak to Mary. Then the Lord announced to the other angels in Heaven that at last the time for man's Redemption had come, and all the celestial spirits were filled with joy and thanksgiving, and they sang: "Holy, Holy, Holy, art Thou, Lord God. . . ."

Accompanied by thousands of resplendent angels, Gabriel descended from the highest Heaven, delighted to obey God's epochal command. His appearance was that of an exceedingly handsome young man with wavy blond hair, and his bright features radiated a divine light. His whole bearing was pleasing, yet also godlike and majestic. He wore a rich diadem on his head and a cross on his breast, and his vestments glowed in various striking colors.

Directing his flight toward Nazareth in Galilee, Gabriel arrived at Mary's modest little cottage as night was falling, when as usual she retired to pray in her small, bare room.

The Blessed Virgin was now fourteen and a half years old. While taller than other girls of her age, she was perfectly proportioned. Her beautiful face with its clear and somewhat brownish complexion was more oblong than round. Under her broad forehead, her dark eyes were large and serious and at the same time wondrously beautiful and gentle. Her straight nose, her small mouth with lips neither thin nor thick—all her features were so symmetrical and so ideally modeled that no other human being has ever had such perfection of form. Her clothes were very humble and poor in appearance, yet spotlessly clean and neat, of a dark silvery color somewhat like ashes, and she wore them without pretense, but with the greatest modesty.

Taking a low narrow table on which was a roll of scriptural writings, Mary placed it in the center of the room. Then she knelt on a little cushion and crossed her hands on her breast. And with growing fervor, her eyes lifted toward Heaven, she began to pray for the coming of the Saviour.

That night I prostrated myself devoutly in prayer, and with the most intense love I begged the Lord that He might deign to let me live long enough to see His Mother with my eyes, serve her with my hands, bow my head before her in reverence, and place myself completely at her service.

I began to meditate on the great power of God: how the angels and all creatures serve Him, and how indescribable and immense is His glory. And while I was marveling over this, all of a sudden I perceived three wonderful things:

I saw a star, but not like those that shine in the sky—I saw a light that was greater and brighter than the sun, yet unlike any light in this world.

And I inhaled a scent, but not one that comes from plants or anything of that kind—it was an utterly sweet and almost ineffable scent which completely filled my soul and made me thrill with joy.

Then I heard a voice, but not a human voice—and suddenly there appeared before me the Angel of God in the form of a most beautiful youth, yet not one of flesh and blood.

Recognizing him as an envoy of God, Mary with her usual humility wished to bow reverently before him. But Gabriel would not allow it. Instead he bowed profoundly before his Queen.

And he said to me:

"Hail, full of grace, the Lord is with thee. Blessed art thou among women!"

When I heard this greeting at first I was indeed very frightened, for I wondered whether it might be an illusion. I asked myself what it might mean and why he uttered such a greeting, because I knew and considered myself unworthy of it or of anything good, although I realized that nothing was impossible with Almighty God.

And now while Mary modestly kept her eyes lowered before the Archangel, the Lord began to make her understand interiorly that He had chosen her for His Mother.

From the midst of this light I heard a voice saying to me: "Thou art to give birth to My Son!" And it added: "Know in truth that I want others to have for thee the reverence which for

*love of Me thou didst want to have for someone else. I want thee
to be My Son's Mother and Giver, so that thou wilt not only
have Him, but thou wilt also be able to give Him to whomever
thou wishest. . . ."*

When I heard this I was so overcome with fear and wonder
that I could hardly hold myself up, and I was about to faint
when some angels came and raised me up and strengthened me.

Then Gabriel said:

"Do not be afraid, Mary, for thou hast found grace with God.
And behold thou shalt conceive in thy womb and shalt bring
forth a Son. And thou shalt call His name Jesus. He shall be
great, and shall be called the Son of the Most High. And the
Lord God will give Him the throne of David His father, and He
shall be king over the House of Jacob forever. And of His Kingdom there shall be no end."

As she slowly grasped the full significance of this tremendous grace, Mary raised her humble heart to God, and in
the secret of her soul she lovingly begged Him to give her
His help in such a crucial moment, for her intuition told
her that in order to test her faith and hope and charity
in this mystery, the Lord had purposely left her without
any other aid than the resources of her human nature.

*I still did not believe myself worthy. And so I did not ask the
Angel why or when, but I asked how it could happen that my
unworthy self should become the Mother of God:*

"How shall this happen, since I do not know man?"

And at the same time Mary interiorly mentioned to the
Lord her vow of perpetual chastity and the mystical
espousal that He had celebrated with her.

And Gabriel answered:

"The Holy Spirit shall come upon thee, and the power of the
Most High shall overshadow thee. And therefore the Holy One
to be born shall be called the Son of God.—And behold, Elizabeth thy kinswoman also has conceived a son in her old age,
and she who was barren is now in her sixth month . . . ." And
the Angel answered me as I had said to myself: ". . . For nothing shall be impossible with God."

After I heard these words, without doubting at all that what he said was true, I felt in my heart an exceedingly fervent desire to be the Mother of God. I prostrated myself on the ground, and on my knees, with my hands joined, I worshipped God, and my soul cried forth with love:

"Behold the handmaid of the Lord—Be it done to me according to thy word!"

Now a celestial light filled Mary's little room, dissolving the ceiling and revealing the Heavens. In a dazzling beam could be seen a brilliant figure of the Blessed Trinity. The Holy Spirit appeared in a winged form. Masses of flame shot out like wings on His right and left. Then three intense rays flashed and darted into the right side of the Virgin, and she became entirely suffused with a glowing light.

As soon as I had spoken those words, the grace of God overwhelmed me—never had I felt such bliss and joy in my soul! And then in that ecstasy God the Father gave me His Son, and my Son was instantly conceived in my womb by the Holy Spirit. He took flesh in my most pure body. And an inexpressible rapture filled my soul and my whole body. And I humbled myself in every way, for I knew that the One whom I bore in my womb was the Almighty.

In the same instant of this miraculous conception, Mary was rapt in a marvelous vision in which the Holy Trinity revealed to her the mystery of the hypostatic union of the Divine and human natures in the person of the Eternal Word, and confirmed her in the title and rights of Mother of God. She was also shown in this vision the future mysteries of the life and death of her Son, the Redeemer of mankind.

Lost in humility and burning love, Mary adored the Lord and gave Him her fervent thanks for having thus favored her and the whole human race. She offered herself as a willing sacrifice in the rearing and service of her Son throughout His life on earth. And for this purpose she prayed for new graces and light in order that she might be guided in all her actions as becomes the Mother of God. And the Lord answered her:

"My Dove, do not fear, for I will assist thee and guide

thee in all things necessary for the service of My only-begotten Son."

Meanwhile the Archangel Gabriel had departed; and just as the radiant channel of light above Mary's room vanished, a number of closed white roses, each having a small green leaf, dropped slowly down over the Holy Mother of God, who remained utterly oblivious to everything around her.

Thus toward dawn on a beautiful spring morning in the flower-covered hills of Galilee did Almighty God consecrate to Himself a pure and humble Jewish girl of Nazareth, making her and her modest home a new sanctuary and fulfilling in her the words of the Prophet-King: "The Most High hath sanctified His own tabernacle. God is in the midst thereof. . . ."

All the heavenly spirits witnessing this great mystery, in union with the happy young Mother of God, blessed and praised the Lord in the name of the whole human race, which was still ignorant of this greatest of all God's gifts. However at that magic hour the Lord infused into the hearts of some of the just men on earth a new feeling of extraordinary joy and inspiration, though each one thought that he alone experienced this inner renewal of spirit. And throughout the whole of nature there was a remarkable stir and movement on that blessed morning when Nature's God became man.

On coming back to herself in her room, Mary's first act was to kneel in humble and profound adoration of the Word Incarnate within her womb. Then after a long interval the Holy Mother of God arose and went to her little altar against the wall, where for some time she prayed standing. Only toward sunrise did she lie down on her bed to rest.

SPEAKING OF THE ANNUNCIATION, THE BLESSED VIRGIN SAID TO ST. ELIZABETH OF SCHOENAU:

"Do you know why God did this? Because I had believed in Him and because I had humbled myself."

CHAPTER NINE

THE VISITATION

O N THE DAY after the Annunciation Mary's many guardian angels appeared before her visibly, and with deep humility they adored their incarnate King in His Mother's womb, saying to her: "Now, O Lady, thou art the true Ark of the Testament. We wish to obey thee as servants of the supreme Lord whose Mother thou art." And indeed when Mary was alone, they helped her in her household work, and whenever she ate alone they served her the modest meals which she took at her poor table.

Now at times God sent a number of birds to visit His Mother. Greeting her with lively movements, as if wishing to congratulate her, they divided into harmonious choirs and chirped and sang sweetly for her. They also brought her flowers in their beaks and dropped them onto her hands and then waited until she asked them to sing. When she told them to praise and give thanks to their Creator with her, they all bowed low on the ground to worship the Lord and to honor His Mother. Sometimes in bad weather birds came to her for protection, and she gave them food and shelter.

Three days after the Annunciation the Lord revealed to Mary in a vision that the son whom her cousin Elizabeth had already conceived was destined to be a great prophet and forerunner of the Messias, and that it was God's Will that Mary should visit her in order that both mother and child might be sanctified by the presence of their Redeemer. Although going out in public and leaving her home for a trip of several days into the mountains of Judea meant a real sacrifice to Mary, she gladly thanked God for this opportunity to serve Him and then asked St. Joseph for his permission. He still knew nothing about the Annunciation, and now Mary told him only that the Lord had informed her that Elizabeth was with child, and that she felt obliged to visit her. Joseph willingly agreed to her plans, and having borrowed a lowly donkey and prepared some provisions consisting of a little fruit, bread, and a few fishes, they were ready to leave. But first Mary knelt at St. Joseph's feet and, despite his hesitation, insisted that he give her his blessing. Then, raising her eyes and her heart to the Lord, she arose and they set out, accompanied by her numerous invisible guardian angels.

Many times during this tiring four days' journey Mary dismounted and urged Joseph to ride, but he never accepted her offer, though now and then he did allow her to walk with him. Often she conversed spiritually with her angels about the divine mysteries, and at other times she spoke with Joseph about the coming of the Redeemer. To his profound wonderment and joy, her words filled him with an entirely new understanding and love for God, and she realized that the Word Incarnate was giving him unusual graces.

In the course of this trip Mary and Joseph had many opportunities to practice charity, for the Blessed Virgin could not remain idle at the sight of want. Some innkeepers received them kindly, while others were rude. Whenever she could, Mary visited the poor and the sick, consoling and sometimes curing them. One poor girl who was ill with a bad fever was suddenly healed in Mary's presence, and for the rest of her life she never forgot the beautiful young lady who helped her.

At last the holy couple reached the little village of Ain-Karem in the Judean hills five miles west of Jerusalem. As they approached the house of Zacharias, which was situated in the midst of a lovely garden on an isolated slope, St. Joseph hastened ahead in order to announce their visit, calling out to those within the house:

"The Lord be with you and fill your souls with divine grace!"

St. Elizabeth, who was tall and past middle age, with a small face and very sweet features, had been forewarned by the Lord Himself that Mary of Nazareth had set out to visit her, although the mystery of the Annunciation had not yet been revealed to her. Elizabeth immediately came out to welcome her cousin, who as the younger in years hastened to greet her, saying:

"The Lord be with you, my dearest cousin."

They met near a fountain and clasped hands affectionately. At this moment the Blessed Virgin became as it were suffused with a mystic light, and a bright ray went forth from her to Elizabeth and had an extraordinary effect on the latter, as she replied:

"The same Lord reward you for having come in order to give me this pleasure."

Holding hands they crossed the garden to the house, where St. Elizabeth again welcomed her cousin and invited her to enter. Once inside, they threw their arms around each other and remained for some time in a warm embrace. Then Mary said in a most friendly way: "May God save you, my dearest cousin, and may His Divine Light give you grace and life!"

At the sound of Mary's voice, Elizabeth was filled with the Holy Spirit, which revealed to her the Mystery of the Incarnation, the unique dignity of Mary, and her own son's sanctification. Rapt in joy she looked reverently at the Holy Mother of God—then, stepping back a little and lifting her hands, she exclaimed with an expression of deep humility, happiness and inspiration:

"Blessed art thou among women and blessed is the fruit of thy womb! And how have I deserved that the Mother of my Lord should come to me? For behold, the moment that the sound of thy greeting came to my ears, the babe in my womb leapt for joy! And blessed is she who has believed, because the things promised her by the Lord shall be accomplished."

Mary humbly referred these words of praise to the Creator.

I was similarly moved by an extraordinary joy in my heart, so that I spoke words about God that I myself did not devise, and my soul could hardly contain itself with joy.

Crossing her hands on her breast, Mary intoned in the sweetest and softest voice:

"My soul doth magnify the Lord.

"And my spirit hath rejoiced in God my Saviour.

"Because He hath regarded the humility of His handmaid: for behold from henceforth all generations shall call me blessed.

"Because He that is mighty hath done great things to me, and holy is His name.

"And His mercy is from generation unto generations to them that fear Him.

"He hath showed might in His arm: He hath scattered the proud in the conceit of their heart.

"He hath put down the mighty from their seat: and hath exalted the humble.

"He hath filled the hungry with good things: and the rich He hath sent empty away.

"He hath received Israel His servant: being mindful of His mercy.

"As He spoke to our fathers: to Abraham and to his seed for ever."

Thanks to a divine inspiration, St. Elizabeth was able to recite the *Magnificat* at the same time as Mary.

While Elizabeth marveled at the fervor of the Holy Spirit that

spoke through me, I likewise marveled at the grace of God in her,
and we praised God together.

Then St. Elizabeth offered herself and her whole family and all her house for the service of the Mother of God, asking Mary to take as a quiet retreat the room which she herself was accustomed to use for her prayers. The Blessed Virgin accepted with humble thanks, and used the room for meditation and sleeping; and no one ever entered it except the two cousins. Mary also offered to serve Elizabeth as a maid, for she said that this was the purpose of her visit.

When toward evening the two holy women came forth after a long friendly talk about the heavenly mysteries that were to be accomplished in them, as soon as the Blessed Virgin saw her cousin's husband Zacharias, a tall and handsome old priest, she asked him for his blessing, which he gave her without saying a word, for he had been stricken dumb six months earlier in the Temple when he had doubted the angel's prophecy that Elizabeth would bear a son.

Three days later St. Joseph returned to his work in Nazareth, as Mary planned to spend three months with her cousin. During this time, in addition to all her usual prayers, the Blessed Virgin busied herself by sewing and preparing swaddling clothes for her cousin's baby. And whenever she could, despite Elizabeth's protests, Mary swept the house and her own room, and washed the dishes with the servants. One of the latter was a very irritable and nervous woman who easily gave way to anger and even to cursing. But as a result of her growing love and reverence for Mary, she soon became kind, meek and self-controlled. And a vain, sensual neighbor who dropped in to see what she called "this guest who gives herself such holy airs," after staring at the Blessed Virgin with impertinent curiosity, went home and began to weep sincerely over her sins and evil intentions. Naturally the holy Mother of Mercy also prayed for all such persons whom she met, and thus usually obtained their conversion.

Every evening Mary and Elizabeth recited the *Magnificat* together, standing facing each other in Mary's room, with their arms crossed on their chests and their veils lowered over their faces. Sometimes they spent nearly all night praying together. Mary always arose at midnight for her prayers. A few times St. Elizabeth merited to see the Mother of God in ecstasy, raised above the ground and radiant with supernatural splendor and beauty.

Often during the intense heat of these early summer months, Mary went with Elizabeth and Zacharias into their lovely garden in the evenings, and they all took a light supper outdoors and then went for a walk by moonlight in the surrounding fields and hills before retiring for the night. But they always arose before sunrise.

During the third month of the visit, St. Elizabeth begged her young cousin, whom she loved deeply, to stay with her at least until the birth of Zacharias' son. "Let me see my child in your arms, dear Mary," she pleaded. "Do not deny this consolation to me nor this great happiness to my son." With her usual prudence, Mary agreed that they should both pray to know God's Will. And the Lord said to her:

"My Dove, assist My servant Elizabeth at her childbirth. And after her son shall be circumcised, return to thy home with Joseph. And continue to pray to Me for the salvation of souls."

A few days later, while Mary prayed fervently in her room for both mother and child, with only moderate pains St. Elizabeth gave birth to a fine baby son, who was destined to be the holy Forerunner of Christ. After he was wrapped in the swaddling clothes made by Mary's own hands, the Blessed Virgin came into her cousin's room and took the babe into her arms. The newborn child already had the use of reason by a special grace, and knowing that Mary bore in her womb the Word Incarnate, he gazed at her with great love and adored his Lord in her with intense humility and thanksgiving. Holding him in her arms, Mary offered him to the Eternal Father and prayed for him and for his future ministry. Then, while St. Elizabeth looked

on with keen joy, Mary lovingly caressed the saintly child—
but she did not kiss him, as she wished to keep her chaste
lips untouched for her own divine Son.

Naturally this extraordinary birth after so many years of
childlessness was generally considered almost a miracle,
and numerous friends and relatives came to congratulate
Zacharias and Elizabeth, whose joy and gratitude were touching. Then in a private talk Mary informed her cousin that
neither she nor her husband was destined by God to live
very long and that they should therefore be still more generous in their charity to the poor, for the Lord would take
care of their son. And she helped her good hosts prepare
and distribute numerous gifts to the poor.

Eight days after his birth, the baby boy was circumcised,
and during the discussion as to his name, his father
Zacharias wrote on a tablet: "His name is John." In that
very moment, at Mary's prayer, he recovered the use of
his voice and joyfully broke forth into the inspired canticle, the *Benedictus:*

"Blessed be the Lord, the God of Israel, because He has
visited and wrought the redemption of His people . . . that,
delivered from the hand of our enemies, we should serve
Him without fear, in holiness and justice before Him all
our days. And thou, child, shalt be called the prophet of
the Most High, for thou shalt go before the face of the
Lord to prepare His ways, to give to His people knowledge
of salvation through forgiveness of their sins, because of
the loving kindness of our God. . . ."

A few days later St. Joseph came to accompany Mary
back to Nazareth. Then the Blessed Virgin said a sad
farewell to her dear cousin and her husband. Kneeling
before Zacharias, she took his hand and begged him to
bless her and to forgive her for all her faults while in his
house. The old priest, who knew now that she was the
chosen Mother of the Messias, was deeply moved, and
giving her his blessing he said: "In thee let all nations
know their God, and through thee let the name of the
Lord of Jacob be glorified." Next Mary consoled St. Eliz-

abeth, who was heartbroken at seeing her leave, and taking the child John in her arms again, Mary gave him many mystic blessings and graces, while he whispered to her: "You are the Mother of God Himself—may your intercession never fail me!" And he kissed her hand three times. Then, after St. Joseph had also bid farewell to his good friends, Mary kneeled before him for his blessing, and they set out on their journey home.

During this four-day trip the Blessed Virgin mercifully healed a poor woman who was partly possessed by evil spirits, and she also converted to a better life an innkeeper who received her and Joseph kindly. Because she was now in her third month with child, she was more easily fatigued. And now she prayed more than ever that the Lord might assist St. Joseph with special graces and understanding when he became aware of her condition, as would inevitably happen soon. For she knew that she could not explain God's holy secret to him until the Lord Himself allowed her to do so.

CHAPTER TEN

TRIALS

WHEN the Blessed Virgin and St. Joseph returned to their home in Nazareth after their visit to St. Elizabeth, Mary proceeded to set her house in order and to clean it, with the help of her angels, while St. Joseph applied himself to his carpentry work.

Now Lucifer and his devils were sorely puzzled by Mary's exceptional holiness. However, they did not think that she was the Virgin chosen to be the Mother of the Messias, because besides having a husband she was also extremely poor and modest in her way of living. Nevertheless Satan was enraged against her, due to her sanctity, and he therefore decided to send seven legions of his devils to tempt her in each of the seven capital sins. But Mary was warned by the Lord, who said to her: "My spouse and My dove, I will be with thee in battle, since I am in thy virginal womb. I wish that thou confound these enemies before I appear in the world, and I trust this victory to thy fidelity and thy love."

Mary was deeply moved as she replied: "My Lord, I belong entirely to Thee. Thou hast condescended to be my Son. Do with Thy servant whatever shall be to Thy greater glory. For if Thou art in me, and I in Thee, who shall be powerful enough to resist Thy Will? Give me strength."

Then while Mary was praying alone, left only to her natural force, God allowed the first legion of devils to tempt her to pride. To make her stop praying, they tried to terrify her by howling and roaring at her. But Mary did not change her position or show any fear. She simply repeated the words of the Psalm: "Who is like unto God, who dwells on high and looks down upon the humble in Heaven and on earth?" Then the devils changed themselves into resplendent angels and tried to convince Mary that they came from God in order to congratulate and praise her, but they gave themselves away when they promised to select her as the Mother of God! The Blessed Virgin, prostrate on the floor, withdrew within herself and quietly yet firmly continued to pray and adore the Lord.

Next the second legion of demons tried to tempt her to avarice by offering her great wealth in gold and jewels, telling her that God wanted her to distribute it to the poor, since it was far better for a holy person like her to have all these riches than to leave them to be misused by wicked sinners. Mary did not argue with the devils. She merely prayed these words of the Psalmist: "I have acquired for my heritage and for my riches the keeping of Thy testimonies and Thy laws, my Lord."

When the third group of devils sought to tempt the Blessed Virgin to impurity, she renewed her vow of chastity with such fervor and merit that her enemies were driven from her presence like a cannonball from a cannon.

Then the fourth legion did all they could to provoke her to anger. They posed as some women whom Mary knew and shouted outrageous insults and threats at her and stole the things she needed most. But Mary saw through their tricks and utterly disregarded them. Then one of the devils took on the appearance of a woman of Nazareth and told an easily influenced neighbor that Mary had criticized and slandered her. The deceived woman, who often lost her temper, hastened to go and insult Mary to her face. The Blessed Virgin calmly allowed her to pour forth all her anger and then spoke to her in such a kind and humble way that soon the woman's heart softened and she apologized. Mary warned her against letting herself be stirred to anger by the devil, and after giving the poor woman some alms dismissed her in peace. Even the demons were astounded, for they had never seen anyone react that way.

The fifth legion had no success at all in tempting Mary to gluttony.

Then the spirits of envy gave her a long list of natural blessings and spiritual favors which God had bestowed on others but denied to her. They also induced several prosperous persons to describe to her the happiness of those who are rich and well off and fortunate in worldly things. But Mary simply told them that they should thank the Lord for all they had and use it well, while she judged herself quite unworthy of such favors.

Finally the last legion of devils tried to tempt her to idleness by making her feel tired and dejected, suggesting that she postpone certain prayers and good deeds on account of weariness, so that she might do them all the better after having rested. They also sent people to bother her and take up her time in order to prevent her from doing good. But Mary prudently detected these plots and did not allow the devil to keep her from her prayers and good works.

By now Lucifer was so enraged against Mary that he himself strove with all his might to hurt her and the Child in her womb, for he feared that anyone born of her would naturally be a great enemy of his. Therefore, assuming the form of a horrifying monster, he rushed at the Blessed Virgin. Howling and shooting forth fire and fumes from his mouth, he sought to terrify her. But though Mary saw and heard him, she remained as unmoved as if he were nothing but a gnat. Then, in order to poison her mind, the Father of Lies began to recite every falsehood and heresy known to history concerning God and His Truth. But Mary firmly proclaimed the various truths opposed to these errors and sang hymns of praise to the Lord. When she prayed to God to prevent the devils from spreading false teachings so freely throughout the world, the Lord did in fact set narrower limits to the demons' activities.

In one last attempt Lucifer stirred up a bitter quarrel over property among Mary's neighbors by taking on the appearance of a woman known to them and by convincing them that Mary was the true source of all their trouble. Consequently the entire group went to St. Joseph's home and harshly accused Mary of disturbing their peace. Instead of defending herself, Mary humbly and patiently begged her neighbors to forgive her if she had offended them, and then she pacified them by proving that none of them had really done anything against the others. Finally, after another useless attack by all the demons together, Mary was allowed to command the defeated devils to return to Hell. And as a reward the Lord Himself appeared to her with all her angels and honored her, while she joyfully and modestly praised the Author of all good.

Now that the Blessed Virgin was in her fifth month of pregnancy, one day when St. Joseph saw her coming out of her oratory, he could not help noticing the evident change in her condition, which she did not once try to conceal. But he was completely unable to explain what he saw so clearly. Naturally, because he loved his dear wife so tenderly, he felt a keen stab of grief in his heart. Yet, as he was a holy and just man, he withheld his judgment, though he began to worry over the matter more and more. He dreaded the terrible thought that he might be forced to give her over to the authorities to be stoned, according to the Law of Moses. But he did not dare to speak to her about this delicate subject, since she did not volunteer any information. And so he turned to the Lord in frequent and fervent prayers, saying: "Most High God, my grief is almost killing me! My reason proclaims her blameless, while my senses accuse her. What shall I do? Why does she conceal this matter from me? Yet I withhold my judgment. . . . Receive my tears as an acceptable sacrifice. I do not believe that Mary has offended Thee. Govern Thou my mind and my heart."

Meanwhile St. Joseph's suffering was known to Mary, and it filled her affectionate heart with intense compassion for him. But she felt obliged to keep God's great secret to herself until He gave her permission to reveal it to anyone. With deep wisdom and confidence, she resigned the whole matter into the hands of Divine Providence. And she sought to comfort her good husband in his trouble by serving him with still more devotion and thoughtfulness. She served him at table, offered him a chair, and often she knelt before him. All the time, with the Word Incarnate in her womb, she was growing in health, gracefulness and loveliness.

St. Joseph, on the contrary, was so troubled in mind and heart that he was wasting away from weakness and emaciation. Mary spoke to him anxiously about his health and urged him to take some rest and recreation. And in great sorrow she prayed fervently to the Lord to console her unhappy husband.

After bearing his tribulation patiently and nobly for two months, St. Joseph finally came to the sad conclusion that the best thing for him to do was to absent himself, and he decided to leave his home that same night at midnight. After packing some clothes in a bundle, he prayed to God: "O Lord, I find no other way to restore my peace. . . . I do not believe my wife an adulteress. So I will withdraw from her and pass my life in a desert. Do not forsake me, my Lord!" And prostrating himself on the ground he made a vow to go to the Temple in Jerusalem and offer up a sacrifice in order that God might help and protect Mary. Then he took a brief rest.

Meanwhile Mary, knowing what he was planning to do, also prayed to God: "I beseech Thee, Lord, not to permit him to carry out this decision and leave me!"

And the Lord answered her: "My dearest dove, I shall presently visit My servant Joseph with consolation. And after I shall have revealed to him by My angel the mystery which is now unknown to him, thou mayest tell him openly about all I have done with thee. I will fill him with My Spirit, and he will assist thee in all that will happen." This divine promise greatly relieved Mary.

Now the Lord mercifully sent the Archangel Gabriel to St. Joseph while he slept, and though Joseph did not see the angel, he distinctly heard the inner voice say to him: "Do not be afraid, Joseph, son of David, to take to thee Mary thy wife, for that which is begotten in her is of the Holy Spirit. And she shall bring forth a Son, and thou shalt call His name Jesus. For He shall save His people from their sins."

Understanding this great mystery for the first time, St. Joseph awoke with the overwhelming realization that his wife Mary was actually the Mother of the Messias. He was filled with joy and at the same time with sorrow for having doubted her. Prostrating himself on the floor, he humbly gave thanks to God for having revealed this Mystery to him. Then he began to blame himself for all that had happened, exclaiming: "O my heavenly wife, how could your unworthy slave have dared to doubt your faithfulness? How is it that I have not kissed the ground that your feet touched? Woe is me—all my thoughts were open to her sight . . . also that I intended to leave her! O my Lord and God, give me strength to ask her forgiveness, so that for her sake Thou mayest pardon my great fault!"

Then, shedding tears of repentance, St. Joseph unwrapped his bundle, went out of his room, and began to scrub the floors on which Mary walked, and to do other chores that he had formerly left to her, for he resolved henceforth to be her servant in all things.

Early that morning when he knew that Mary had finished her first prayers and meditation, he went to her room and threw himself on his knees before her with the deepest reverence saying: "My spouse, Mother of the Eter-

nal Word, I beseech you to pardon my audacity. I am certain that none of my thoughts are hidden to your heavenly insight. Great was my presumption in deciding to
leave you instead of serving you as the Mother of my Lord.
But you know that I did it all in ignorance. Now I consecrate my heart and my whole life to your service. I will
not rise from my knees until I have obtained your pardon and your blessing."

Raising him to his feet, Mary knelt before him and said
with tender joy and love: "My master and my husband, I
should ask you to forgive me for the sorrow and bitter-
ness which I have caused you. As much as I wanted to, I
could not on my own account give you any information
about the Holy Sacrament hidden within me by the power
of the Almighty. But I will always be your faithful servant.
The Lord has not made me His Mother in order that I
should be served in this life, but in order that I should
be the servant of all and your slave. That is my duty."

As St. Joseph raised her from her knees, the pure and
humble Mother of God was filled with the Holy Spirit. All
aflame and transfigured in a mystical ecstasy, she recited
the *Magnificat*. Seeing her surrounded by a bright radiance of heavenly light, St. Joseph with profound humility
and reverence bowed his head and adored his Lord in
her womb. And God looked down upon good St. Joseph
with kindly favor and accepted him as His foster father,
filling his pure heart with holy graces.

CHAPTER ELEVEN

MARY AND JOSEPH IN NAZARETH

AFTER LEARNING that Mary was the chosen Mother of God, St. Joseph was changed spiritually into a new man. He resolved henceforth to act toward her with much greater reverence. Whenever he passed her or spoke to her alone, he respectfully genuflected, and he would no longer let her serve him or clean the house or wash the dishes. As she protested, he did these chores during the time which she spent in contemplation. Therefore in her humility Mary appealed to the Lord, and St. Joseph's guardian angel was sent to tell him: "Exteriorly allow her to serve thee, and interiorly treat her with the highest reverence. Always worship in her the Lord of all creation. It is His Will and His Mother's to serve and not to be served, in order to teach the world the value of humility."

The modest home of the holy couple contained only three rooms: St. Joseph's bedroom, his workshop, and Mary's room. In the latter was a couch which Joseph had made. Now when he came to talk with her in her room, he often found her in ecstasy raised above the ground, or conversing with her angels, or prostrate on the floor in the form of a cross. At such times he heard heavenly melodies and noticed a marvelous fragrance, which filled him with deep spiritual joy.

Mary's outer garments were of a gray color. Underneath she wore a cotton tunic. Nothing that she wore ever became soiled or worn, and she always kept herself immaculately clean. She ate very sparingly and took no meat, though she prepared it for Joseph. She usually ate cooked vegetables and bread, fruit and fish.

St. Joseph and Mary now frequently read and discussed together the various prophecies in Holy Scripture concerning the Messias, especially all that related to His birth. But out of consideration for her husband, the Blessed Virgin did not dwell on the Redeemer's sufferings and death. Often during these conversations, St. Joseph would become so moved by Mary's inspiring words that with tears of joy in his eyes he would exclaim:

"Is it really possible that I shall see my God in your arms, and hear Him speak, and touch Him—that He will live with us—that we shall eat at the same table with Him and talk with Him? I do not deserve this good fortune, which no one can ever deserve! Oh, how I regret that I am so poor!"

Then Mary answered:

"My master and husband, the Lord is coming to redeem the world and to guide men on the path to life eternal, and this is to be done by means of humility and poverty. In humility and poverty He wishes to be born, to live, and to die, in order to break the chains of greed and pride in the hearts of men. That is why He chose our poor and humble home and did not want us to be rich in passing goods, which are but vanity and which darken the understanding."

When St. Joseph asked Mary to instruct him in the various virtues and in the love of God, she did so with touching humility and skill, often by putting questions to him which of themselves suggested the right answers. She also taught him how to make his daily labor more a practice of virtue than mere manual work.

Although both St. Joseph and Mary performed work for others, they never demanded any wages or set a price on their labor. As they worked not for gain but for charity or to supply a need, they left the payment to their employers and accepted it as a freely given alms rather than an earned reward. Joseph learned this perfect degree of sanctity in economic matters from Mary.

Several times during this period they found themselves so poor that they even lacked necessities, for they were extremely generous in their gifts to the needy and they never stocked up food or clothing for the future. In her faith and humility Mary blessed the Lord for this poverty, which was a source of profound spiritual consolation to her. But she asked God to supply Joseph's wants. And the Lord heard her prayers. Sometimes He moved their neighbors to bring them gifts or to pay off a debt. At other times St. Elizabeth sent them presents, which Mary always acknowledged by sending in return some work of her hands. On rare occasions she commanded her friends, the birds, to bring some fish or fruit or bread, and St. Joseph marveled when he saw the birds come down and place this food in her hands.

One day it happened that they had nothing at all to eat at mealtime. So Mary and Joseph each retired to their room and persevered in prayer, thanking the Lord for this privation and begging Him for help. Meanwhile angels prepared the table and set on it fresh white bread and fish and fruit and a wonderfully sweet and nourishing jelly. When they called the holy couple in to this truly Heaven-sent meal, the Blessed Virgin and her husband wept tears of humble gratitude while they sang hymns of praise and thanks to God.

As Mary's pregnancy was now far advanced, one day she said to St. Joseph:

"My master, it is time that we prepare the things necessary for the birth of my holy Son. If you give me your permission, I will make the various clothes ready. I have already woven a piece of linen for His first swaddling clothes. Now please try to find some woolen cloth of soft texture and plain color for the other coverings. Later on I will weave a seamless tunic for Him. But let us pray to the Lord together for guidance in treating Him worthily."

Then as they knelt in prayer, each heard a Voice saying:

"I have come from Heaven to earth in order to exalt humility and discredit pride, to honor poverty and scorn riches, to destroy vanity and establish truth, and to enhance the value of labor. Therefore it is My Will that exteriorly you treat Me according to the humble position which I have assumed, as if I were your natural child, and that interiorly you love and revere Me as the Man-God, Son of My Eternal Father."

Soon in exchange for his work Joseph obtained two pieces of woolen cloth of the best quality available, one white and the other gray. Of these Mary made the first little robes for her Son. From the linen which she had already woven as a present for the Temple, beginning the first day in her home in Nazareth, she made the swaddling clothes. While doing this work for the Child in her womb, she remained on her knees all the time and often shed tears of devotion and love. From some flowers and herbs which St. Joseph gathered, she extracted fragrant essences and sprinkled them over the clothes. Then she folded them neatly and laid them away in a chest, saying to herself:

"My sweetest Love, when shall my eyes enjoy the light of Your divine face? When shall I as Your mother receive my Beloved's tender kiss? But how shall a poor insignificant worm like myself ever be able to treat You worthily? Look graciously upon me and let me take part in all the labors of Your life, since You are my Son and my Lord."

And then one day St. Joseph, while away from home on an errand, heard that a recently proclaimed Roman edict ordered all heads of families in Palestine to be registered on the tax lists in their native cities. When he sadly told Mary this disturbing news, she answered reassuringly:

"Do not let this edict cause you any concern, for all that

happens to us is ordained by the Lord, and in all events
His providence will assist and direct us."

"Nevertheless," said St. Joseph anxiously, "please pray
that I may not have to be separated from you, for my
heart would not have a moment's peace away from you,
and I dare not leave you alone without help. But your
delivery is too near for me to ask you to go with me to
Bethlehem, for I fear to place you in any risk, because of
your condition and my poverty—I would be heartbroken
if the Nativity should occur on the way amid inconve-
niences that I could not alleviate. . . ."

Mary obediently presented St. Joseph's petitions to God,
although she already knew that her divine Son was to be
born in Bethlehem. And she received the following answer
to her prayer:

"My dearest dove, accompany My servant Joseph on the
journey. I shall be with you and I shall assist you with
paternal love in the tribulations you will suffer for My
sake. Although they will be very great, do not fear."

Her heart being thus prepared for what lay ahead, Mary
calmly told St. Joseph that she was going to travel with
him. He was filled with joyful consolation, and thanking
the Lord, he said to her:

"My Lady, now my only source of grief will be the hardships you will have to undergo. But in Bethlehem we shall
find friends and relatives, and there you will be able to
rest from the journey."

Mary said nothing about the trying circumstances which
she knew the Lord had decreed for His birth, though she
fully realized that they would be far different from what
Joseph expected. She always kept to herself all the secrets
of God which she was not told to reveal. Instead she now
said to her good husband, quietly and humbly:

"My master, I will accompany you with great joy. And
we will make this journey as poor people, in the name of
the Lord, for He will not despise poverty, which He has
come to seek with so much love. Relying on His help, we
will go with confidence to Bethlehem."

CHAPTER TWELVE

THE JOURNEY TO BETHLEHEM

AT SIX O'CLOCK on a cold, wet, mid-winter morning, the Blessed Virgin and St. Joseph set out from Nazareth on their journey to Bethlehem. Mary was mounted sidesaddle on an unpretentious little donkey, and St. Joseph guided the animal with his right hand, holding his staff with his left. Two bags hanging on the beast's right side contained their provisions: some bread, fruit and fish, and the linens which Mary had lovingly prepared for her baby. Ten thousand angels marched along with them in dazzling forms visible only to their Queen. She and St. Joseph alternated with this heavenly choir in singing canticles and hymns of praise to God.

The first evening they found themselves in a windy, uninhabited valley. After a long day on the rough road, the Blessed Virgin, who was suffering keenly from the cold, told St. Joseph that they would have to stop there for the night. So he pitched their little tent under a great old turpentine tree near a fountain. God miraculously warmed Mary, and she placed her hands in her husband's to share the warmth with him.

Then they took some supper. Poor St. Joseph was very kind to Mary, and suffered much to see her in pain. He tried to cheer her by describing enthusiastically the excellent lodging they were sure to have in Bethlehem.

The next morning at half past five they went on. By noon the donkey became tired, so Mary dismounted and continued on foot. Soon they arrived at a farm and rested a while.

After another hour's climb through the hills, they came to a fine-looking inn comprising several buildings with gardens. Here they were received by the owner's wife, and remained all the next day, as it was the Sabbath. Some women with their children came to visit Mary and were deeply impressed by her wisdom and reserve. They were also very touched when they watched her instruct their children in religion. She explained it to the little ones so lovingly that they could not take their eyes away from her face. St. Joseph spent the afternoon walking through the gardens with his host, whom he greatly edified by his simple piety.

The following day they traveled over twelve miles and spent the night with some hospitable shepherds. On this trip they avoided the great, crowded, caravan roads as much as possible, and also they detoured around the city of Jerusalem to the east, though this took them much longer.

The next night, in a cold rain, they came to an isolated house. St. Joseph knocked on the door and asked for shelter. Without opening, the heartless man within shouted that he was not running an inn and they should leave him alone! They went on until they found a shed, where Joseph prepared a resting place for Mary. Then he fed the donkey, and after a light supper and prayers they took a few hours' sleep.

The last night they spent in a large farmhouse, though the owner's wife, who was young and conceited, treated them coldly because she was jealous of Mary's beauty (thirty years later Our Lord found her all bent over and blind, and after reproaching her for her vanity and heartlessness He healed her). Here St. Joseph was warned that Bethlehem was very crowded, but he replied that he had friends there and was quite sure of being well received.

Toward the end of the trip they made many stops, as Mary found traveling more and more trying. Nevertheless, knowing the secrets of the souls she met, she prayed for them and assisted the sick and afflicted by asking her holy Son to come to their aid.

They arrived at Bethlehem about four in the afternoon and made their way through the crowds to a large building where public officials were taking the census and levying taxes. Mary rested in the court, and several women generously gave her something to eat. St. Joseph went into a big room, where he was asked his name and occupation. He replied that he owned no property, but lived from his manual labor.

Later, as the sun was sinking, they began to look for a lodging. While Mary waited at the end of a street, Joseph went down it from house to house, knocking at the doors of his relatives and acquaintances, but he was admitted nowhere and in many places he met with harsh refusals and insults. Each time he came back to Mary, he was more and more upset. She knew that the hearts and houses of men were to be closed to them. And although to expose her condition at her young age to the public gaze was more painful to her modesty than their failure to find a lodging, still she meekly followed her husband through the crowds.

At one end of the village they found a big tree, and under the shelter of its spreading branches Mary waited and rested for a long time, first standing and then sitting with her legs crossed under her. Many people passed by and stared at her as she sat there so patiently and humbly in her long, white dress and veil, with her hands folded on her breast and her head lowered.

Finally, about nine o'clock, St. Joseph came back, utterly overcome, crying and trembling with heartbreaking sorrow. Mary consoled him tenderly. Then he told her of a shepherds' shelter outside the town. And she said:

"That will be perfectly satisfactory to me. Let us lovingly embrace poverty, dear Joseph, and go gladly wherever the Lord guides us."

Upon entering the bare grotto which the shepherds used as a stable, they both knelt and thanked the Lord, and Mary was filled with joy at being at last in this holy place. She immediately set about cleaning the cave with her own hands, out of humility and reverence. St. Joseph hastened to do likewise, and the angels helped them. Next he started a fire, as it was very cold, and they ate a frugal supper, their souls overflowing with happiness at the thought of the impending Incarnation.

CHAPTER THIRTEEN

THE NATIVITY

AFTER RECITING some prayers together with Mary, St. Joseph filled the manger with straw and moss and placed a cloth over it. Then he withdrew to the entrance of the cave. Looking back, he saw the holy Mother of God praying on her knees, surrounded by flames of dazzling supernatural light. Filled with reverent fear, he threw himself down on the ground and was soon rapt in an ecstatic sleep.

Mary was kneeling, with her eyes raised to Heaven and her hands joined on her breast. Her countenance emitted rays of light, like the sun incarnadined, and shone in indescribable earnestness and majesty, all inflamed with burning love of God. Her body became so spiritualized with the beauty of Heaven that she seemed no more a human and earthly creature.

Toward midnight a channel of brilliant light came down from the highest Heaven and terminated in sparkling fire at the Blessed Virgin. In it was an extraordinary movement of celestial glories which took on the forms of choirs of angels.

Then, in the twinkling of an eye, the infant God was born, glorious and transfigured as on Mount Thabor.

There the God-Man lay, naked, utterly clean and pure. And from Him radiated such marvelous light and splendor that the sun could not be compared to it. The angels could be heard gently singing canticles of wonderful sweetness.

When the holy Mother of God perceived that she had been delivered—for her child came forth without any pain or injury to her—she immediately bowed her head, placed a cloth over His tiny body, and adored Him with the greatest respect and reverence, saying:

"Welcome, my God, and my Lord, and my Son!"

Then the divine Child suspended the effects of His transfiguration and assumed the appearance of one capable of suffering. The Babe now moved, shivered with cold, and stretching forth His little arms, cried out.

Bending down, Mary tenderly clasped Him to her heart and with great joy warmed Him against her cheek and breast, while thousands of angels knelt and adored their incarnate Creator.

Nearly an hour after the birth, Mary called St. Joseph. Awakening and coming near, he perceived his Saviour in her arms and at once prostrated himself on the ground with the deepest devotion and humility. Only at her bidding did he rise. And with touching joy and gratitude he kissed the Babe's feet, and held the little Jesus in his arms, pressing Him to his heart, while tears of happiness moistened his cheeks.

Then, sitting on the ground, Mary laid her Son in her lap, and while St. Joseph handed her the linens, she began carefully and lovingly to wrap the divine Child in swaddling clothes, drawing them tight on His small body.

Next she and Joseph gently placed the Infant in the manger.

At this point an ox from the neighboring fields entered the cave with the ass. They both approached the crib, knelt down before it, and breathed over it, as if to warm the Baby.

Mary and Joseph were so affected by this act that they

could not restrain their tears.

For a long time they remained on their knees beside the crib, adoring the Christ Child and praising and thanking God. Later St. Joseph took some blankets and made a resting place for Mary beside the manger.

CHAPTER FOURTEEN

THE ADORATION OF
THE SHEPHERDS

AT THE holy hour of the Nativity of the Saviour, an extraordinary wave of rejoicing was manifest in Nature in many parts of the world. Many animals leaped with exultation. Flowers raised their faded stems. Plants and trees took on new life and gave forth sweet scents. A number of new springs flowed abundantly.

The thrilling and consoling news of the birth of the Messias was immediately announced by the holy angels to a small number of chosen souls. The Archangel Michael brought it to the patriarchs and prophets in Limbo, as well as to St. Ann and St. Joachim, and they all rejoiced together. Another angel informed St. Elizabeth and her baby St. John, who clearly expressed his joy by waving his little arms. His mother at once sent one of her servants to Bethlehem with some money and linen for Mary. The mystery of the Saviour's birth was revealed to the holy old priest Simeon and to Anna, Mary's former teacher, in the Temple in Jerusalem. In the Orient each of the three Magi was enlightened by angels concerning the Incarnation of the Redeemer of mankind, which they had long expected, and perceiving the mystic star, they set out on their pilgrimage to the Crib of the newborn King of kings. All good men everywhere felt a new supernatural joy at this time, and many of them believed that the Saviour had at last come into the world.

But of all the human race those who merited to be the first to see the Christ Child were the poor, humble, and devout shepherds of Bethlehem. During this holy night, three of their leaders, while watching over their flocks in the fields about a mile from the grotto of the Nativity, noticed with amazement a strange, luminous cloud hovering above the hill in which the cave and manger were located. And as they were staring up at the sky, all of a sudden a bright light came down toward them, bathing them in its celestial radiance. Then within the light they perceived the splendid Archangel Gabriel in human form, and at first these simple men were filled with intense fear, until Gabriel said to them reassuringly:

"Do not be afraid, for behold, I bring you good news of great joy for all the people. For there has been born to you today in the town of David a Saviour, who is Christ the Lord. And this shall be a sign to you: you will find an infant wrapped in swaddling clothes and lying in a manger."

While he was speaking, the radiance around him became still brighter, revealing seven other great angels of extraordinary beauty and then a whole multitude of the heavenly host, all praising God and chanting in sweet harmony, to a soft and joyful melody:

"Glory to God in the Highest, and on Earth Peace to Men of Good Will!"

After singing this lovely canticle, the angels went to two other groups of shepherds at some distance and brought them the same wonderful news. And these good men said to one another eagerly:

"Let us go over to Bethlehem and see this thing that has come to pass, which the Lord has made known to us!"

But first they thoughtfully set about collecting suitable presents.

Only toward dawn did they find the grotto-stable and knock timidly at its entrance. St. Joseph very obligingly opened the door and welcomed them. They told him what the angels had announced to them during the night, and they said that they had come to offer their gifts and veneration to the divine Child. At the same time they gave St. Joseph a number of young goats and chickens, which he accepted with humble gratitude and placed in a side-room off the stable.

Then he led the shepherds into the grotto, where the Blessed Mother of God was sitting on the ground beside the crib in which the beautiful Babe of Bethlehem was lying. And as they gazed down at the tiny Jesus, He looked up at them, and from His radiant little face and eyes a mystical current of divine love streamed forth and touched the sincere hearts of those poor but fortunate men, changing and renewing them spiritually and filling them with a new grace and understanding of the mystery of the Incarnation and of the Redemption. "And when they had seen, they understood what had been told them concerning this Child." Still holding their shepherd's staffs in their hands, they very humbly knelt down before the Infant Jesus and prostrated themselves on the ground, weeping tears of joy as they adored their God. For a long time they were so deeply moved with supernatural happiness that they could not say a word. Finally they began to sing together the words and melody which the angel had taught them.

Meanwhile the lovely Mother of God modestly observed all that they did and felt, for she also saw into their inmost hearts. And when they had finished singing their beautiful hymn, she spoke to them, urging them to persevere in the love and service of the Lord. They stayed in the cave from dawn until noon, when Mary graciously gave them something to eat. As they were about to leave, she allowed each of them in turn to hold the divine Babe for a moment, and each one, as he reverently gave the Child back to her, wept tears of sweet joy and gratitude. Then

they left, filled with heavenly consolation and understanding, "glorifying and praising God for all that they
had heard and seen, even as it was spoken to them."

"But Mary kept in mind all these words, pondering them
in her heart."

"And all who heard marveled at the things told them
by the shepherds." The following day the latter returned
with their wives and children, bringing gifts of eggs and
honey and cloth. The men helped St. Joseph to make
the grotto somewhat more habitable, and some devout
women who had known him as a boy in Bethlehem
brought firewood and did some cooking and washing for
the Holy Family.

Once during these happy days after the Nativity, while
Mary and Joseph were alone, absorbed in contemplating
the Christ Child, their donkey came into the stable and
suddenly knelt down on its forelegs and bowed its head
to the ground before the Babe in the crib.

Most of the time the loving Mother of God held her
divine Son in her arms. Whenever she took Him up, she
first made three genuflections and humbly kissed the
ground before kneeling at the crib and touching the tiny
Jesus. And when she thought that she should nurse Him,
she first asked His permission. All her angels remained
present and visible to her until the Flight into Egypt, and
on rare occasions she gave her Baby into the hands of the
Archangels Gabriel and Michael. She would not sleep
except when the Lord Himself commanded her to do so.
With her angels and with St. Joseph, she often composed
and sang beautiful hymns in honor of the holy Child. And
she often gave her good husband the intense pleasure of
hearing her refer to Jesus as "our Son."

Many times in caressing her beloved Son, she humbly
kissed His feet, and she always asked His consent before
kissing His sacred face. And often He returned her affection by putting His little arms around her neck.

At such times Mary said to Him:

"O my Love, sweet Life of my soul, who art Thou, and

who am I? What return shall I make for the great things
which Thou hast done to me?"

SPEAKING OF THE NATIVITY, THE MOTHER OF GOD SAID TO ST. BRIDGET OF SWEDEN:

*"And when I gave birth to Him, I brought Him forth with-
out pain, just as I had also conceived Him with such great joy
of soul and body that in my rapture my feet did not feel the
ground on which they were standing. And as He had filled my
soul with happiness on entering my body, so did He again come
forth in such a way that my whole body and soul exulted with
indescribable joy and in such a way that my virginity was not
impaired.*

*"How overwhelmed I was when I perceived and gazed at His
beauty, and when I realized that I was not worthy of such a
Son. And then, too, when I looked at the places where the nails
would be driven into His hands and feet, how my eyes filled with
tears and how my heart was torn with grief! And when my Son
saw the tears in my eyes, He was sad unto death.*

*"But then, when I contemplated the power of His Divinity, I
regained confidence, for I knew that it was His Will and that it
would be for the good, and I made my whole will conform to His.*

"Thus my happiness was ever mixed with sorrow."

—AND TO VENERABLE MOTHER MARY OF AGREDA:

*"Who would be so hardened as not to be moved to tenderness
at the sight of their God become man, humiliated in poverty,
despised, unknown, entering the world in a cave, lying on a
manger surrounded by brute animals, protected only by a poverty-
stricken Mother, and cast off by the foolish arrogance of the world?
Who will dare to love the vanity and pride which was openly
scorned and condemned by the Creator of Heaven and earth in
His actions? No one should despise the humility, poverty and
indigence which the Lord loved and chose for Himself as the very*

means of teaching the Way of Eternal Life. Few there are who stop to consider this truth and this example, and as a result of this rank ingratitude only the few reap the fruit of these great mysteries."

CHAPTER FIFTEEN

THE CIRCUMCISION

DURING the first days after the Nativity, whenever Mary thought of the painful ceremonial operation known as Circumcision, which the Law of Israel prescribed for every male child on the eighth day after birth, she suffered intensely. Although she had received no intimation of God's Will, in her humility and prudence she refrained from asking either the Lord or her angels whether her divine Son had to submit to this purifying rite. When she spoke of it to St. Joseph, they both wept tears of compassion.

Then one day while Mary was kneeling in prayer, the Lord said to her:

"My Daughter, do not let your heart be afflicted because your Son is to be subjected to the pains of circumcision. I have sent Him into the world as an example. Therefore resign yourself to the shedding of His Blood."

Whereupon the Blessed Virgin prayed:

"Supreme Lord and God, I offer to Thee this most meek Lamb. But if His pains may be mitigated at the expense of my suffering, Thou hast power to effect this exchange. . . ."

Rising from prayer, she told St. Joseph that since the time for the Circumcision was near and they had not received any orders to the contrary, it seemed necessary that they should comply with the Law. She also informed him that the rite was to be performed in the usual way, except that she herself would hold the Child. Then with reference to the name to be given to the Infant Saviour during the ceremony, St. Joseph said:

"The holy angel told me that your sacred Son should be called Jesus."

And Mary answered:

"The same name was revealed to me when He assumed flesh in my womb, and we will propose this name to the priest."

While they were conversing thus, innumerable strikingly beautiful angels in human form, clothed in shining white garments, descended from on high, each holding on his breast a shield on which was engraved the word Jesus. Their two leaders, the holy Archangels Michael and Gabriel, said to Mary:

"This is the Name of your Son, which the Blessed Trinity has given Him as the sign of salvation for the whole human race. But now He is to shed His Blood in receiving it, since it is that of the Saviour. This will be the beginning of His sufferings in obedience to His Father's Will. We have come to accompany Him and to minister to Him until He ascends into Heaven."

St. Joseph also witnessed this marvelous sight, and both he and Mary were filled with supernatural joy and admiration.

On the eighth day therefore, after having duly prepared everything in the stable, St. Joseph went to Bethlehem and returned with a dignified, elderly priest and his two assistants. At first, the priest was somewhat astonished and shocked at the primitiveness and poverty of the Holy Family's home. But the young Mother of God welcomed him with such modesty and grace that he was soon moved to deep respect and devotion toward such a saintly person.

And when he saw the divine Child in her arms, his soul was filled with tender mystic reverence for the adorable Babe of Bethlehem.

The ceremony was to take place at the entrance to the grotto, not far from the crib. St. Joseph lighted two candles, and the priests began to recite some prayers. When the old priest asked Mary to give her Son to the two assistants and to withdraw a bit so that she should not have to witness the painful sacrifice, the Mother of God hesitated, torn between her spirit of humble obedience on the one hand and her love and reverence for Jesus on the other. Finally she meekly requested to be allowed to stay and to hold her Son in her arms, as she did not wish to leave Him at such a moment. She asked only that the operation be performed as delicately as possible on account of the Child's unusual sensitiveness.

The priest consented, and Mary then unwound her Baby's swaddling clothes and drew from her bosom a linen towel which she had placed there in order to warm it, as the weather was very cold that day. After sitting down and spreading out this towel on her lap, she placed her Child on it, and the priest then proceeded to perform the ceremony of Circumcision with a small flint knife, while St. Joseph recited the ritual prayer:

"Blessed be Jehovah the Saviour. He hath sanctified His well-beloved from the womb of His Mother and hath written the Law in our flesh. He hath signed His Son with the sign of His Covenant, that He may impart to Him the blessings of Abraham our father."

To which the assistants responded:

"Blessed be He whom Thou hast chosen for Thy child!"

Now, with infinite love, the divine Son of God offered up to His Father in Heaven the sacrifice of this first shedding of His Precious Blood as a pledge that He would one day give it all for the Redemption of mankind. True to His human nature, the tiny Babe of Bethlehem cried as other children do, though His tears were caused more by supernatural sorrow over the hardheartedness of men than by His physical pain, which was intense.

As usual His holy Mother perceived and felt all that He was doing and suffering, and she too wept. When the rite was over, in mutual love and compassion the Child clung to His Mother while she tenderly caressed and comforted Him as she wrapped Him again in His swaddling clothes.

After some more prayers, the priest asked the parents what name they wished to give the Child. Both Mary and Joseph now said at the same time:

"Jesus is His name!"

Then, while the old priest recited a prayer, a luminous angel appeared before him and showed him the name Jesus written on a piece of wood. Profoundly moved and shedding tears of supernatural joy, the priest inscribed the Holy Name on a parchment register. And under the inspiration of divine grace, he exclaimed:

"I am convinced that this Child is to be a Prophet of the Lord! Take great care in raising Him, and let me know how I can relieve your needs."

The ceremony being completed, Joseph and Mary gratefully offered a light meal to the priests and two shepherds who had also been present. And when the visitors left, Mary gave the old priest some candles as a gift. The three priests were good and devout men, and they later attained salvation.

When the Holy Family was alone again, as the Infant Jesus was crying from pain, Mary withdrew to the end of the grotto with Him, and, sitting down, she lowered her veil and soothed Him by nursing Him, weeping quietly as she did so.

During the day some poor persons came to the stable and St. Joseph generously gave them alms. But among them were some wandering beggars who insulted and cursed him because they were not satisfied with his presents.

That night Jesus' pain was so severe that He could not rest, and He often cried. So Mary and Joseph took turns walking up and down the grotto with Him. In moments when they were not grieving over His suffering, they sang canticles of praise and joy in honor of the Holy Name of Jesus.

A few days later St. Elizabeth came with an old servant to pay the Holy Family a visit. Mary was overjoyed when she affectionately embraced her cousin, whom St. Joseph respectfully welcomed. Elizabeth wept as she reverently and lovingly clasped the Infant Jesus to her breast.

Mary and Elizabeth now had several long, intimate talks together, sitting side by side next to the crib. The Blessed Virgin told her cousin all that she and St. Joseph had experienced, and when she described the trouble they had had in finding a lodging, St. Elizabeth wept a great deal. And after the Mother of God had told her about the miraculous birth of her Son, Elizabeth said to her:

"The birth of my John was indeed quite painless, but it certainly was very different."

After St. Elizabeth left, various visitors came to see the Infant Jesus, bringing gifts. But Mary asked a woman who helped her to distribute most of these presents among the poor families in Bethlehem.

CHAPTER SIXTEEN

THE ADORATION OF THE MAGI

THE MOTHER of God knew by supernatural enlightenment that on the night of the Nativity an angel
had been sent to announce the birth of the Saviour of
mankind to the three Magi Kings of the East, and she also
knew that they would soon come to adore the Infant Jesus
in the stable, for which she had a real affection. Yet when
St. Joseph suggested that they move to a more comfortable dwelling in Bethlehem, Mary simply answered, without revealing the mystery:

"My husband and master, wherever you wish to go, I
will follow with great pleasure."

Just then the holy Archangels Michael and Gabriel
appeared to them both and said:

"Divine Providence has ordained that three kings of this
world shall come from the East in search of the King of
Heaven, and shall adore the Word Incarnate in this very
place. They are already ten days on the way and will shortly
arrive."

Joseph and Mary therefore set about preparing the grotto
for the visit of the Kings, and during the following days

the Blessed Virgin saw in visions the Magi traveling together across the deserts east of the Holy Land.

The three Kings, whose names (according to tradition) were Gaspar, Balthasar and Melchior, ruled over what is now Iraq and Iran. Gaspar of Mesopotamia, the youngest, was light brown in appearance, Balthasar of Parthia was dark brown, while Melchior of Media, the oldest, was rather stout and had an olive-colored complexion. All three were unusually just and honorable men who were also great scholars and students of religion. Through their knowledge of the Old Testament prophecies and of certain traditions of their own peoples, they believed in the coming of the Saviour of mankind. And because they were kind and generous and good men, on the night of the Nativity they earned the privilege of being told by the angels in a dream that the long-awaited King of the Jews had just been born, that He was the Promised Redeemer, and that they were chosen by the Lord to seek Him and to honor Him. Though each one received this revelation separately, each was made aware that it had also been given to the other two. The three Kings awoke at the same hour of the night, filled with extraordinary joy, and prostrating themselves on the ground they humbly thanked and worshipped Almighty God. Then they decided to leave immediately for the Land of Israel in order to adore the divine Child. Without delay they prepared gifts and procured the necessary camels, provisions and servants for their journey.

As each King set out that evening, he suddenly perceived a beautiful mystic star, which was formed by the angels, and in this star he saw a symbolic vision of a Virgin and a Child with a cross, who was the King of a heavenly city and whom all the kings on earth worshipped. The star then guided the three Magi in such a way that within a few days they came together, Melchior having traveled more rapidly than the others from his more distant kingdom. All three, who were already intimate friends, after conferring about their revelations became still more inflamed with devotion for the newborn King, and they now pursued their trip together, always under the guidance of the star, which they could see as clearly during the day as at night. Each King was accompanied by four or five relatives and friends and a large number of servants, all riding on camels, dromedaries or horses, and consequently the caravan consisted of about two hundred persons. The journey across the deserts, mountains, and rivers of Chaldea and Syria took nearly a month, despite the fact that the camels and horses were unusually fleet-footed. The whole caravan traveled in perfect order, and everyone seemed filled with simple joy and devotion. At times, while contemplating the mystic star, the good Kings spontaneously composed and sang lovely canticles, with words such as: "Beyond the mountains we yearn to kneel at the feet of the newborn King!"

At last, after crossing the river Jordan, they arrived before the walls of Jerusalem, which, because it was the capital of Israel, they thought was the logical birthplace of the new King of the Jews. However, they were already disturbed by the fact that, contrary to their expectations, they had observed no signs of rejoicing among the people over the birth of the Messias. Also as they approached the great city, the star almost faded from their sight. At the city gate they questioned some of the guards, saying:

"Where is the newly born King of the Jews? For we have seen His star in the East and have come to worship Him."

But to their astonishment, the guards and other Jews indicated that they knew nothing about the birth of a new King of Israel. Then at the request of the Magi, messengers were sent to arrange an interview with King Herod in his palace. And while they were waiting, the three Wise Men became very discouraged and only recovered some of their confidence after a period of silent prayer.

Herod having agreed to see the Kings the following morning, the caravan camped for the night in a large courtyard. But the Magi could not sleep. Instead they wandered through the city with guides, and studied the sky as though they were looking for the star. They thought that perhaps Herod wanted to hide the Child King from them.

Actually Herod too was so deeply troubled that he could not sleep, and during the night he summoned the high priests and doctors of the Law to meet with him. And he inquired of them where the Christ was to be born. Unrolling their scriptures and pointing to a passage in the Book of Micheas, they said to him:

"In Bethlehem of Judea, for thus it is written through the prophet."

Becoming still more disturbed and fearful for his throne, Herod thereupon resolved to have the Infant King secretly put to death. Taking some of the priests with him, he went out onto a porch and tried in vain to see the star of the Magi. Meanwhile the scholars urged him to pay no attention to the fantastic stories of the Eastern rulers, for they insisted that, if the Messias had indeed been born, the fact would already be known both in the Temple and in the Palace. Realizing how unpopular he was among the people, Herod decided to keep the whole matter quiet.

He therefore received the Magi, in secret, at dawn the following morning in a large hall in which refreshments and bouquets of flowers had been prepared for his guests. After having made them wait a while, he entered, accompanied by several doctors of the Law, and proceeded to question the Wise Men closely concerning the time when the star had first appeared to them and concerning all that they knew about the Infant King. Then Gaspar described the vision which they had had of a Virgin and a royal Child whom the kings of the earth adored, because His kingdom was greater than all the kingdoms of the world. After telling them about the prophecy referring to Bethlehem, Herod hypocritically pretended that he too wished to adore the Infant King, and he said to the Magi:

"Go and make careful inquiry concerning the Child, and when you have found Him, bring me word, that I too may go and worship Him."

Leaving the king very ill at ease, and without taking any

of his refreshments, the Magi set out with their caravan for Bethlehem. Soon after they had passed out of the city gate, they again perceived the star and burst into cries of joy and happy songs. Then they camped for awhile and said some prayers, and all of a sudden a spring of clear, fresh water gushed out of the ground before their eyes. Taking this as a good omen, they built a small pool and let their animals drink their fill. The three Kings now ate their first meal since leaving Jerusalem. Later in the day they continued on their way over the hills of Judea to Bethlehem.

When they arrived in the City of David toward evening, the star disappeared again, and they felt somewhat anxious. They were directed to the Valley of the Shepherds as a suitable place for the caravan to camp overnight. After their servants had put up a large tent and had begun to unpack provisions, the three Kings suddenly perceived the star shining with extraordinary brightness over a nearby hill. Then a beam of fiery light descended from the star onto the grotto, and in this ray the Magi saw a vision of the holy Child. Reverently taking off their headdress, they slowly walked over to the hill and found the entrance to the stable. Gaspar pushed the door open and caught sight of the humble Mother of God sitting with the Infant Jesus at the far end of the cave, which was filled with a heavenly light. Both Mother and Child were just as the Kings had seen them in the vision a month before.

St. Joseph and an old shepherd now came out of the grotto, and the Magi told him very simply and modestly that they had come to worship the newborn King of the Jews and to offer Him their gifts, whereupon Joseph welcomed them with touching friendliness and cordiality. Then, accompanied by the shepherd, they returned to their tent in order to prepare for the solemn ceremony by which they planned to honor the Saviour. And after having assembled their gifts and put on their great, white, silk cloaks, they set out for the grotto in an orderly procession with their relatives and servants.

When Mary knew that the Magi were approaching, she asked St. Joseph to stay at her side, and she calmly awaited them, standing with her Son in her arms, her head and shoulders covered with her veil, in perfect modesty and beauty, with a celestial light shining in her countenance and shedding over her a majesty that was more than human, even amid the extreme poverty of the stable.

After taking off their sandals and turbans, the three Kings entered the grotto. At their first sight of the Mother and Child, they were overwhelmed with reverence and admiration, and their pure hearts overflowed with joyful devotion. By a special permission of God they also perceived the multitude of resplendent angels who were attending the King of kings. Then the three Magi simultaneously prostrated themselves very humbly on the ground and fervently worshipped the divine Infant, acknowledging Him as their Lord and Master and as the Saviour of all mankind.

When they arose, Mary sat down, holding Jesus on her lap. And the Kings approached her, for they wished to kiss her hand, as they customarily did to the queens in their countries. But the Queen of Heaven and earth modestly withdrew her hand and said:

"My spirit rejoices in the Lord, because among all the nations He has called you to behold the Eternal Word Incarnate. Let us therefore praise His Name!"

Then she uncovered the upper part of the Christ Child's body, which was wrapped in red and white swaddling clothes, and with one hand she supported His head, while she put her other arm around Him. The Infant Jesus had His tiny hands crossed on His chest, as if He were praying, and all His features seemed to radiate joy and love.

Seeing the divine Babe of Bethlehem thus, the three Kings fell on their knees before Him and again adored and worshipped Him. Their hearts became inflamed with a burning mystical devotion for Him. And in a fervent, silent prayer they offered to the Christ Child their kingdoms, their peoples, their families, all their possessions, and their own selves. They humbly begged Him to rule over their souls and thoughts and all their actions, to enlighten them and to give happiness, peace and charity to the world. Tears of joy and devotion ran down their cheeks, while all they could say was:

"We saw His Star—we know that He is to reign over all kings—and we have come to worship Him and to offer Him our gifts."

Then Gaspar took from a purse hanging at his waist a number of small gold bars and laid them at Mary's feet. Next the copper-skinned Balthasar placed a golden censer with green incense on a table in front of Jesus. Finally Melchior came forward and left on the table a lovely little flowering shrub which gave forth myrrh.

As each gift was presented, the divine Infant smiled and waved His arms in a very lovable way, while Mary nodded with touching humility and spoke a few words of simple heartfelt gratitude to each of the three Kings. Then they congratulated St. Joseph on his good fortune in being chosen as the husband of the Mother of the Messias, and expressed their profound sympathy over the dire poverty in which the Holy Family was living.

After the Magi had been in the stable for three hours, they withdrew, and their servants were allowed to enter in groups of five and to adore the Child Jesus. Meanwhile, outside the grotto, the Magi and their relatives stood around a great old tree and joyfully chanted their evening prayers. Then they went to their tent, where St. Joseph and some of the shepherds had prepared a light supper for them consisting of bread, fruit, vegetables and honey. As he sat there eating with the good Kings, Joseph was so happy that his eyes filled with tears. And when he returned to the grotto, he and Mary were overflowing with a joy that they had never known before, as at last they saw how Almighty God had brought to His Incarnate Son the honors and gifts that were due to Him.

The next day the Magi generously distributed food, clothing and money among the needy families of Bethlehem, and they sent their servants to the grotto with many choice presents, which Mary set aside for charity. The Kings planned to return to Jerusalem the following morning, and so they now went to say farewell to the Holy Family.

First they consulted the Blessed Virgin concerning many mysteries of faith and the practice of religion in their daily lives and duties. Her words were so filled with divine truth that the Wise Men were deeply moved and wished that they did not have to part from her. When they presented some gems of great value to her, Mary respectfully refused them. They also offered to have a comfortable house built for her, but she humbly thanked them without accepting.

When at last the Kings had to leave, the Mother of God allowed each of them to hold the Christ Child in his arms, and as each did so, his face became transfigured with joy and he wept tenderly. At the door they very fervently begged Mary and Joseph to pray for them. Then, in order to make them happy, Mary suddenly unwound her long yellow veil and handed it to Gaspar. The three Magi bowed low before her and gratefully accepted this precious relic, and when they looked up, their hearts were thrilled with reverence and love as they contemplated the full heavenly beauty of both Mother and Child.

After chanting their evening prayers, the Kings and their attendants retired for the night—until, about midnight, an angel warned them in a dream to leave at once for the East without passing by Jerusalem.

Within less than an hour the caravan had quietly packed up all its equipment, and after a last, touching farewell to St. Joseph, the Magi silently vanished into the night, guided by an angel.

THE BLESSED VIRGIN SAID
TO VENERABLE MOTHER MARY OF AGREDA:

"My daughter, great were the gifts which the Kings offered to my most holy Son, but greater still was the affection with which they offered them and the mystery concealed beneath them. I wish

you also to offer up similar gifts. For I assure you, my dearest, that there is no more acceptable gift to the Most High than voluntary poverty. There are few in the world who use temporal riches well and offer them to their Lord with the generosity and love of those holy Kings. You too can make such an offering of the things necessary for sustenance, giving a part to the poor. Your ceaseless offer, however, must be love, which is the gold; continual prayer, which is the incense; and the patient acceptance of labors and true mortifications, which is the myrrh. All that you do for the Lord, you should offer up to Him with ardent affection."

CHAPTER SEVENTEEN

THE PURIFICATION

AFTER THE DEPARTURE OF THE MAGI, the Mother of God said to St. Joseph:

"My master, dispose of all the offerings of the Kings as belonging to my Son and to yourself—I deserve nothing."

Together they divided the gifts into three parts: one for the Temple (the incense and myrrh and some of the gold), another for the priest who had circumcised the Child, and the rest for the poor.

A devout woman whom Mary had helped urged the Holy Family to move into her modest home, and they humbly accepted her invitation. Sadly they took leave of the holy stable, after cleaning it thoroughly.

During the days that remained before the Purification, when alone with His beloved Mother, the Infant Jesus often murmured to her:

"My Dove, My Chosen One, My dearest Mother, make thyself like unto Me!"

When the poor women and children of Bethlehem came to visit Mary, she gave them gifts and tactfully instructed them in the knowledge of God, the mysteries concerning the expected Messias, and the practice of virtues in everyday life. Sometimes their superficial talk about such matters was so full of confusion that it made St. Joseph smile secretly, yet he continuously marveled at Mary's patience, firmness and gentleness in leading these poor people to the truth, as well as at her great humility and reserve.

When the fortieth day after the Nativity drew near, the Immaculate Mother of God did not hesitate to subject herself to the general Hebrew law requiring the purification of mothers and the presentation of first-born sons in the Temple at Jerusalem. For she saw in the soul of her divine Son that He wished to offer Himself as a living victim to the eternal Father in the Temple.

Consequently Mary and Joseph gratefully took leave of the good woman who had sheltered them, and went with Jesus to the cave of the Nativity for a last visit. Having gently placed the Christ Child on the ground at the very spot where He was born, they both knelt and prayed fervently together, and they did the same where He had been circumcised.

Then, as usual before a journey, Mary asked her husband for his blessing, and on this special occasion for his permission to make the trip on foot and with bare feet. But St. Joseph replied kindly yet firmly:

"May the Son of the eternal Father, whom I hold in my arms, give you His blessing! You may travel to Jerusalem on foot, but not barefooted, because of the weather."

Prostrating herself on the ground for the last time in the grotto of the Nativity, with all her heart Mary thanked the Infant Jesus for the marvelous blessings which He had given to Joseph and herself and to all mankind in the stable of Bethlehem, and she prayed to God that this holy place might always be revered by Christians.

Rising to her feet, she covered herself with her cloak and took her Baby into her arms, pressing Him to her breast to protect Him from the cold winter wind. Then, after the Infant God had visibly given them His blessing, Joseph and Mary set out for Jerusalem, accompanied by a donkey bearing their few belongings and the gifts for the Temple. Some of the good shepherds bade them a sad and touchingly affectionate farewell.

During the five-mile journey, the weather was unusually severe. Cold, sleety winds made the Child Jesus shiver and weep.

Toward evening, having traveled slowly with several resting periods, the Holy Family reached the city gate of Jerusalem and found a welcome lodging in the humble home of a devout old couple without children. Then, at Mary's suggestion, St. Joseph went alone to the Temple and made an anonymous donation of the myrrh, incense and gold, in order to avoid any ostentation of wealth at the ceremony the following day.

The holy Mother of God spent the night before the Purification in fervent prayer. Speaking to the Eternal Father, she said:

"My Lord and my God, a festive day for Heaven and earth will be that on which I offer the living Victim to Thee in Thy Temple. In return, this is what I ask of Thee, my Lord: pour forth Thy mercies upon mankind, pardoning sinners, consoling the afflicted, and helping the needy! My soul shall magnify Thee forever. . . ."

That night, the holy man Simeon, a very old and thin priest with a short beard, was kneeling at prayer in a tiny cell of the great Temple in Jerusalem. The Holy Ghost, who dwelt in him, had already revealed to him that he was not to die until he had seen the promised Messias. Now while he was praying in ecstasy, an angel appeared to him and told him to observe carefully the first child presented to the priests the next morning, for that child would be the Saviour of the world for whom he longed so much. The angel also informed Simeon that he would die soon afterward. The old man was inflamed with joy.

The holy matron Anna was likewise favored with a vision concerning the Purification, and she rejoiced greatly, because she had been one of Mary's teachers during her stay in the Temple as a girl.

Before dawn the Holy Family left their lodging in Jerusalem and went to the Temple, accompanied by thousands of invisible chanting angels. At the entrance of the Women's Court, Mary knelt and humbly presented herself to God with His Son in her arms. She was dressed in a light-blue robe, over which she wore a long, yellow mantle and a white veil.

The simple and devout old priest Simeon, who had been waiting for several hours already, could no longer restrain his impatience. Moved by the Holy Spirit, he went to meet his Lord, and in the hallway he caught sight of both Mother and Child surrounded by a wonderful light. After saying a few words to Mary, with the greatest joy he took the divine Child into his arms and pressed Him to his heart. Then he quietly withdrew into another part of the building, while Mary was led by a woman to the Temple Court. St. Joseph had given the basket with the two turtledoves to Anna and then passed through another door to the men's section.

In the large ceremonial hall everything was prepared. On the walls many lamps hung in pyramid form. Several priests had placed in front of the altar a long table covered with a white cloth on which rested a cradle-like container and two baskets.

Simeon came to Mary and led her to the table, where she placed in the cradle the Child Jesus, who was wrapped in a long sky-blue veil. Then she was led back to the grilled-in women's section, in which about twenty mothers with their first-born sons were waiting their turn.

The holy Temple now seemed to be filled with a heavenly light. Almighty God was present there. And above the Child the Heavens seemed to open before the throne of the Holy Trinity.

Simeon and three other priests, having put on their ceremonial vestments, took their places around the table and prayed over the Babe. Then Anna gave Mary the basket with her offerings of fruit and coins, and Simeon again led her to the table. One of the priests took up the Child, raised Him toward Heaven and turned to Simeon, who placed Him back in the Virgin's arms and recited over them both some prayers from a rolled manuscript. Then Simeon led Mary back to Anna, who accompanied her to the women's section.

After these ceremonies were over, Simeon came to Mary and received the Infant Jesus from her hands. Then, raising his eyes to Heaven in an ecstasy of joy, he offered the Child to the eternal Father, glorifying God for having fulfilled the promises, and saying:

"Now Thou dost dismiss Thy servant, O Lord, according to Thy word, in peace: because my eyes have seen Thy salvation, which Thou hast prepared before the face of all people:

"A light of revelation to the Gentiles, and a glory for Thy people Israel."

St. Joseph had come to join Mary, and he listened with deep respect to the inspired words of the old man. Simeon blessed them both. Then addressing himself to Mary, who was luminous like a heavenly rose, he added:

"Behold, this Child is destined for the fall and for the rise of many in Israel, and for a sign that shall be contradicted. And thy own soul a sword shall pierce, that the thoughts of many hearts may be revealed."

At the moment when the priest mentioned the sword and the sign of contradiction, which were prophetical of the Passion and death of the Lord, the Child Jesus bowed His head, thereby ratifying the prophecy and accepting it as the sentence of the eternal Father pronounced by His minister. All this was understood by Mary, and she began to feel sorrow, for as in a mirror her spirit was made to see the mysteries included in this prophecy. All these things remained indelibly impressed on her memory.

Anna the Prophetess was also inspired and proclaimed the Child's Mother blessed.

Mary then humbly kissed the hand of the priest and again asked his blessing, and she did the same to Anna, her former teacher. Then with St. Joseph and her divine

Child she returned to her lodging.

Not long afterward both Simeon and Anna passed away in peace.

THE BLESSED VIRGIN SAID TO ST. BRIDGET OF SWEDEN:

"I did not need purification, like other women, because my Son who was born of me, made me clean. Nevertheless, that the Law and the prophecies might be fulfilled, I chose to live according to the Law. Nor did I live like worldly parents, but humbly conversed with the humble. Nor did I wish to show anything extraordinary in me, but loved whatever was humble.

"On that day (of the Purification) my pain was increased. For though by divine inspiration I knew that my Son was to suffer, yet this grief pierced my heart more keenly at Simeon's words. And until I was assumed in body and soul to Heaven, this grief never left my heart, although it was tempered by the consolation of the Spirit of God. Let not, then, this grief leave thy heart, for without tribulation few would reach Heaven."

—AND TO VENERABLE MOTHER MARY OF AGREDA:

"My daughter, the doctrine and example contained in this Mystery will teach thee to strive after the constancy and expansion of heart by which thou mayest prepare thyself to accept blessings and adversity, the sweet and the bitter, with equanimity.

"How persistently the human heart forgets that its Teacher and Master has first accepted sufferings, and has honored and sanctified them in His own Person!

"Remember the sorrow that pierced my heart at the prophecies of Simeon, and how I remained in peace and tranquility, even though my heart and soul were transfixed by a sword of pain.

"Seek ever to preserve inward peace.

"Full of trust in me, whenever tribulation comes over thee, fervently exclaim:

" 'The Lord is my light and my salvation: whom shall I fear?' "

CHAPTER EIGHTEEN

THE FLIGHT TO EGYPT

AFTER the Purification, Mary and Joseph decided to stay in Jerusalem for nine days in order to renew their offering of the Child Jesus and to acknowledge their gratitude for the great blessing which God had given them. Every day therefore, from noon until midnight, they prayed humbly in an obscure corner of the Temple.

On the fifth day the Lord said to Mary:

"My Spouse and My Dove, you cannot finish the nine days' devotion. Herod is seeking the life of the Child. In order to save your Son's life, you must flee with Him and Joseph into the land of Egypt. The journey is long, hard and very tiring. Suffer it all for My sake, for I am and always will be with you."

The Mother of God answered meekly:

"My Lord, dispose of me according to Thy Will. I ask only that Thou permit not my Son to suffer and that Thou turn all pains and hardships upon me."

But as she left the Temple with the Infant Jesus in her arms, Mary's compassionate heart was filled with sorrow for Him, and she wept.

At home in their two rented rooms she prudently kept the disturbing news to herself, since she had not been told to reveal it to her husband. St. Joseph noticed that she was troubled, but he thought that it was due to Simeon's prophecy.

That night, while Joseph was sleeping, an angel in the radiant form of a young man appeared in his room and said to him:

"Arise, and take the Child and His Mother, and flee into Egypt, and remain there until I tell thee. For Herod will seek the Child to destroy Him!"

Taking Joseph by the hand, the angel raised him up, and vanished. As St. Joseph dressed hurriedly, he was greatly worried for Mary's sake and for the safety of the Child Jesus. He lit his lamp and after knocking on the door of his wife's room, humbly asked her whether he could come in. Then, upon entering, he said to her anxiously:

"My Lady, God wills that we should be tried further, for His holy angel has announced to me that we must flee to Egypt with the Child, because Herod is planning to take His life. Prepare yourself, my dear wife, to bear the hardships of the journey, and tell me what I can do to alleviate them."

"My husband and master," replied Mary calmly, "if we have received from God such great blessings and graces, it is fitting that we should joyfully accept temporal suffering. Wherever we go, we carry Our Lord with us, and He is our comfort and our country. So let us proceed to fulfill His holy Will."

Then she went to the crib at the foot of the bed, where the Infant Jesus was sleeping, and falling on her knees she awakened Him and took Him in her arms. At first the divine Babe wept a little, but when Mary and Joseph asked Him for His blessing, He gave it to them visibly.

After St. Joseph had hurriedly packed their few belongings on the donkey that had traveled with them from Nazareth, the Holy Family left Jerusalem shortly before midnight on their long and dangerous trip to Egypt.

Mary held in her arms the Infant Jesus, who was well wrapped in swaddling clothes and supported by a large piece of linen which was tied around His Mother's neck. The Blessed Virgin wore a long cloak that covered her and the Child, and also a wide veil.

Although Mary and Joseph were filled with anxiety for Jesus, they felt greatly encouraged when, as they went through the city gate, all the splendid angel protectors of the Mother of God again appeared in bright human forms and changed the night into day for them.

As the Holy Family journeyed southward in the direction of Bethlehem, Mary longed to visit and again venerate the holy grotto of the Nativity, but her angels informed her that such a delay would be dangerous. Then, with St. Joseph's permission, she sent one of the angels to warn St. Elizabeth to hide with her son John in the desert around the town of Hebron, where they were then living.

The Holy Family spent their first night in a cave in the hills south of Bethlehem, off the regular caravan route. They were thirsty and exhausted, and Mary was so sorry for her Child that she wept. But at her prayer a spring of clear water suddenly gushed forth, and a wild goat came to them and allowed Joseph to milk it.

Late the next day, as they were crossing the desert near Hebron, they ran out of water, and both Mary and Joseph suffered keenly from thirst.

St. Elizabeth and John were then hiding in a cave on a hill nearby. Suddenly John felt that his Lord was close and was suffering. He fell on his knees and prayed fervently with his arms extended.

St. Elizabeth sent one of her servants with generous gifts of money, food and clothing to the Holy Family, which he overtook near Gaza. There they rested briefly, while Mary shared these gifts with the poor and healed several sick and crippled women.

Then the Holy Family set out on the long and difficult journey across the great desert between Palestine and Egypt. While it was still dark, they had to pass through a stretch of ground infested with many dangerous snakes which slithered toward them and reared up, hissing menacingly, but did not harm them.

During the first night in the desert the Holy Family rested at the foot of a small sand dune. After they had eaten and after Mary had nursed her Babe, St. Joseph made a sort of tent with his cloak and some sticks in order to protect the Mother and Child from the wind, and he slept near them on the ground, resting his head on the sack that contained their belongings. Mary now perceived that Jesus was offering up to His Father all their hardships, and she did likewise, praying with Him and with her angels most of the night.

Within a few days the poor travelers had exhausted all their small provisions of fruit and bread and water, although they tried to make their supply last longer by not eating several times until nine o'clock at night. And while they were thus suffering from hunger and thirst and fatigue, a strong wind and sandstorm arose. Finally, at Mary's fervent prayer for her Son and her husband, the Lord commanded her angels to serve them some nourishing food and drink.

During the long journey, while Mary walked or rode on the donkey, always holding her divine Son in her arms, she often thanked Him for having made her His Mother. Three times a day she nursed Him, and whenever they stopped for a rest she caressed Him tenderly. A few times the Infant Jesus wept tears of love and compassion for mankind, and Mary would weep too. Often Mother and Son conversed mystically.

At other times St. Joseph would talk with Mary, frequently asking her what he could do for her or Jesus. Sometimes he would humbly and devoutly kiss the feet of the divine Child and take Him in his arms and beg Him for His blessing. Thus the Holy Family passed the ten days of their flight across the barren desert, consoling and cheering one another in mutual kindness and love.

Several times, when they were resting, a great number

of birds came flying toward Mary and entertained her by perching on her shoulders and hands, chirping affectionately and joyfully. Then she urged them to be thankful to God for their beautiful plumage, their freedom in the air, and their daily food on the ground, and she joined them in singing lovely lullabies for the Infant Jesus. And often she sang hymns of praise to the Lord with her angels.

Once when the travelers were completely lost and did not know which way to go, Mary and Joseph were deeply troubled for a moment. But after they had prayed fervently for help, some wild animals came toward them in a friendly manner and ran off in a certain direction, thus indicating the right way.

One evening the Holy Family arrived at the camp of some highway robbers, who were at first inclined to treat them cruelly. But when the leader looked at the Infant Jesus, somehow his hard heart was deeply touched, and he ordered his men not to harm the travelers. Taking them into his hut, he had his wife give them some food and settle them comfortably in a corner.

At Mary's request the woman brought her a large container filled with water, in which the Blessed Virgin gave her Son a bath and washed His swaddling clothes. Meanwhile the chief robber said to his wife:

"That is no ordinary child—He is a holy Baby. Ask His Mother to let you bathe our leprous son in the water she has used. Perhaps it will heal him. . . ."

But before the woman said a word, Mary urged her to wash her sick son in the water. Then the mother brought in her three-year-old boy, whose leprosy was so advanced that it covered all his face and body. Yet as soon as he was placed in the water that Jesus had used, which was now clearer than it had been before, the sick boy's skin became perfectly smooth and healthy.

His mother was almost beside herself with joy and gratitude. She tried to kiss Mary and Jesus, but the Mother of God gently held her off and did not let her touch either of them. The father told all his men about the miracle, and they crowded into the hut and stared at the Holy Family with awe.

Later Mary had a long talk with the mother, who promised that she would stop living from crime as soon as she could.

That night Mary hardly slept at all. She remained sitting on her bed, praying.

The next morning when the Holy Family left with some new provisions, the robber chief gratefully said good-by to them and exclaimed with deep emotion:

"Remember me, wherever you are!"

(Thirty-three years later his robber son said to the Man crucified beside him on Calvary: "Lord, remember me when Thou comest into Thy Kingdom!" And that time—again due to Mary's prayers—Jesus healed his soul.).

Within a few days, although nearing the end of their trip, the Holy Family was once more utterly exhausted and suffering intensely from hunger and thirst. While they were resting on a sand dune, Mary prayed again for help, and a spring of water began to flow beside her. After they had quenched their thirst, she bathed the Infant Jesus in the water. Then, as they approached the delta of the Nile, they camped under a tall date tree, which at Mary's prayer bent over so that they could pick and eat its fruit. That night they spent in the shelter of a great hollow sycamore tree.

Finally, after ten days of torture on the endless sands of the desert the Holy Family reached the fertile land of Egypt.

OUR LORD SAID TO ST. BRIDGET OF SWEDEN:

"By My flight to Egypt I showed the infirmities of My Humanity and fulfilled the prophecies. I gave too an example to My disciples that sometimes persecution is to be avoided for the greater future glory of God. That I was not found by My pursuers, the counsel of My Divinity prevailed over the counsel of man, for it is not easy to fight against God."

—AND THE BLESSED VIRGIN SAID TO VENERABLE MOTHER MARY OF AGREDA:

"I was not alarmed in my exile and prolonged journey. Since I trusted in the Lord, He provided for me in the time of my need. Even when help is somewhat delayed, it will always be at hand at a time when it will do most good. Thus it happened with me and my husband in the time of our destitution and necessity."

CHAPTER NINETEEN

THE HOLY FAMILY IN EGYPT

AFTER THE Holy Family had fled from Palestine, King
Herod, "seeing that he had been tricked by the Magi,
was exceedingly angry," and he gave a secret order to his
officers in Bethlehem to kill all male children under two
years of age. The Slaughter of the Innocents took place
in a large courtyard of a palace to which the mothers and
children had been summoned. Executioners armed with
swords and spears proceeded to cut the throats or pierce
the chests of the infants and to throw their bodies onto
a pile, before the eyes of the helpless and frantic mothers, who screamed and tore their hair.

While this frightful atrocity was occurring, Mary and
Jesus in Egypt were mystically aware of it. With heartbroken anguish Mary joined her divine Son in praying for
the souls of the murdered children and for their grieving
parents. Jesus asked His Father to reward these first fruits
of His own Passion with the crown of martyrdom, and His
request was granted.

Although the Blessed Virgin was very anxious to know
how young John the Baptist had escaped the massacre, she

refrained from asking the Lord to enlighten her. But He soon informed her that St. Elizabeth and John had escaped from Herod's soldiers by hiding in a cave in the desert, where they were now living under the greatest hardships. Mary therefore immediately obtained the permission of Jesus to send them provisions by means of her angels.

A few years later, when John was only four years old, his saintly mother died peacefully, assisted by Mary's angels, who also helped to bury her in the desert. Young John was then supported by a holy hermit who often visited him. The Forerunner of Christ grew up in the wilderness, living a hard and solitary life of ever-increasing prayer and mortification. He received his education, not from men, but directly from the Holy Spirit. His only companions were the wild animals of the desert, with whom he was on friendly terms. The birds especially loved to come and perch on his shoulders or on his staff, while he talked to them familiarly. Often too he conversed with angels, humbly yet with all the innocent frankness of a deeply religious boy.

When the Holy Family entered the pagan land of Egypt, the Infant Jesus in the arms of His Mother raised His eyes and hands to the Eternal Father and asked for the salvation of its inhabitants. And as they arrived at the town of Heliopolis or City of the Sun, He used His divine power to drive the demons from the idols in the temples. Some of the idols then crashed to the ground and broke into many pieces, causing a great commotion among the people.

St. Joseph found a poor and humble three-room house at a small distance from the town. Upon entering this new home, the Mother of God knelt on the ground and kissed it with profound humility, thanking the Lord for giving them this place of rest after their long and hard journey. She dedicated all that she was to do there to the glory of God, and she offered to take upon herself all the trials and labors of their exile. Then she set about cleaning the rooms.

During the next three days the Holy Family was so completely destitute that they had to live on whatever St. Joseph could beg for them. Then he succeeded in obtaining work in his trade as a carpenter. But he was not well treated by the persons who employed him. Looking upon him as a foreigner and a refugee, they paid him whatever they pleased. Sometimes after a whole day's work he was not able to bring any money home. As the house was without any furniture, he soon made a couch for Mary and a cradle for Jesus, as well as some low tables and stools. Of the three rooms, they assigned one to the Mother and Child, and the other two to St. Joseph as his bedroom and workshop.

The Holy Family adjusted themselves to their poverty calmly and even joyfully. However, Mary decided to help in earning their living. She therefore began to do needle-work for some good women in the Jewish colony, and soon her reputation for skill and quality work spread, so that she was never in want of employment. But she always refused to do any frivolous fashion pieces, although her attitude aroused criticism among some of her customers. While she sewed, the Infant Jesus lay quietly in His cra-dle beside her.

Due to the many hours which she now spent at this work, she had to devote more of the night hours to prayer and contemplation. Her divine Son was greatly pleased with her zeal and acceptance of poverty, and wishing to lessen her labor, one day He said to her:

"My Mother, I wish to make a rule for your daily life and work. From nightfall you will take some sleep and rest. From midnight until dawn We will praise the Eter-nal Father together. Then prepare the necessary food for yourself and Joseph, and afterward give Me food and hold Me in your arms until noon, when you will place Me in the arms of your husband, to give him some refreshment in his labors. Then retire and return to your work until it is time to prepare the evening meal. And pray contin-ually to the Eternal Father for sinners."

Mary and Joseph had the Infant Jesus with them as they took their meals. Whenever St. Joseph wished to caress the divine Child, he humbly asked Mary's permission. And taking the little Jesus in his arms, he was so filled with tender joy and love that he forgot all his hardships or even considered them easy and sweet. Both Mary and Joseph often received such heart-warming consolations from Jesus that they gladly accepted all their trials for love of Him.

While the Holy Family was in Egypt, they joyfully celebrated the first anniversary of the Annunciation, and later of the Nativity. On each occasion Mary prepared for the anniversary by nine days of prayer, and celebrated it by prostrating herself before the Infant Jesus in the form of a cross, begging Him to thank the Eternal Father for all the graces which the gift of His Only-Begotten Son was bringing to her and to the whole human race. Then, inflamed with the love of God, she rose up and sang beautiful hymns alternately with her angels, to honor her Son.

Until this time the Divine Child had spoken only to His Mother and only when alone with her. Now when He reached the age of one year, He decided to break His silence and speak to His foster father. One day, therefore, when Mary and Joseph were talking together with deep reverence about the marvelous goodness of God as manifested in the Incarnation, the Child Jesus, resting in His Mother's arms, said to St. Joseph in a clear voice:

"My father—"

Upon hearing the Infant God call him "father," Joseph, his heart thrilling with new love, gratitude, and joy, fell on his knees before Jesus and while tears ran down his cheeks, thanked Him for such a grace and begged Him to enlighten him and enable him in all things to fulfill God's holy Will.

Then Jesus continued:

"I have come from Heaven upon this earth in order to be the Light of the world and in order to rescue it from the darkness of sin, to seek and to know My sheep, as a good shepherd, to give them the nourishment of eternal life, to teach them the way to Heaven, and to open its gates, which had been closed by their sins. And I desire that you both be children of the Light, which you have so close to you."

Now Mary placed Jesus in the cradle, and kneeling before Him said:

"My Son and sweetest love of my soul, Thou hast been oppressed for a long time by the swaddling clothes. Tell me, my Lord, what shall I do to place Thee freely on Thy feet?"

"My mother," replied the Child Jesus, "on account of the love which I bear toward men, the swathings of My childhood have not seemed irksome to Me, for when I shall be grown up I shall be bound and delivered to My enemies to be put to death. I wish to possess only one garment during all My life, for I seek nothing more than what is sufficient to cover Me. Clothe Me, My Mother, in a tunic of a lowly and ordinary color. This alone will I wear, and it shall grow with Me. Over this garment they shall cast lots at My death. . . . Men shall see that I was born and wish to live poor and destitute of visible things which, being earthly, oppress and darken the heart of man. I shall not have anything to do with visible things except to offer them up to the Eternal Father, renouncing them for His love, and making use of only so much as is sufficient to sustain My natural life, which I will afterward yield up for man's sake. By this example I wish to impress upon the world the doctrine that it must love poverty and not despise it."

But Mary replied:

"My Son and my Lord, Thy Mother has not the heart to allow Thee to go barefoot at this tender age. Permit me, my Love, to provide some kind of covering to protect Thy feet. I also fear that the rough garment which Thou askest of me will wound Thy tender body if Thou wearest no linen beneath."

"My Mother, I will permit a slight and ordinary covering for My feet until the time of My public preaching, for I must do that barefooted. But I do not wish to wear linen."

Mary therefore set about at once preparing her Son's robe. She obtained some natural and uncolored wool, and spinning it very finely with her own hands, she wove it on a small loom into a one-piece garment without any seam. At her request its color was changed to a unique mixture of brown and silver-gray. She also made a half tunic as undergarment and a pair of strong sandals.

When all was ready, after humbly asking her Divine Son's permission, Mary carefully and lovingly clothed Him and set Him on His feet. Although she had taken no measurements beforehand, the robe fitted Him perfectly, covering His feet without hindering Him in walking, and the sleeves extended to the middle of His hands. The collar was round in front and somewhat raised around the neck. Our Lord never took off this robe until His executioners tore it off at the Scourging and the Crucifixion, for by divine power it continually grew with Him, adjusting itself to His body. Nor did it ever become worn in appearance or lose its color, and it always remained spotlessly clean.

Then Mary gently placed the Infant God on His feet for the first time, and He took His first steps on this earth. He was by far the most beautiful Child who has ever lived. Upon seeing Him standing there in His plain and humble robe, the angels marveled, while Mary and Joseph were filled with new love and joy.

The Mother of God continued to nurse her Son until He was a year and a half old. Then He began to take frugal meals of broth mixed with oil, and some fruits and fish. He never asked for food, and later He ate all His meals with His Mother and foster father. Then Mary always waited for Him to give the blessing at the beginning and thanks at the end of each meal.

Now that the Child Jesus could walk, He began to retire and spend certain hours in prayer in His Mother's room. As she silently wondered whether she should stay with Him at such times, He said to her:

"My Mother, remain with Me always in order to imitate Me in My actions, for I have chosen you as the vessel and model of all perfection."

Mary therefore frequently joined Him in praying for mankind. And sometimes when the divine Child meditated on the ingratitude with which men would receive the Redemption, she saw Him weep and even perspire blood, and then she would sorrowfully wipe His little face. At other times she saw Him resplendent with heavenly light and surrounded by sweetly chanting angels.

Within a few years a number of children began to gather around the young Jesus, for He soon won their hearts by His kindness and qualities of leadership. They often came to visit Him, and He took them to drink at a fountain behind the house which Mary had discovered. With words full of life and strength He instructed His little friends in the knowledge of God and the virtues, and His informal teaching made such a deep impression that all these boys later became great and saintly men.

One day, as soon as He was strong enough, while Mary was praying in her room, the Child Jesus took a pitcher and filled it with water at the fountain. When she saw Him bringing it to her, she was profoundly moved. And from that day Jesus always thoughtfully carried water for her whenever she needed it, without her having to ask for it. He also helped St. Joseph, handing him his tools or pieces of wood. When He was old enough, the boy Jesus took His Mother's needlework to her customers in town and brought back some bread. Occasionally, after a trip to town, He wept over the suffering and sinning which He had seen in the city. He then began to visit the sick in the hospitals with His Mother, seeking out those who were most afflicted in order to cheer and console them. Attracted by His charity and sanctity, they often gave Him gifts, which He refused or accepted only for distribution among the poor.

The merciful Mother of God did not hesitate to tend to the festering ulcers and sores of the women, and she often changed their bandages with her own hands, while comforting the suffering patients. Frequently she healed them, and St. Joseph was given power to cure some of the men. When a severe pestilence devastated the town, Jesus, Mary and Joseph nursed and healed many of the victims.

As a result, the Holy Family became very popular among the people, especially among the poor, and a large number of men and women came to them for advice and instruction. In order to honor His Mother, Jesus told her to teach them the laws of the one true God. Speaking therefore to each individual in a way suited to his or her personality and problems, she urged them to give up their sinful ways of living in order to serve and worship the Lord in purity and in truth. Her gentle and modest manner and her penetrating messages were so moving and inspiring that many of her listeners were converted to a better life and eventually became Christians. St. Joseph also helped in instructing the men in his own plain and sincere way. Thus the Holy Family sowed in Egypt the spiritual seed that was later to develop into many generations of holy Christians, saints, martyrs and hermits.

THE BLESSED VIRGIN SAID
TO VENERABLE MOTHER MARY OF AGREDA:

"My daughter, I came into Egypt, where I knew no relations or friends, in a land of foreign religion, where I could offer no home or protection or assistance to my Son, whom I loved so much. It can easily be understood, then, what tribulations and hardships we suffered. Thou canst not understand with what patience and resignation we accepted them. It is true, I grieved much to see my husband in such necessity and want, but at the same time I blessed the Lord to be able to suffer them. In this noble patience and joy of spirit I wish thee to imitate me whenever the Lord offers thee an opportunity. My most holy Son chose poverty and taught it by word and by example. This same doctrine I taught and practiced during all my life. I wish thee to love and diligently to seek after this poverty."

CHAPTER TWENTY

THE RETURN TO NAZARETH

SOME TIME after King Herod's death, God the Father decreed that the Holy Family should return to Palestine. Mary learned of this decision one day while she was praying with Jesus, but neither of them made it known to St. Joseph. The good foster father of Our Lord had been very sad lately because he had not been paid for his work, and he often begged God on his knees to help his family in their growing need. Then one night during his sleep an angel appeared to him and said:

"Arise, and take the Child and His Mother, and go into the Land of Israel, for those who sought the Child's life are dead."

Upon awakening, St. Joseph immediately told Mary and Jesus about the Lord's command, and they both answered that God's Will must be done. They therefore decided to leave Egypt without delay. They distributed their furniture among the poor, and St. Joseph packed their few belongings on their faithful donkey which had come from Palestine with them. As the news of their departure spread, many of their Jewish and Egyptian friends gathered around

149

them and said good-by with touching sorrow.

When the Holy Family, accompanied by Mary's many angels, set out to cross the desert again, they were wearing light head-coverings made of bark, as protection against the sun. Mary had sandals, and Jesus wore bark shoes. Often they had to stop and shake the sand out of His shoes, and sometimes He was so tired that He had to ride on the donkey. All three suffered a great deal on this long trip, although occasionally the divine Child miraculously provided strengthening food for them.

When they reached Palestine, hearing that the new King was cruel, St. Joseph was afraid to settle in Bethlehem, as he had hoped to do. And after an angel warned him one night in a dream, the Holy Family followed the coast, passed Mount Carmel, and arriving at last in Nazareth, went to their former home, which had been cared for in their absence by a cousin of St. Joseph. When Mary entered the house with her husband and her Son, she immediately prostrated herself on the ground and fervently thanked the Lord for having led them safely through their long exile and hard journeys.

After they had settled in their home, Mary, who always observed perfect order in all her arrangements and habits, set up a rule of life for herself, so that she could again spend much time in prayer. St. Joseph took up his carpentry work, humbly rejoicing in the knowledge that he was laboring to support God Himself and His beloved Mother.

Young Jesus, besides helping Joseph and Mary whenever He could, soon became the most popular boy in Nazareth. All His young friends, among whom were His future Apostles John and James the Elder, loved Him so much that they tried hard not to displease Him. When a child was disobedient, the parents would therefore say: "What will little Jesus think of you? How sorry He will be!" Sometimes they even brought their naughty sons to Him and asked Him to make them good. Then with striking simplicity and kindness, while playing with His young friends, Jesus would urge them not to hurt their parents anymore. He would also persuade them to pray with Him to the good Lord to give them the strength to change. Then He would inspire them to go home, admit their faults, and sincerely ask their parents to forgive them.

At this time Jesus was a slender boy and rather tall for His age. Though somewhat pale, He had a clear complexion, and His handsome face was radiant with health. He had a broad and high forehead, and His dark-brown hair, which was parted in the middle, fell to His shoulders.

Soon after their return from Egypt, the Lord resolved to test Mary's love for Him by seeming to treat her coldly and impersonally for awhile. Therefore without any warning Jesus began to be very reserved with His Mother, speaking to her only rarely and very gravely. Most of the time He avoided her company, and when she came to Him or when they were at meals together, He would neither speak to her nor even look at her. Naturally Mary was deeply disturbed, for with her usual humility she feared that somehow she had offended God through some fault. She therefore examined her conscience minutely and racked her memory for some evidence of ingratitude. Although she could find not even one slight venial sin, nevertheless she humbled herself more than ever and acknowledged that she deserved such treatment. Yet with ardent longing she begged the Lord in unceasing prayer to pardon her and restore her to His favor. This trial lasted thirty days. Then one day as Mary knelt at the feet of Jesus, He said to her with great tenderness:

"Arise, My Mother."

And His words had such a profound effect on her that she was rapt into a prolonged ecstasy, in which many divine mysteries were revealed to her. When she came out of her trance and adored her Son, she was again privileged to contemplate His holy soul, as before. Henceforth until the time of His public ministry, Jesus regularly taught her the truths of the Christian religion which He was later to give to His Church.

CHAPTER TWENTY-ONE

THE BOY JESUS IN THE TEMPLE

IKE ALL the Jews, the Holy Family went to the Temple in Jerusalem at least once a year, to celebrate the Pasch in April. The Boy Jesus first took the long trip when He was eight years old, and He wished that it be made entirely on foot. Often He became tired and overheated, and then with tender compassion His Mother would ask Him to rest, while she gently wiped His face. Some nights they spent in inns and some in the open fields.

In the great Temple, Mary observed how Jesus prayed to His Father in Heaven for the whole human race. And when she thought of her Son's future sufferings in that same city, He would turn to her and urge her to offer up those sufferings with Him for the salvation of men. Several times in the Temple she heard the Voice of the Eternal Father declare:

"This is My Beloved Son in whom I am well pleased."

After Jesus reached the age of twelve, the Holy Family made their yearly pilgrimage to the Temple and spent seven days with friends in Jerusalem. But this time, when Mary and Joseph left the city and were on their way back to Nazareth, the Child Jesus withdrew from them without their knowledge. Not far from the city gate He turned and hastened back through the streets. In His divine omniscience He foresaw all that was to happen, and He offered it up to His Eternal Father for the benefit of souls.

During the next three days, He spent part of His time begging and visiting the hospitals of the poor, consoling the sick and giving them the alms He had received. Secretly He restored bodily health to some and spiritual health to many.

Then, joining some boys, He went to three schools, on each day to a different one. The questions and answers of the twelve-year-old Jesus surprised and irritated the teachers and priests of these schools so much that they decided on the third afternoon to have Him publicly tested in the Temple by their most famous experts, in order to embarrass and humiliate Him. For though they began by applauding the Boy's knowledge, they soon felt a secret envy and jealousy.

They all met accordingly in the great hall of the Temple, where Our Lord often taught later on. It was a vast auditorium in which crowds of people circulated casually, making it hard to recognize as a place dedicated to the service of God. Jesus was seated in a large throne-like chair that He could not wholly fill. Around Him were grouped a number of aged Israelites dressed as priests. He had stepped into their midst with remarkable majesty and grace, and by His pleasing appearance He awakened in these learned men a desire to hear Him. They listened to Him very intently, but with growing fury.

As, on the preceding days, Jesus in His replies had brought in analogies from nature and art, the scholars had taken care to call in some specialists skilled in the various branches of learning. When several of them began to ask Him questions relating to their fields, He told them that profane knowledge was not the proper subject for teaching in the Temple, but that He would nevertheless answer them, because such was the Will of His Father.

They did not understand that He was referring to His heavenly Father, and assumed that Joseph had told Him to show them how much He knew.

In replying to their questions, Our Lord spoke first about medicine, and the way He described the human body aroused the admiration of the foremost doctors. Then He took up several matters pertaining to astronomy, architecture, agriculture, geometry, mathematics and law. He was so skillful in correlating these different subjects with the promises, prophecies and mysteries of their religion, its ceremonies and sacrifices, that His listeners were astounded and embarrassed.

Finally the discussion turned to the coming of the Messias. Most of the Hebrew scholars maintained that He could not yet be due, because He was to come with kingly pomp and free His people by force from the Romans. But the Boy Jesus, by quoting the other prophecies concerning the rejection and death of the Messias, proved that the Prophets had described His two different comings: first to redeem, and then to judge mankind. And by recalling that the people of Israel were now in that very servitude which was foretold as a sure sign of His coming, Jesus demonstrated that the Messias must already be among them. He even reminded them of the visit of the three Magi, seeking the King of the Jews. Thus, while seeming to ask questions, Jesus taught with divine conviction.

The scribes and scholars who heard Him refute their arguments were all at first dumbfounded and then furious with shame. They could not tolerate His teaching them things they did not know, or His explaining the mysteries of the Law better than they could.

Meanwhile, during these three days, Mary and Joseph, their hearts filled with anxiety and self-reproach, had been searching in vain for Jesus among their relatives and friends. Although Mary knew that the time for her Son's Passion had not yet come, still she feared that Archelaus the King might have taken Him prisoner and be mistreating Him. Also she wondered whether Jesus might have gone to live in the desert with John the Baptist. Throughout those three days she neither ate nor slept. Though she often spoke with the angels that always accompanied her, they were not allowed to tell her where they knew Jesus was, and in her humility and prudence she did not ask them.

Since she did not know the cause of her loss, her anxiety was without measure, and yet she bore it with patience, resignation and submission. Not for a moment did she lose her interior or exterior peace, or entertain a discouraging thought. And though her sorrow pierced her inmost heart, she never failed in reverence or ceased her prayers for the human race and for the grace of finding her Son.

One of the women she questioned exclaimed: "That Child came to my door yesterday begging for alms, and I gave Him some—His grace and beauty touched my heart. I was moved to compassion at seeing such a lovely Child in poverty and need."

Later at the city hospital Mary was told of Jesus' visits there. Then the thought occurred to her that since He was not with the poor, He was probably in the House of God and of prayer. Now the holy angels encouraged her and said:

"Our Queen and our Lady, the hour of thy consolation is at hand. Soon thou wilt see the Light of thine eyes. Hasten thy footsteps and go to the Temple."

Just at this moment St. Joseph rejoined her, as they had been searching separately for a while. During all these three days he had suffered indescribable sorrow and affliction, hastening from one place to another. In fact he had been in serious danger of losing his life, if God had not strengthened him and if Mary had not consoled him and forced him to take some food and rest.

Mary and Joseph arrived at the Temple and found Jesus just as He was finishing His last explanation. All the scholars rose in complete amazement and looked at each other, exclaiming: "What a prodigy of a boy!"

Joseph humbly remained silent while Mary approached

her Son and said with reverence and affection, before all those present:

"Son, why hast Thou done so to us? Behold, Thy father and I have been seeking Thee sorrowing."

In a very serious tone of voice Jesus replied:

"How is it that you sought Me? Did you not know that I must be about My Father's business?"

Mary and Joseph did not understand what He said, first because just then they were overwhelmed with joy at finding Him, and secondly because they had not heard Him explaining the Messias' mission. Moreover, during all this time the soul of her Son had again been veiled from Mary's eyes.

For a moment it seemed as if several of the scholars who were so angry at Jesus might do Him some harm. But then the Holy Family quietly went out through the crowd, which opened to let them pass. Soon they had left the city.

When they were alone on the road, Mary knelt before her Son and asked His blessing. With loving tenderness the Boy Jesus raised her from the ground, comforted her, and revealed to her all that He had done in those three days. Later during the journey He also explained to her that the learned doctors had not recognized Him as the Messias because they were inflated and arrogant in their own knowledge, and that their understanding was obscured by the darkness of their pride, for if they had had the humble and loving desire to see the truth, His reasoning would have sufficiently convinced them.

"And His mother kept all these things carefully in her heart."

OUR LADY SAID TO VENERABLE
MOTHER MARY OF AGREDA:

"The Lord absented Himself from me in order that by seeking Him in sorrow and tears I might find Him again in joy and with abundant fruits for my soul. In my great love the uncertainty as to the cause of His withdrawal gave me no rest until I found Him.

"In this I wish that thou imitate me, whether thou lose Him through thy own fault or by the disposition of His Will. For to lose sight of God for the purpose of being tried in virtue and love is not the same as to lose sight of Him in punishment for sins committed.

"So strong are the bonds of His Love that no one can burst them, except thy own free will."

CHAPTER TWENTY-TWO

THE HIDDEN LIFE IN NAZARETH

WHEN THE Boy Jesus returned to Nazareth with Mary and Joseph after the Finding in the Temple, a party was given in His honor by thirty-three of His young friends and relatives, who later became His disciples. The banquet table was decorated with wreaths made of ears of corn and vine foliage, and in front of each child were bunches of grapes and bread rolls. During the meal, young Jesus told His companions a beautiful story about a wedding at which water would be changed into wine and indifferent guests into faithful friends, and then about another kind of wedding at which wine would be changed into blood and bread into flesh as a living bond of love until the end of the world. At the time the boys did not understand what He meant. He also told His young cousin Nathanael that one day He would attend his wedding. Henceforth Jesus was the acknowledged leader of these boys, and He spent much time with them, sitting and talking with them or accompanying them on walks in the country, and all the time teaching them many practical lessons.

As Jesus grew up, He helped St. Joseph more and more

at his carpentry work, and when He reached the age of eighteen He became His foster father's regular assistant, thus giving St. Joseph great pleasure and consolation.

Jesus' bed was a plain, wooden couch that Joseph had made for Him, and He used only one blanket and a small, woolen pillow made by Mary. Yet He would not even stretch out on this hard bed, but rested sitting on it, and when His Mother spoke of getting Him a better bed, Jesus replied that the only couch on which He was to be stretched out would be His Cross. Each evening Mary would kneel before her Son and ask His pardon for not having done all her duty in serving Him and for not having been sufficiently grateful for the blessings of the day. And each morning she likewise asked Him to order her to do what He wished during the day in His service.

Jesus now began to show more gravity in His conduct and conversation with His parents. More and more they observed a certain divine power and majesty in His features, and they caressed Him less. Yet in His relations with them He remained humble and obedient and loving. However, as the time for His public ministry slowly approached, He became more recollected and devoted more time to prayer and meditation.

Every day Jesus, His Mother and Joseph prayed together in Mary's plain and poorly furnished room, the holy room in which the Annunciation had taken place. They prayed aloud, standing with their arms crossed on their chests, in the light of a lamp. And frequently Mary and Joseph prayed silently together. Sometimes they knelt and sometimes each lay face down on the floor with arms extended like a cross. Occasionally when Jesus prayed for hardhearted sinners, Mary saw drops of blood appear on His face, which she would then wipe away with deep reverence and compassion. At other times she perceived Him resplendent with glory, as during the Transfiguration, and surrounded by adoring and chanting angels.

Young Jesus continued to visit the poor and the sick in Nazareth and the neighboring villages, and while influencing for the good everyone whom He met, He secretly helped many persons both spiritually and physically.

Throughout these years of His hidden life, Jesus spent much time teaching His Mother all that she must know and do later for His Church. Soon after the return from Jerusalem when He was twelve, the eternal Father said to Mary:

"We have resolved to make you the closest image and likeness of My only-begotten Son. Be mindful therefore that a great preparation is required of you."

Henceforth Jesus instructed His Mother thoroughly in the new Law of His Gospel and all the mysteries and doctrines of the Catholic religion. Day after day He taught her the meaning and value of the Sacraments and dogmas of the Church, and He described to her the whole history of His Church until the end of the world, together with all its saints and martyrs and doctors and prelates. He also showed her how to apply this knowledge in a practical way to her daily life, so that she might be well prepared to serve Him and His Mystical Body the Church as Divine Providence planned. Mary received these inspiring instructions with profound humility, reverence, gratitude and fervent love, which reached a climax when Jesus explained to her the mysteries of the Holy Eucharist and the Mass. Then she exclaimed:

"My Lord and life of my soul, shall I be so fortunate as to bear Thee once more within my body and soul?"

And Jesus answered:

"My beloved Mother, you shall receive Me many times in the Blessed Sacrament, and after My death and Ascension it will be your consolation, for I shall choose your sincere and loving heart as My most pleasing and delightful resting place."

From that hour Mary humbly and gratefully began to prepare herself in all her thoughts and actions for the time when she could receive Holy Communion, and she prayed fervently that all men might know and appreciate this greatest of all the Sacraments.

By a special privilege granted to the Blessed Virgin by God, after she reached the age of thirty-three—during the hidden life in Nazareth, Jesus being then eighteen—her beautiful physical appearance and perfection remained unchanged during all the rest of her long life. She now strikingly resembled in features and complexion the unique beauty of Christ during His last years on earth, and the Lord allowed Mary to keep that perfection in order that His likeness might be preserved in her as long as she lived.

SPEAKING OF THE HIDDEN LIFE, THE BLESSED VIRGIN TOLD ST. BRIDGET OF SWEDEN:

"As the Gospel says, my Son was subject to His parents, and He acted like other children until He grew up. Nothing unclean ever touched Him, nor was the least disorder ever seen in His hair. When He grew older, He was constantly in prayer. His features and His words were so wonderful and so pleasing that many persons when in trouble used to say: 'Let us go to Mary's Son—He will console us!' As He grew in age, He worked with His hands, and He talked with us so inspiringly about God that we were continually filled with indescribable joy. And when we were in fear, in poverty, and in trouble, He did not produce gold and silver for us, but urged us to be patient, and we were marvelously protected. What we needed was sometimes given to us by compassionate and devout persons, and sometimes came from our work, so that we had what we needed to live on, but nothing superfluous, for we sought only to serve God. At home, with friends who visited us, He talked familiarly about the Law of God and its meanings and types. He also openly disputed with learned men, so that they were astonished and used to say, 'Joseph's Son instructs the Scribes—there is a great spirit in Him!'

"He was also so obedient that when Joseph said to Him: 'Do this' or 'Do that,' He did it at once, for He concealed the power of His Divinity in such a way that it could only be perceived by myself and at times by Joseph. Very often we saw Him surrounded by a wonderful light and heard angels' voices singing over Him.

We also observed that unclean spirits, which could not be cast out by official exorcists, fled at the sight of my Son's presence. Keep this always in your memory, my daughter, and offer sincere thanks to God that He chose to reveal His childhood to others through you."

CHAPTER TWENTY-THREE

THE DEATH OF ST. JOSEPH

AT THIS time, although he was not very old, St. Joseph was worn out in strength and health after twenty years of hard work for his family, and the Lord now ordained that he was to spend his last eight years of life in illness and suffering, in order to increase his sanctity through the practice of patience and resignation. Mary therefore lovingly persuaded him to give up his work, which Jesus had been helping him to perform, often miraculously making it easier for him.

Now Mary gladly volunteered to support the family, as she had done in Egypt, by spinning and weaving linen and wool, with the help of a good and loyal woman friend. Consequently she often spent the greater part of the night at work, although Jesus sometimes enabled her to accomplish a great deal in a short time.

During his last years St. Joseph suffered a series of fevers, violent headaches and a very painful rheumatism which made him weak and helpless. As Mary observed how he bore all his sufferings with humble patience and supernatural love, her affection and admiration for him increased every day, and she joyfully labored for his support and comfort. His greatest consolation was that she should prepare and serve his meals herself, and she often made special efforts to get him choice foods. She would often take off his shoes for him and support him with her arms and console him with kind and inspiring words.

During his last three years Joseph's illness grew worse, and Mary nursed him day and night. Several times she begged the Lord to let her take over her husband's suffering, and when his pains were keenest she obtained her Son's permission to command them to cease for a while. She also ordered her angels to console St. Joseph, which they did by appearing to him in beautiful human forms and speaking to him about God or by singing heavenly hymns for him.

All this time Jesus also helped and encouraged His beloved foster father, whenever He was not engaged in His intensive preparation for His public ministry.

Realizing one day that the hour of St. Joseph's death was very near, Mary went to her Son and said to Him:

"My Lord, I beseech Thee, let Thy servant Joseph's death be as precious in Thy sight as the uprightness of his life has been pleasing to Thee."

And Jesus replied:

"My Mother, your request is granted, for the merits of Joseph are great. I will now assist him and will assign him so high a place among My people that he will be the admiration of angels and of men. With no other human being shall I do as with your husband."

Then for nine days St. Joseph enjoyed the company of Mary or Jesus without interruption, and three times each day the angels comforted him with celestial music and invigorating fragrances.

On the eighth day he fell into an ecstasy that lasted twenty-four hours, during which he was shown clearly many divine mysteries which he had believed by faith concerning the Incarnation and the Redemption, and he was formally commissioned as the messenger of the Saviour to the patriarchs and prophets in Limbo.

When St. Joseph came out of this ecstasy, his face was shining with heavenly light, and he asked Mary to give him her blessing. But instead she indicated that Jesus should bless him, which He did. Then Mary fell on her knees and begged her dying husband to bless her, and after he had done so she kissed his hand tenderly and affectionately. St. Joseph also implored her pardon for all his deficiencies in serving her and requested her prayers in this hour of his death.

Then he spoke these last words to her:

"Blessed art thou among all women, Mary! May angels and men praise thee! And may the Name of the Lord be known, adored and exalted in thee through all the coming ages. I hope to see thee in our heavenly home. . . ."

And turning toward Jesus with profound reverence, St. Joseph tried in vain to kneel, but the Saviour gently took him in His arms, while Joseph said:

"My Lord and my God, give Thy blessing to Thy servant, and pardon the faults I have committed in Thy service. I give Thee my heartfelt thanks for having chosen me to be the husband of Thy Mother! May Thy glory be my thanksgiving for all eternity. . . ."

Jesus then lovingly blessed St. Joseph and said:

"My father, rest in peace and in the grace of My eternal Father, and bring to the saints in Limbo the joyful news of the approach of their redemption."

At these words, in the arms of Jesus, with Mary kneeling and weeping at his feet, in a room brightly lighted by hosts of angels, St. Joseph died a happy and peaceful death.

After Jesus had closed His foster father's eyes, Mary prepared his body for burial with the help of her angels, and as she did so, God enveloped it in a wonderful light, so that she could see only Joseph's lifelike face. The body was wrapped in a white shroud and placed in a narrow bier, which was then carried to a fine tomb given to St. Joseph by a rich man. Only Jesus and a few friends formed the funeral procession, together with a great number of resplendent angels.

THE BLESSED VIRGIN SAID TO
VENERABLE MOTHER MARY OF AGREDA:

"The whole human race has much undervalued the privilege and prerogatives conceded to my blessed husband, St. Joseph. I assure you that he is one of the greatly favored personages in the Divine Presence, and he has immense power to stay the arms of divine vengeance. That which my husband asks of the Lord in Heaven is granted upon earth, and on his intercession depend many extraordinary favors for men."

CHAPTER TWENTY-FOUR

PREPARATION FOR THE PUBLIC LIFE

DURING the four years between the death of St. Joseph and the beginning of Christ's public ministry, the Blessed Virgin did not have to work so much and was able to spend more time in prayer. Jesus and Mary usually took only one meal a day, at about six o'clock in the evening. Frequently they ate nothing but bread, although sometimes Mary added fish or fruit or vegetables. She served her divine Son on her knees.

Often in the privacy of their home Mary would remain prostrate on the ground, adoring her Lord, until He told her to rise, and then with tears of reverence, love and humility she would kiss His feet or hands. She did all the housework for Him with joy and eager zeal, and whenever her angels would begin her tasks before she did, she would order them to stop, so that she could do the work herself. At such times she would say to them: "My friends, permit me to do this work, since I can thereby gain merits which you do not need. I know the value of such work which the world despises, and the Lord has given me this knowledge in order that I may perform it myself and not let it be done by others." At work or in prayer she composed and sang lovely hymns in honor of her Lord.

Once when Mary was almost overcome at the thought of the future ingratitude of men toward their Saviour, Jesus ordered the angels to console her by singing canticles of praise to God for her. Then Christ gave His Mother a still deeper understanding of the mystery of sin and redemption, and He encouraged her by revealing to her the great number of the predestined apostles and saints of the Church.

As the time for His public ministry approached, Jesus and Mary prayed more and more fervently together for the Apostles whom He was soon to call to His service. The Lord also showed His Mother how He was going to conduct His preaching and how she was to co-operate with Him and help Him to found His Church.

Some time after the death of St. Joseph, Jesus and Mary decided to move to an isolated cottage near Capharnaum on the northern shore of the Lake of Galilee. When Jesus began to spend most of His time in prayer and traveling in preparation for His public ministry, some of the inhabitants of Nazareth criticized Him. He therefore accepted this cottage by the lakeside when a man named Levi who lived in Capharnaum offered it to Him, for He would be able to meet there more conveniently with His future disciples. Jesus and Mary made several trips between Nazareth and Capharnaum, transporting their modest belongings on a donkey. Finally they thoroughly cleaned and then closed up their house in Nazareth, although later they stayed there whenever the Saviour preached in Nazareth or its surroundings.

After reaching His twenty-seventh year, Jesus began to mingle more with men and to go away on trips that lasted several days. Often He spent the nights in prayer on the hills of Galilee. During His absences Mary missed Him keenly. When He returned after two or three days without rest or food, He gave His Mother His hand and greeted her with great affection, yet also with grave restraint. Then she lovingly prepared refreshing meals for Him, and He told her about the hidden blessings which had been communicated to many souls.

One day Jesus said to her:

"My dearest Mother, the time has come when, in accordance with the will of My Eternal Father, I must begin to prepare the hearts of certain persons to receive the light of My teaching. In this work I want you to follow Me and assist Me."

Henceforth Mary accompanied Him on many of the short trips which He took to the towns and villages of Galilee. Usually she humbly walked behind her Son along the country paths. And she stood silently praying beside Him during conversations with men and women, while He announced to them the imminent coming of the Messias, assuring them that the Promised One was already in the world and in the Land of Israel. Thus He became acquainted with those whom He knew to be prepared and able to accept the Truth.

In His appearance Jesus showed so much beauty, grace, peace, kindness and gentleness of manner, and His way of speaking was so vivid and strong, that with the help of divine grace many persons decided to give up their sinful ways of life and thus became capable of believing that the Messias had already begun His reign.

In addition, usually accompanied by Mary, Jesus visited the sick and the grief-stricken, especially among the poor. He restored health of body to many, and assisted the dying, giving them true peace of mind. Mary did the same, particularly among the women.

During this preparatory ministry Jesus and His Mother worked alone together, accompanied only by angels. Some of the nights they passed in prayer in the open. Often they begged for their food, and sometimes the angels brought it to them.

Meanwhile in the desert, St. John, the son of Elizabeth and Zacharias, having reached the age of thirty, was com-

manded by the Lord to come forth and prepare the way
for the Messias as a forerunner. John the Baptist was intensely
devoted to the Mother of God, for until he was nine years
old she had regularly sent him food by her angels, and
since then she had often told them to give him news of his
Lord, whom he fervently loved and worshipped from afar.

Now St. John lcft the desert and appeared among the
people of Israel, preaching penance and baptizing on the
banks of the River Jordan. He was clothed in a camel skin,
with a leather belt. His feet were bare, and his features
thin and ascetical. Yet in manner he was graceful, modest and kind, though he could be terrifying to the proud,
the hardhearted and the greedy.

One day, when Jesus was thirty years old, Mary heard a
Voice of marvelous power say to her:

"Mary, My Daughter and My Spouse, offer your Son to
Me as a sacrifice."

Realizing that the time had at last come for the Redemption of mankind through the public life and death of
Christ, she replied generously:

"Eternal King and Almighty God, Lord of all, He is
Thine and so am I. What then can I offer Thee that is
not more Thine than mine? Yet because He is the life of
my soul and the soul of my life, to yield Him into the
hands of His enemies at the cost of His life is a great sacrifice. However, let not my will but Thine be done. I offer
up my Son in order that He may pay the debt contracted
by the children of Adam."

The Blessed Trinity immediately rewarded and consoled
her by a vision in which she was shown the glory and the
good that would result from Jesus' sacrifice and hers. When
she came out of this rapture, Mary was prepared to endure
the pain of being separated from her beloved Son and
Lord.

Jesus therefore called her and said:

"My Mother, give Me your consent to accomplish the
Will of My eternal Father, for the time has come when I
must begin My work for men. Although I must now leave

you alone for awhile, My blessing and powerful protection will remain with you. Later I will return and claim your help and company in My task."

Both Jesus and Mary were so deeply moved in this moment of parting that they were weeping quietly, and the Lord tenderly placed His arms around His Mother's shoulders. Among other things He told her that He would still go to Jerusalem three times for the Passover, and that the third time her heart would suffer cruelly. Then Mary fell at His feet and said with intense sorrow and reverence:

"My Lord, I offer Thee my own will as a sacrifice. And as Thy Mother I ask only that I may be allowed to share Thy labors and Thy Cross."

They went to the door together, and Mary kissed her Son's feet as He gave her His blessing. Then Jesus set out on His journey to the River Jordan, where John was baptizing.

During the absence of Christ, Mary spent nearly all her time in prayer, shut up in her house. Many times each day, in order to practice penance and reverence for God, she genuflected and prostrated herself on the floor, interceding for sinners by her prayers and mortifications. The rest of the time she conversed with her holy angels, whom the Lord had commanded to attend her in visible form. They kept her informed of all her Son's actions and prayers, so that she was able to pray with Him whenever He prayed, in the same posture and with the same words. Meanwhile she continued to visit the sick and the poor in her neighborhood.

In addition to the detailed reports of Jesus' doings which she received from the angels, the Blessed Virgin was also able to witness in visions all the most important incidents of the public life of Christ, no matter where He was at the time. Thus she saw Him being baptized by John and then go up into the mountainous desert and begin His forty days' fast. Mary then locked the door of her house, and entering her little oratory she began to pray and fast with her Son, imitating and co-operating with Him in His work for mankind. After forty days of uninterrupted prayer and fasting, she witnessed the threefold temptation of Christ by Satan, and from her retreat she likewise entered into conflict with the Tempter. When she saw the devil carrying Jesus from place to place she wept, but soon she rejoiced over the victory of the Lord. Then her angels brought her some of the heavenly food which they administered to Jesus at the same time, and with them came a number of birds that had kept Him company during His fast, and they gathered around her and sang sweetly while she ate the miraculous food, which quickly restored her strength, for Jesus had sent it to her with His blessing.

The Saviour now spent several months preaching and preparing some of the men and women who were to become His disciples. In order to imitate Him, Mary left her solitude and devoted nearly all her time to visiting on foot some sick and poor women and children, instructing and healing and consoling them.

When she saw Jesus call to His service His first Apostles, Andrew, John, Peter, Philip and Nathanael, Mary accepted them as her spiritual children in the Lord and prayed fervently for them. The Saviour taught them to revere and admire His Mother even before they met her, and He impressed upon them her extraordinary sanctity and virtue. At the very first words of the Master concerning Mary, St. John conceived a holy love and esteem for her. The five Apostles begged Jesus to let them meet and honor His Mother, and He therefore led them northward to the Lake of Galilee.

As soon as Mary was aware that they were approaching, she set the cottage in order and prepared food for them. When Jesus came near, she waited for Him at the door, and when He entered she prostrated herself on the floor and kissed His feet, while she asked for His blessing. The profound humility and reverence with which the Blessed Virgin received her Son filled the disciples with new devotion and awe for their Master. Feeling a mystical attraction toward the holy Mother of God, they immediately knelt before her and begged her to accept them as her sons and servants. St. John was the first to do this, and Mary welcomed him with special love, because of his extraordinary purity and humility. Then she personally served the meal which she had prepared for them.

That night after the disciples had retired, Jesus prayed with His Mother in her oratory, as formerly, and He spoke to her about the Mystery of Baptism. Because He had already promised her that she would be baptized, she now asked Him whether He would administer the Sacrament to her Himself.

Then, in the presence of a multitude of visible angels, Jesus baptized His Immaculate Mother, and immediately the Voice of the eternal Father was heard saying:

"This is My beloved Daughter in whom I take delight." Next the Incarnate Word declared:

"This is My beloved Mother whom I have selected and who will assist Me in all My works."

And lastly the Holy Spirit added:

"This is My Spouse, chosen among thousands."

THE BLESSED VIRGIN SAID TO ST. BRIDGET OF SWEDEN:

"You are not able to see my Son as He is in Heaven, but let me describe to you His physical appearance as He was in the world. His features were so beautiful that no one looked at His Face without feeling filled with joy and consolation, even when depressed. Yes, even the wicked were free from worldly gloom while looking at Him. Consequently persons suffering from sorrow used to say: 'Let us go and see Mary's Son, and we shall be without our grief at least that long.'

"When He was twenty years old, He reached His full growth in manly stature and strength. He had no superfluous flesh. His muscles were well-developed. And He was powerfully built. His hair, eyebrows and beard were light brown. His beard measured the width of a hand. His forehead was neither prominent nor retreating, but straight and erect. His nose was well-proportioned,

neither large nor small. His eyes were so clear and pure that even His enemies enjoyed looking at Him. His lips were not thick but light red. His chin did not jut out and was not overlong, but pleasing and finely proportioned. His cheeks were moderately full, and His complexion was a clear white mixed with fresh red. He held Himself straight and erect, and there was not a spot on His whole Body."

CHAPTER TWENTY-FIVE

THE WEDDING AT CANA

AFTER HIS return to Galilee with His first disciples, Jesus and His Mother were invited to Cana near Nazareth to attend the wedding of a young couple whom they knew. The bride came from Bethlehem and was related to St. Joseph's family. Her father, who now lived in Cana, was a wealthy man who had charge of the transportation of mail and owned a number of inns and warehouses with large stables. His wife was quite lame. The groom was a prosperous young man from Capharnaum whose parents were dead and who was related to St. Ann.

The Blessed Virgin urged Jesus to accept the invitation, and He not only promised to attend the wedding, but also undertook to be responsible for some of the arrangements and for the supply of wine. Our Lord considered this wedding of great importance for several reasons. He wished to begin His public ministry by sanctifying and blessing the institution of marriage. He wanted to strengthen and to unite His new disciples by performing His first public miracle among them. And He wished to refute the unjust criticism which had arisen against Him during His prolonged

absence from home, to the effect that He was neglecting
His work, His Mother and His relatives.

The numerous guests who had been invited to the wedding traveled to Cana in several parties. The Blessed Virgin went the shortest way along the narrow paths across
the hills, accompanied by some women friends, for they
preferred to avoid the caravan road in order to be alone.
Jesus took a longer route with about twenty-five of His followers, as He wanted to stop and instruct them on the
way and also to speak to the people in certain villages.
Thus Mary reached Cana first, after a walk of several hours,
and she helped in the preparations for the wedding. When
Jesus arrived, she went out to meet Him with the bride
and her parents, who greeted Him with marked respect.
The bridegroom's aunt invited Jesus and Mary to stay in
her large house.

Jesus Himself planned all the details of the wedding
festivities, deliberately combining serious considerations
and spiritual instruction with the various entertainments.
When He announced the program for the next few days,
He explained that the guests were free to enjoy themselves in the traditional festive ways, but that they should
also grow in wisdom as a result of their recreation.

On the second day after His arrival, all the guests—the
men on one side and the women on the other—went out
to a lovely meadow in which there were trees and a stream.
Some of the guests walked up and down, talking together,
while others played various games. Jesus organized a game
in which the men, sitting in a circle on the ground, tossed
different fruits to one another according to certain rules.
As He watched them play, His expression was one of friendly
seriousness, and several times He said a few well-chosen
words which made a deep impression on the men and
aroused their admiration. Later He distributed the prizes
to the winners with fitting individual comments.

While the younger guests competed at running and
catching fruits tied to the branches of the trees, in another
part of the field the women were playing a game with

fruits as prizes, which the Blessed Virgin watched, sitting between the bride and the aunt of the groom.

That evening Jesus preached in the temple before all the guests, who now numbered over one hundred. He spoke of pleasures which are permissible, of the motives with which one might indulge in them, of their limitations, and of the caution and restraints that must accompany them. Then He spoke of marriage, of the mutual obligations of husband and wife, of continence and chastity, and also of spiritual marriage. When He was through and all the guests had left, the bride and groom remained with Him, and He gave them some private instructions.

Later in the evening, after a banquet, there was a dance. First the young couple danced alone, and then some of the guests joined them in a series of calm, rhythmical movements by which they formed various figures. None of the future Apostles took part, nor did the married women, but some of the disciples did. The whole atmosphere was one of quiet and restrained gaiety and good cheer.

The wedding ceremony took place at nine o'clock the next morning. The bride was dressed and adorned by her maids and companions. Her costume was very similar to the one which Mary had worn on her wedding day. She also had a crown, but it was more richly decorated.

In the solemn and colorful procession from the house of the bride to the temple, the young couple was accompanied by children carrying floral wreaths and playing musical instruments, as well as by all their relatives and guests. The ceremony was performed by the priests at the entrance to the temple. The Blessed Virgin had already presented the two rings to Jesus for His blessing, and now she gave them to the bride and groom, who exchanged the rings. The chief priest, taking up a sharp instrument, lightly cut the pair's ring fingers and let flow into a cup filled with wine, two drops of the groom's blood and one of the bride's. After the couple had drunk the wine, they destroyed the cup. After the ceremony, clothes and other objects were distributed to the many poor persons who had gathered to see the wedding. And when the newly married couple returned to the festival hall, Jesus Himself welcomed them and said to them and to all the guests: "The Peace of the Lord and His Light be with you!"

Before the banquet, Jesus organized another remarkable game for the men in the garden. He placed various flowers, plants and fruits around a large table on which there was a pointer that rotated on a pivot until it stopped before the prize of the person who had twirled it. In this game, which the men now began to play, nothing occurred by mere chance. Each prize somehow had a definite significance related to the qualities and faults of its winner. And as each of the players in turn won his particular prize, Jesus made a brief and profound comment. Yet the personal application of His words was grasped only by the man to whom they were directed. The others found in them merely some broadly edifying teaching. But the individual himself was deeply moved and felt that Jesus had indeed seen into the most secret thoughts of his heart and conscience.

When the bridegroom won a very striking exotic fruit, Jesus spoke about marriage, chastity, and the hundredfold fruit which purity produces. And as the Master handed him his prize, the young man was stirred to the depths of his soul. He turned pale and, without anyone noticing it, he underwent a mystical purification in which he was supernaturally liberated from the unclean lusts of the flesh. At the same time the bride, who was sitting among the women at some distance, had a fainting spell and experienced something similar, while the Blessed Virgin held her in her arms and helped her to revive. Thereafter both the boy and the girl seemed definitely brighter and purer in appearance. The other disciples, after they had eaten the fruit which they won, felt their predominant passion awake and struggle for mastery within them, but when they used their will power and resisted the impulse, they conquered it and thereby became greatly strengthened against future temptations.

When the game was over, everyone went in to the wedding feast in a spacious hall with three long, narrow tables at which the guests reclined, the women remaining apart from the men. Jesus had the seat of honor at the head of the middle table, with the relatives of the married couple. The groom served his guests, assisted by the steward and several servants, while his wife and some maids served the women.

When the bridegroom brought the carving knife to Jesus, the Master reminded him that at the banquet when they were boys, after the Finding in the Temple, He had predicted that He would attend the youth's wedding. The young husband now became very thoughtful as he recalled what Jesus had said then, for he had completely forgotten this incident of his childhood.

Jesus gave the guests an instructive talk while carving the lamb. He spoke of the lamb being separated from the flock and led to be killed. Then He explained how, in the process of roasting, the flesh was purified by fire. The carving up of the parts, He said, symbolized the way in which the followers of the Lamb of God must leave those to whom they are attached by bonds of flesh and blood. While distributing the pieces of meat to the guests, who were eagerly listening to His instructions, He said that just as the lamb had been taken from its companions and had been put to death in order to provide food for many persons, so too he who wished to follow the Lamb of God must leave his home and neighborhood and family, and put his passions to death, for then he could become, through the Lamb of God, a source of spiritual food by which he could unite his fellow men with one another and with the Father of all in Heaven.

Throughout the banquet, as during the whole wedding celebration, Jesus was very cheerful, while taking every opportunity to give the guests helpful instruction. He also spoke about relaxations and pleasure at social gatherings, remarking that a bow must not remain bent all the time and that the soil must from time to time be refreshed by rain.

During the festivities the Blessed Virgin had spoken

only when she was asked a question or when it was really necessary. At all times she gave a good example to the women around her by remaining perfectly recollected and composed. In her Son's presence she listened attentively to all that He said, and then she meditated on His words.

During the banquet Jesus and His Mother ate some of the food, though with great moderation and without showing outwardly their unusual abstinence. Then, as the second course, consisting of bird meat, fish, honey, fruit and pastry was being served, Mary noticed that there was no more wine. She therefore immediately went to Jesus, who was instructing the guests, and whispered to Him:

"They have no wine."

She also reminded Him that He had promised to supply the wine.

The divine Saviour, who had just been speaking of His heavenly Father, replied aloud, with calm and loving, yet impersonal majesty:

"What is that to you and to Me, woman? My hour has not yet come."

Then Mary understood that Jesus was waiting for His Eternal Father's permission to perform His first great public miracle. Feeling entirely relieved of her anxiety for the guests and trusting that Almighty God would reveal the Lord's power at the right moment, she went to the worried servants and said to them with quiet modesty and confidence:

"Do whatever He tells you."

Then, having done her part as intercessor for others, the Mother of God humbly returned to her place among the women.

A moment later Jesus told the waiters to bring the water jars to Him and to turn them upside down. The servants brought in six large, stone jars which were so heavy when full that two men had to carry them. That they were now empty was evident when they were turned upside down. Then Jesus said to the waiters:

"Fill the jars with water."

When the six jars, filled to the brim with water, were

brought back from the well in a nearby cellar, Jesus arose, went to them, and blessed them. Then, returning to His seat at the table, He said to the servants:

"Draw out now and take to the chief steward."

The men did as He commanded. When the chief steward, who had been absent from the hall momentarily and did not know where they had obtained the wine, drank what St. John, an eyewitness, called "the water after it had become wine," he went to the bridegroom and exclaimed in surprise: "Every man first sets forth the good wine, and when they have drunk freely, then that which is poorer in quality. But you have kept the good wine until now!"

When the bridegroom and the bride's father tasted the miraculous wine, they too were amazed, for the servants were insisting that they had just filled the jars with nothing but water from the well. Then all the guests drank the new wine and fell silent from awe and reverence as they realized that they had indeed witnessed a striking miracle wrought by the Master, Jesus of Nazareth.

Now the Saviour gave them a long talk on the deeper significance of what had taken place. Among other things He said that the world gives the strong wine first and then the poorer, but it was not so in the Kingdom of His Father. There pure water was changed into excellent wine, to demonstrate that negligence and lukewarmness should give place to love and zeal. He mentioned the party in His honor when He was twelve years old, which many of His present listeners had attended as His childhood friends. He reminded them that He had spoken then of bread and wine and of a wedding at which the water of lukewarmness would be changed into the wine of love and enthusiasm. All those promises, He said, had now been fulfilled. And He predicted that they would witness still greater miracles, that He would celebrate several Passovers with them and at the last one He would change bread and wine into His Flesh and Blood, and thus He would remain with them until the end, to strengthen and to console them. And He added that after that Last Supper they would see things happen to Him which they would not even believe if He revealed them now.

All the men and women listening to Jesus were filled with awe and wonder. They were utterly changed in their attitude toward Him as a result of the miracle which they had witnessed and also due to the extraordinary qualities of the miraculous wine. As St. John observed, Jesus had "manifested His glory, and His disciples believed in Him."

His new followers and His relatives were now suddenly convinced of His power, His dignity, and His divine mission. Henceforth they believed with firm faith that Jesus was indeed the promised Messias.

At the same time they had become better men and women, more devout and more united among themselves. Thus by performing this miracle on the first occasion when His closest future Apostles and disciples were gathered together, Jesus had succeeded in strengthening their faith in His leadership and their willingness to follow Him.

After the banquet the young bridegroom went to Jesus and spoke to Him very humbly in private. He said that he now felt himself dead to all carnal desires, and that if his bride consented, he wished to live in continence with her. His wife then came to Jesus and said the same thing.

The Master took them both aside and spoke to them about marriage and chastity in terms of sowing and reaping supernatural merit. He explained the rich fruit of the life of the spirit and mentioned the prophets and saints who had lived in continence and made of their bodies a pleasing sacrifice to the Father in Heaven. Thus they had brought many sinners back to God and had inspired numerous followers who in turn formed holy spiritual families and communities.

The young bride and groom now decided to take a vow of continence, and they resolved to live as brother and sister for three years. Then they knelt before Our Lord, and He gladly gave them His blessing.

CHAPTER TWENTY-SIX

MARY DURING
THE PUBLIC MINISTRY

WHEN JESUS and Mary returned to their home in Capharnaum after the wedding at Cana, the Saviour explained to His Mother in a long talk one evening that His time had come and that He planned to leave for Judea and to celebrate the Pasch in Jerusalem. Then He would call His Apostles to join Him and would preach still more openly. Consequently, He predicted, He would be persecuted and His enemies would stir up opposition to Him in Judea and Galilee. Then Jesus described to Mary the principal events of His public ministry and explained how she and the other women were to cooperate in it.

The Blessed Virgin wept at the thought of the great dangers to which her Son would be exposed on account of the intense feeling which His recent teaching and miracles were arousing among His enemies, for she had been informed of all the rumors and slanders that were being circulated against Him by persons who would not dare to utter them in His presence.

That evening the Saviour also gave a talk in the Synagogue of Capharnaum, in which He explained the story of Elias and the rain cloud in terms of the coming of the Messias bringing new life to all who accepted His teaching. He declared that whoever was thirsty could now drink and whoever had prepared his field could now receive refreshing rain. He spoke so impressively that all His listeners, and especially Mary and the holy women, were moved to tears.

A few days later Jesus traveled to Jerusalem with some of His first disciples. The women went there separately, and the Blessed Virgin stayed in the house of Mary Mark, the mother of one of the disciples. It was at this time that the Saviour first drove the merchants from the Temple. During these eight days Jesus hardly saw His Mother, for He was staying with Lazarus in Bethany outside the city. Mary did not go out, but spent her time praying for her Son, as the evil intentions of His enemies alarmed her.

In fact, after the Sabbath the Pharisees decided to arrest Jesus, and they went to seize Him in Mary Mark's home. But when they found only His Mother and the holy women there, they rudely insulted them and ordered them to leave the town. Deeply troubled by this harsh treatment, the Blessed Virgin and the other women fled to the sisters of Lazarus in Bethany. Soon afterward they returned to Galilee.

The Saviour visited His Mother briefly in Capharnaum on His way northward to Tyre and Sidon. And during His absence Mary received visits from the holy women and some of the disciples, who brought her news of her Son. Several times she refused to see persons from Nazareth and Jerusalem whose only motive was curiosity. A very old servant woman was living with the Blessed Virgin, but she was so weak that Mary had to serve and take care of her. The house which they occupied was very much like its neighbors and quite roomy. They were hardly ever alone now that this home had become the Master's headquarters. The Mother of God did not own any land or cattle, and she was supported by the gifts of her friends. Besides the many hours that she spent in prayer, she worked at sewing, spinning, and knitting with small wooden needles. She did her own housework, and she often instructed and encouraged the other women.

At this time Mary was very youthful looking, tall, and delicately built. Her forehead was very high, her nose rather long and her eyes quite large and usually downcast. Her lips were a beautiful red, while her complexion seemed rather dark, yet lovely, and there was a light, natural rose tint in her cheeks. She far surpassed all the other women in her unique heavenly beauty, for, although some of them may have had certain external features that were more striking, the Blessed Mother of God outshone them all because of her indescribable simplicity, modesty, sincerity, kindness and gentleness. She was so entirely pure in soul and body that she reflected in a marvelous way the image of God in His creature. The only person whom she resembled at all in her bearing was her divine Son. The expression of her features revealed her innocence, gravity, wisdom, peace and holiness. Her whole appearance was one of true sanctity and nobility, and yet she also seemed like a simple child. She was always serious and very quiet, and often very pensive. Even when she wept, her grief did not spoil the loveliness of her features, for the tears just flowed softly down her calm face.

When Jesus returned to Capharnaum alone, having sent His disciples ahead, Lazarus came out to meet Him and washed His feet in the vestibule of Mary's house. As the Master entered the big central room, the men bowed low before Him. He greeted them and went up to His Mother, holding out His hand to her. She also bowed humbly and lovingly. Since He had begun His public ministry, she treated Jesus as a mother might treat a son who was a great prophet or ruler. She never embraced Him in public now, but only extended her hand when He offered His. When they were alone, however, Jesus always embraced Mary upon arriving or leaving. But in the presence of others they treated each other with such restrained and holy affection that everyone who saw them was deeply touched. Next the Saviour greeted the other women, who sank onto their knees before Him, as He gave His blessing to all who were there. Then He calmed the fears of His disciples, who were greatly disturbed by the recent arrest of John the Baptist.

The next day, when Jesus told His Mother that He intended to go back to Judea, she wept. But He consoled her and assured her that He would accomplish His mission, for the sorrowful days had not yet come. Then He urged her to persevere in prayer for His work. Before leaving, He predicted to her and to His disciples that Mary Magdalen would soon be converted and would become a model of virtue. Meanwhile, He said, they should all pray for her and take a loving attitude toward her.

During the three years of the Lord's public ministry, the Blessed Virgin accompanied Him on many of His trips through the towns and villages of the Holy Land. And like Him, she always traveled on foot, enduring all the fatigue and hardships involved in such journeys. Sometimes she became so exhausted that Jesus had to restore her strength miraculously. At other times He obliged her to rest for several days in one of the inns which the holy women established for the Master and His Apostles at strategic locations in Galilee and Judea.

Mary always listened to her Son's sermons with profound reverence, and by her rapt attention to His words she inspired others to appreciate His teaching. When He spoke, she also prayed fervently that God's grace might enter into the minds and hearts of His listeners, for she felt an intense sorrow that the Redeemer of mankind should not be known and loved by all men.

The Blessed Virgin treated her Son's followers, and especially His Apostles, with remarkable prudence, charity and wisdom. As a mother she took care of them and looked after their needs and comfort. But above all she helped them by her prayers, her example and her advice. Often in the beginning, when she knew by mystic intuition that they were experiencing some doubt or temptation, she immediately went to them and helped them. The Lord also infused into the souls of His disciples a supernatural reverence and love for His Mother, which grew as they came to know her better. Whenever they talked with her, they found that they left her presence filled with new joy and consolation.

Mary had a special affection for Peter, because she knew that he was destined to be her Lord's vicar, and for John, because he was to be given to her as a son and protector on Calvary. John soon became the most beloved disciple of both Jesus and Mary on account of his truly extraordinary chastity, simplicity, gentleness and humility. The Blessed Virgin always considered him the most faithful of her Son's followers. He too experienced an ever-increasing love and devotion for his Master's holy Mother, and consequently he soon excelled all the others in his eagerness to honor and serve her in every possible way.

John sought to be in her company as much as he could and to do her housework for her. He faithfully reported to her all the miracles and conversions which Jesus accomplished when she was absent. He always referred to her as "The Mother of Our Lord Jesus," and after Christ's Ascension he was the first to call her "The Mother of God." His devotion to Mary was so evident that the other Apostles often asked John to intercede with her for them. It was because of his profound love for Mary that John earned the distinction of becoming the Beloved Disciple of Jesus, and it was through her that he received the marvelous insight into the Mysteries of Christianity which he manifested in his inspired writings.

The Blessed Virgin also interested herself in a special way in the women whom Jesus converted and who accompanied Him and His Apostles on some of their trips. She used to gather these good women around her and instruct them privately in Christ's teachings. And most of all by her own example she taught them to practice the new religion of charity by visiting and helping the sick, the

poor, the imprisoned and the afflicted. Often while nursing sick women and children with her own hands, Mary
prayed to Jesus to cure them—and He gave her the power
to do so. Thus she secretly healed many persons, restor-
ing sight to the blind and even bringing the dead back
to life, yet in such a hidden way that all the glory was
attributed to her Son, in whose name she performed
these miracles.

Once, when Jesus was preaching in Samaria, the parents of a crippled nine-year-old boy begged Mary to intercede for him with her Son, and she did so, as was her
custom in such cases. Jesus told the parents to bring the
boy to Him, and taking him by the hand, the Saviour
raised him from his stretcher. Then the boy joyfully ran
to his astounded and grateful parents—he was completely
healed.

By her prayers and by her apostolate, Mary obtained a
remarkable number of conversions, for the salvation of
souls was the primary aim of all her efforts. She achieved
such success by proceeding with great patience, gentleness and charity, overlooking the imperfections of the
newly converted, and enlightening them gradually with
touching humility and kindness.

While maintaining all due moderation and reserve, both
Jesus and Mary conversed and ate and traveled with the
disciples with such human naturalness that no one doubted
that the Master was a true man. Yet everyone, even His
enemies, honored Mary in a special way as the Mother
of the Messias. However, the Blessed Virgin did not have
very much to do with anyone except the sick and the
ignorant. She never sought after anyone, but most of the
time she remained alone, quietly recollected and absorbed
in prayer.

One afternoon in Capharnaum, when Jesus had been
preaching for several hours in the open courtyard of Peter's
house, Mary and the other women prepared a meal for
Him and for His disciples. But as Jesus continued to teach,
the Blessed Virgin and some of her relatives went to the

edge of the crowd, intending to urge Him to come and take some food. However, since she was unable to make her way through the crowd, Mary requested that her message be passed along to Him from person to person. Soon a Pharisee standing near Jesus called to Him:

"Your Mother and Your brethen are outside, asking for you."

The humble Mother of God immediately prayed that Jesus should turn the attention of the crowd away from her.

The Master looked at the Pharisee and said:

"Who is My Mother and who are My brethren?"

Then grouping the Apostles together and assembling the disciples around them, Jesus held His hand over the Apostles and declared:

"Behold My Mother!"

And stretching His hand over the disciples, He continued:

"Behold My brethren! For all those who do the will of My Father in Heaven are My brother and sister and mother."

Then He went on preaching without taking any food, but He sent His disciples to get the nourishment which they needed.

On another occasion a woman named Leah, whose sister-in-law the Saviour had cured of a hemorrhage, upon seeing Mary approach and hearing Jesus say "Blessed are the pure of heart . . ." exclaimed with spontaneous enthusiasm:

"Blessed is the womb that bore Thee and the breasts that nursed Thee!"

But Mary heard her and prayed to Jesus to divert this praise from her. Granting her silent request, the Master said quietly:

"Rather, blessed are they who hear the word of God and keep it!"

As Jesus continued His instruction, Leah went to Mary, greeted her respectfully, told her of the miraculous cure, and declared that she had resolved to dedicate her wealth to the apostolate of the Messias. The Blessed Virgin conversed with her in a low tone, and soon withdrew.

Once during the course of a particularly profound and important talk which Jesus gave to His closest Apostles and disciples, He referred to His Mother with striking reverence, calling her the purest and holiest of God's creatures, a vessel of election, for whose coming devout men and the prophets had prayed for thousands of years.

During His first conversation with Mary Magdalen, soon after her conversion, the Saviour spoke to her about His Mother and explained how Mary had always been pure and immaculate. Then He praised the Blessed Virgin to Magdalen in terms which He had never used before to anyone, and finally He urged her to go to Mary, unite herself closely to her, and obtain from her the guidance and consolation which she needed. The merciful Mother of God welcomed Magdalen with tender affection and kindness, for she knew how powerful the repentant girl's love for God would be, that it would earn for her a place of honor at the foot of the Cross, and that she would become a world-famous example of God's forgiving mercy toward great sinners. All the rest of her life, therefore, Mary encouraged and guided Magdalen in her penance, and the two became very close friends in their mutual love and service of the Lord.

During the imprisonment of John the Baptist, the Blessed Virgin frequently sent her angels to comfort him and to bring him food. And when the day of his martyrdom came, she knelt before Jesus and with tears in her eyes begged Him to help His Forerunner at the hour of his death. The Saviour promised to do so, and immediately took Mary with Him to John's prison cell by a miraculous and invisible flight. They found the Baptist chained and lying on the ground, severely wounded from three cruel beatings. When John perceived first the heavenly light and then the presence of Jesus and Mary, he was so overcome with emotion that he could not utter a word for several minutes. Then he joyfully knelt before them and asked for their blessing. After giving it to him and healing his wounds, the Saviour and His Mother remained with him for some time. Among other things, Jesus said to him:

"John, My servant, how eager you are to be persecuted and to offer your life for the glory of My Father, even before I Myself begin to undergo My sufferings! You are soon to enjoy the happiness of dying for My Name. I offer your life to the Eternal Father in order that Mine may still be prolonged."

John replied with humble fervor and love:

"My Lord, I am altogether unworthy of this new blessing. I offer my life for Thee, my Beloved, in the joy of my heart. And, O Mother of my Saviour, turn thy loving eyes in mercy upon thy servant."

At that moment several soldiers and executioners entered the cell. St. John the Baptist faced them and said: "I am ready."

And while he knelt in prayer, they quickly cut off his head, in the invisible presence of his Lord and the Mother of God, who offered this holy victim to the Eternal Father.

During the last year of His public ministry, the Saviour decided to prepare His three closest followers, Peter, James and John, for the shock of His Passion by revealing to them beforehand the divine glory of their Master whom they were soon to see scourged and crucified. Almighty God decreed that Mary also deserved to share this privilege, because she was destined to share her Son's Passion in a spiritual way and then to become the guide of the infant Church. Therefore, while some of the angels brought the souls of Moses and Elias to the Mount of the Transfiguration, others were commissioned to carry the Blessed Virgin there.

Unlike the Apostles, Mary witnessed the dazzling glory of Christ's Transfiguration without the least fear or disturbance. On the contrary, she was profoundly strengthened and enlightened while contemplating the glorious divinity of her Son. As long as she lived, she never lost the inspiring impression caused in her soul by that vision of His glory, and this memory greatly consoled her whenever she was separated from Him, especially during the years after His Ascension. On the other hand, it also made her feel all the more intensely the terrible sufferings that He experienced in His Passion, which was slowly approaching.

CHAPTER TWENTY-SEVEN

JUDAS

IT WAS the Saviour's custom to introduce His newly converted disciples to His Mother, for there was a tacit understanding between Jesus and Mary that she would take His followers into her heart and into her prayers as her own children and as the brothers of Christ, thus becoming their spiritual Mother just as she was His natural Mother. Because this mystical adoption was holy and supernatural, Jesus always performed the introduction with great solemnity, and the Blessed Virgin accepted His Apostles with touching seriousness and affection.

Among the new disciples whom the Master introduced to His Mother during the second year of His public ministry was a good-looking young man with black hair and a reddish beard, whose name was Judas Iscariot. This charming and clever twenty-five-year-old businessman was the illegitimate son of a dancer and an army officer. He was always very well-dressed and eager to oblige. However, he talked too much and liked to make himself appear important. He was intensely ambitious for fame, wealth and honors. Seeing that the people were beginning to accept Jesus of

Nazareth as the promised Messias and future Ruler of Israel, and noticing that the wealthy Lazarus was providing for the expenses of the growing new movement, Judas became interested in the teaching of the Master, and one day he asked to be admitted as one of the followers of Jesus.

Looking at Judas kindly, yet with indescribable sorrow, the Saviour replied prophetically:

"You may have a place among My disciples—unless you prefer to leave it to another. . . ."

Judas proved to be extremely active and zealous, and thus he soon earned a place among the twelve Apostles. Both Jesus and Mary, although they knew that he would later betray his Master, nevertheless loved him and treated him with the same affection as the other Apostles. In fact the Blessed Virgin even spoke to him and listened to him more kindly than to all the rest.

But unfortunately, Judas began to criticize the human faults of his associates, while complimenting himself on his own perfection. He was especially jealous of the popularity of John.

When Mary perceived that Judas was thus opening his heart to sinful feelings which were destroying his charity toward God and men, she spoke to him privately about it in a very tactful and gentle way. But he hypocritically denied that he had such thoughts and went so far as to reproach her for correcting him, because he had already lost his first reverence for his Master's holy Mother. As a result of this grave sin of ingratitude which seriously offended God, Judas fell from the state of grace. Then he began to yield to a growing dislike for both Mary and Jesus and for the hardships of his work as an Apostle.

The merciful Mother of God spoke to him again, urging him to restrain himself and humbly ask the Lord to forgive him. She also offered to intercede for him and to do penance for him, if only he would repent and amend his life. But in his pride Judas lied to her, denying his guilt. Nevertheless, the Saviour and His Mother continued to treat him with the same friendly love as before.

When Jesus announced that one of the Apostles would have to take charge of the alms which were being donated for their support and for the poor, Judas immediately decided to obtain this appointment, and he asked John to intercede with Mary for him. But when John did so, the Blessed Virgin did not mention it to her Son, as she knew that Judas was moved only by greed and ambition. Then the unhappy Apostle went to her directly, and she said to him:

"Consider well what you are asking, Judas, and examine your intentions. The Master loves you more than you love yourself. Seek to grow rich in humility and poverty. Rise from your fall, and I will give you a helping hand, and my Son will show you His loving mercy."

But Judas turned away, feeling enraged and insulted, and resolved to ask Jesus to make him the group's treasurer. When he did so, the Saviour said to him:

"Judas, do not be so cruel to yourself as to seek the poison which may cause your death!"

However, as the ambitious Apostle insisted, the Lord let him have what he wanted. But contrary to his expectations, Judas did not receive considerable amounts of money, because the Master and His disciples accepted only very small sums. When Judas saw the Saviour refuse several large donations, and when he noticed that the Blessed Virgin continually gave generous gifts to the poor, he became so angry and resentful that he began to be tempted with the idea of abandoning Jesus and even of betraying Him to His powerful enemies, who seemed increasingly determined to destroy the new movement by doing away with its Leader.

CHAPTER TWENTY-EIGHT

PRELUDE TO THE PASSION

MEANWHILE the day arrived when Our Lord had to leave Galilee for the last time. As He told His Mother that He must now go to Jerusalem and suffer His Passion there, she was deeply troubled and wept quietly. The Saviour supported her on His breast and consoled her lovingly and gently. He explained to her that He must now fulfill the mission for which His Father had sent Him into the world and for which she had become His Mother, and that she must therefore continue to be strong and brave, in order thus to strengthen and edify His followers. Then Jesus and Mary prayed together to the Eternal Father, and the Mother of God thought:

"Oh, if only I could receive the pains and sorrows that await Him, and suffer death so as to save His life! Accept, Heavenly Father, the sacrifice of my grief and affection, which I offer in union with Him, in order that Thy holy Will may be fulfilled. O children of Adam, begin at last to take heed of the harm caused by your sins!"

Since her divine Son would soon leave her to return to His Father in Heaven, the force of Mary's love for Jesus increased a thousandfold, and she experienced an intense longing to be in His presence as much as possible. The beauty and purity of her soul also refreshed the Saviour so much that He too loved to be with her, for her mere presence repaid Him for all His labors. At this crucial time the Lord and His Mother began to distribute the graces of conversion and healing more generously than ever among the poor and suffering.

Later, while Jesus and Mary were staying at the home of Lazarus in Bethany, near Jerusalem, after the sensational miracle of the raising of Lazarus from the tomb, Judas gave way to anger and even hatred for Jesus when the Master defended Mary Magdalen for having anointed His feet with an expensive perfume. It was then that Judas decided to plot the arrest of Christ with the Pharisees.

Knowing his secret thoughts, the Blessed Virgin called Judas aside on the night before Palm Sunday, and with tears of compassion in her eyes she explained to him the terrible danger which threatened his soul if he persisted in his evil intentions. She urged him to take vengeance on her if he were offended at his Master, and she offered him some presents which Magdalen had given her. But her kind words had no effect on Judas, who merely showed his cold anger by a sullen silence, though he did accept the gifts.

Mary then went to Jesus and cast herself weeping at His feet. She knew that He was now beginning to suffer His bitter sorrow unto death, and she wanted to share it with Him and thus console Him. Together they prostrated themselves on the ground and prayed for sinners, offering themselves as willing victims for the salvation of mankind.

Just before midnight the Eternal Father and the Holy Spirit appeared to Jesus and Mary, surrounded by a multitude of angels. Then the Father formally accepted the sacrifice of the Son, in order that humanity might thus obtain pardon through the satisfaction of divine justice upon the Innocent Victim. And addressing the Blessed Virgin, the Eternal Father said:

"Mary, Our Daughter and Spouse, I desire that you ratify this sacrifice of your Son for the redemption of men."

The Mother of God replied:

"O Lord, I offer Him and myself entirely as a sacrifice
to Thy divine Will, but I beseech Thee to permit me to
suffer with Thy Son and mine!"

The heavenly Father raised up Jesus and Mary from the
ground and said:

"This is the fruit of the blessed earth which I have
desired."

Then He exalted the Saviour in His humanity and placed
Him in Heaven on His right, while the Mother of God rev-
erently uttered the first words of the 109th Psalm: "The
Lord said unto my Lord: 'Sit thou at my right hand. . . .'"
And the Eternal Father intoned the rest of the Psalm's
mystic prophecies, which were now about to be fulfilled.

Throughout the following day, while Christ the King,
riding into Jerusalem on a donkey, received the enthusi-
astic acclamations of His followers, the Blessed Virgin
remained in retirement in Lazarus' home in Bethany,
although by visions she was able to watch the thrilling tri-
umph of her Son. She noticed how sad He was as He
gazed at the Holy City and wept over its approaching
destruction, and she perceived the extraordinary gravity
and serene majesty of His countenance during the solemn
procession. On this occasion she heard the Voice of the
Eternal Father in Heaven declare:

"I have glorified, and I shall glorify again!"

A few days later the heart of Judas had become so filled
with evil that he made arrangements with the Pharisees
to betray his Master to them at the earliest opportunity.
Returning to Bethany, he inquired of the Apostles and
even of Jesus and Mary what their plans were for the next
few days. When he questioned the Blessed Virgin, she
replied quietly and sadly:

"Who can penetrate, O Judas, the secret judgments of
the Most High?"

Henceforth she no longer warned him, though with Jesus

she continued to tolerate his presence and to pray for him. But when alone with her angels, Mary let her heartrending sorrow overflow. And, as the Master repeated to His friends in Bethany His predictions that His Passion was near, they too became profoundly sad.

During this last week, while Jesus was teaching nearly every day in the Temple in Jerusalem, His Mother frequently prayed with the holy women under the trees in the garden of Lazarus. Sometimes they stood together, sometimes they knelt, or again they sat apart, meditating in silence. One morning the Master gave a special instruction to all the women.

During His last talk with His Apostles in a private room of the Temple, when He spoke of leaving them, Peter asked whether He would take with Him His Mother, whom they all loved and reverenced so much, and Jesus answered that she would remain with them for some years, and He also said many other things in praise of her.

The next day, while instructing about thirty of His disciples in Bethany, He revealed to them that His holy Mother would suffer with Him in her compassionate heart all the cruel torture of His Passion, that she would mystically die His bitter death with Him, but that she would still have to survive Him for about fifteen years.

During these days between Palm Sunday and Holy Thursday, the Saviour passed every moment He could spare with His Mother, who was inexpressibly sad. He disclosed to her many divine mysteries concerning the Redemption, and He told her all that she was to do during His Passion and death. In these talks He spoke to her with a new reserve and majesty, for now the tenderness and caresses of a son toward his mother had ceased.

CHAPTER TWENTY-NINE

HOLY THURSDAY

AT DAWN on Holy Thursday Jesus called Mary to Him and said to her:

"My Mother, the hour decreed by My Father for the salvation of the human race has now arrived, and we must subject our wills to His. As My true Mother, give Me your permission to enter upon My suffering and death. Just as you consented of your own free will to My Incarnation, so I now desire that you also consent to My death on the Cross. This sacrifice is the return which I ask of you for having made you My Mother."

These words pierced Mary's loving heart with the sharpest pain which she had hitherto felt. Looking at her divine Son, she remembered how He had obeyed her for so many years, and she recalled all the blessings which He had given her throughout their thirty-three years together. And she realized that now she had to lose Him and give Him up to a cruel death at the hands of His enemies.

Prostrating herself before Him and kissing His feet, she replied:

"My Lord, I offer myself and resign myself, in order that

in me, just as in Thee, the Will of the Eternal Father may be fulfilled. The greatest sacrifice that I can make is that I cannot die with Thee. O my Son and Lord, give Thy afflicted Mother strength and courage. Admit her as Thy companion so that she may share Thy Passion and Cross and so that the Eternal Father may receive the sacrifice of Thy Mother in union with Thine."

Then, knowing that the Saviour intended to institute the Most Blessed Sacrament of His Body and Blood before He died, Mary humbly begged Him to allow her to receive Him in the Holy Eucharist, for which she had longed and had been preparing herself for many years. The Lord then promised her that He would secretly give Himself to her in Holy Communion when He instituted It, and He instructed her to follow Him to Jerusalem that evening with the holy women and to prepare them for the shock of His death. He also told her exactly when and where He would first appear to her after His Resurrection. Like a devoted Son, Jesus now thanked her for all her love, while He embraced her with His right arm and pressed her to His breast. Finally, as unutterable sorrow filled His Sacred Heart and her Immaculate Heart, Jesus lovingly gave His Mother His blessing and left her. At His command her many guardian angels attended Mary in visible form and strove to console her in her overwhelming grief.

That afternoon the Blessed Virgin and the holy women went to Jerusalem together, and she instructed them so inspiringly that during the Passion some of them showed more courage and faithfulness to their Master than many of the Apostles. Mary Magdalen had resolved with all the fervor of her passionate nature to accompany and assist her Lord's holy Mother, no matter what happened, and she faithfully fulfilled her resolution.

Upon arriving at the hall in which the Last Supper was to take place, Mary prostrated herself on the floor and adored her divine Son, and He told her to occupy an adjoining room with the holy women. Going into that room, they reclined around a low table. Magdalen was opposite the

Blessed Virgin. During the meal, while Jesus was encouraging and consoling His Apostles, even Mary seemed more cheerful. When John, the Beloved Disciple, was reclining on the bosom of Jesus, the Lord revealed to him many mysteries concerning His Mother, and it was then that He privately commissioned John to take charge of her after the Passion. In visions Mary saw with what sincere love the Master humbly washed the feet of His Apostles and especially of His betrayer, Judas. Yet when occasionally one of the women came to her and attracted her attention by a little pull at her veil, the Blessed Virgin turned to her in a touchingly simple and kind way. Frequently she urged them all to persevere in faith and prayer.

Then, knowing that the moment of her First Holy Communion was near, the Mother of God became absorbed in meditation as she contemplated the sacred drama of the Institution of the Holy Eucharist, in close spiritual union with her Son's prayers and actions. At the climax of this beautiful and moving ceremony, immediately after the Consecration, while Mary was reverently adoring her divine Son in the Blessed Sacrament, in the presence of God the Father and God the Holy Spirit, Our Lord took a particle of the Consecrated Bread and gave it to the invisible Archangel Gabriel, who brought it to Mary, without anyone else being aware of what was happening. When she saw Gabriel approach, she humbly received her Eucharistic Lord with reverence and fear and joy, giving thanks to God with all her heart.

Later, when Jesus was about to leave the Cenacle with the Apostles, Mary rose and went to meet Him at the door. Magdalen and another woman begged Jesus not to go to the Mount of Olives, for it was reported that He would be arrested there. The Master comforted them with a few words. Then He came face to face with His Sorrowful Mother, who threw herself at His feet and worshipped Him.

Looking down at her with divine majesty and also with the overflowing love of a son, the Lord said to her:

"My Mother, I shall be with you in tribulation. Let us

accomplish the Will of the Eternal Father and the salvation of men!"

Then, as Mary made a silent offering of her grieving heart to God, He gave her His blessing, and stepping quickly past her, He set out for Gethsemani.

CHAPTER THIRTY

THE PASSION

B Y SPECIAL favor of the Lord, the Blessed Virgin was able to see in visions everything that happened to her Divine Son during His Passion. Thus she was able to cooperate with Him in His redeeming suffering for mankind by uniting the prayers and sacrifices of her Immaculate Heart to those of His Sacred Heart. Throughout His Passion, Our Lord derived almost His only consolation from the love and holiness of His Mother.

When the Saviour and His Apostles left the Cenacle for Gethsemani, the Blessed Virgin went to the home of Mary Mark with Magdalen and several of the holy women. On the way they met Lazarus, Nicodemus and Joseph of Arimathea, who reported that they knew of no immediate steps being planned against Jesus. But Mary described to them Judas' sudden departure from the Cenacle, and she expressed her fear that he intended to betray his Master that same night. Actually, she had witnessed in vision the plotting of Judas and the Pharisees.

As the Redeemer began to pray in the Garden of Gethsemani, His Mother likewise retired to a private room and begged the Eternal Father that she might be allowed to feel all the physical and spiritual pain and torture which her Son was about to undergo. The Holy Trinity granted her prayer.

As though in response to her loving self-sacrifice, Jesus in Gethsemani turned toward her, and they mystically exchanged unspoken messages of mutual sympathy and encouragement. Then the Saviour went to His three sleeping Apostles, and He especially urged them to console and to comfort His Mother during the days ahead, after His death, which He described to them. Later, during His bloody sweat, Mary sent some of her angels to Him with a towel, so that He might wipe and dry His holy face.

When Judas betrayed his Master with a kiss, the Blessed Virgin prayed fervently for his conversion, and then she interceded for the soldiers as they were thrown unconscious to the ground by the invisible power of God; subsequently they all became Christians. Judas, however, refused to cooperate with the rich graces which the Mother of God obtained for him, and she wept bitterly over his tragic fate.

She also prayed especially for the Apostles of Christ as they fled in fear of their lives. In this dark hour of her Son's arrest, when His closest followers abandoned Him, Mary united in her valiant heart all the faith and holiness and worship of the Christian Church, for she alone preserved perfect hope and love and adoration for the Incarnate Lord. And as His enemies began to insult and mistreat Him, she correspondingly increased her praise of the suffering God-Man, thus making reparation for the sacrilegious sins of evil men.

When the soldiers arrested and bound Jesus, His Mother felt on her wrists the same pains caused by the ropes and chains on His flesh. Similarly she felt on her delicate body all the blows and kicks and falls which He suffered while being dragged to the palace of the High Priest.

At this time the Blessed Virgin went out into the dark streets with some friends, as they wanted to find out what was going to be done to Jesus. They were able to watch the procession of the guards and their victim from a distance. Mary was speechless with grief. The little group of holy women tried to avoid the crowds that were gathering, and often they were obliged to hide in an alley while a band of Jesus' enemies passed by. Several times Mary and her friends were insulted as women of bad character, and more than once they heard men curse or slander her Son.

Then the holy women went to the home of Lazarus' sister, Martha, in the western part of the city, where John met them and told them all that had happened since the Master had left the Cenacle. Although they were deeply upset, each tried to help and console her neighbor. At intervals other messengers came and knocked lightly at the door, bringing further discouraging news.

Meanwhile Jesus had been led before the High Priest, and His first trial had begun. One of the points over which the various witnesses argued bitterly among themselves was the legitimacy of His birth.

As soon as John the Beloved Disciple, who had gained admittance into the judgment hall, heard Caiphas declare that Jesus deserved death, he gave his Master a compassionate look which meant: "Lord, You know why I am leaving," and he hastened to Martha's house nearby, in order to break the sad news gently to the Blessed Virgin and to console her in this terrible moment.

After hearing John's distressing report, Mary and the holy women yearned to be as close as possible to their suffering Lord, and so they insisted that John should lead them to the judgment hall at once.

Mary Magdalen, who was almost out of her mind with grief, staggered with the others through the moonlit streets, sobbing and wringing her hands. Again they were frequently insulted by the enemies of Jesus.

The Blessed Virgin endured it all in silence, like her Divine Son, who at the same moment was being mocked and struck in the High Priest's palace. But her inner suffering in sympathy with Him was so intense that occasionally her companions had to support her in their arms. Once when they met a friendly group who greeted Mary as "the most unhappy and afflicted Mother of the Holy One of Israel," the Blessed Virgin thanked them earnestly for their kindness.

Near the palace of Caiphas they had to pass by a yard where some cursing laborers were hammering away at the Cross for the newly condemned Criminal. Nevertheless, Mary prayed with a grieving heart for the wretched men.

John conducted the holy women to a corner of the outer court of the judgment hall. The Mother of God knew that her Son was just on the other side of the closed door, and she longed to be with Him.

Seeing in vision how Peter denied his Master three times, she wept and prayed fervently for him, and her prayers earned him the grace of an almost immediate repentance.

Suddenly the door of the hall opened, and Peter rushed out, weeping bitterly. In the glare of the torches he recognized John and Mary. His conscience was already deeply stirred by the penetrating look which Jesus had just given him, and now he trembled as the Blessed Virgin said to him:

"O Simon, what about my Son? What about Jesus?"

Being unable to speak or to endure Mary's questioning eyes, Peter miserably turned away. But Mary approached him and said in a voice choked with emotion:

"Simon, are you not going to answer me?"

Then Peter exclaimed:

"Mother, do not speak to me! Your Son is suffering cruelly. They have condemned Him to death—and I have shamefully denied Him three times!"

As John came near to speak to him, Peter ran off and made his way to a cave on Mount Olivet. Because of his perfect contrition, Mary obtained that God should soon forgive him, and she sent one of her angels to console him invisibly.

When she heard Peter's words, the Mother of God sank onto the stone pavement for a moment. Then, wishing to go still closer to her Son, she rose up and was led by John to a spot where she could hear the sighs of Jesus and the insults and blows which He was enduring.

While Magdalen was now too completely upset to control the violence of her grief, by a special grace the Blessed Virgin appeared marvelously dignified and majestic in her ever-increasing suffering, although she seemed to be more like a dying than a living person.

Some men in the crowd coming out of the palace recognized her and exclaimed roughly:

"Isn't that the Galilean's Mother? Her Son will certainly be crucified, though not until after the Festival—unless He is really the greatest of criminals!"

As Jesus was now dragged to a filthy underground prison cell to spend the hours until dawn, Mary and the holy women sadly returned to Martha's home. The Mother of God prayed still more fervently for her Son and by her intercession prevented His drunken jailers from torturing Him.

After sunrise Caiphas sent Jesus to Pilate. Although John warned the Blessed Virgin that it would break her heart to see her Son after He had been so defiled and disfigured as to be nearly unrecognizable, Mary took her mantle and veil, and said firmly:

"Let us follow my Son to Pilate. My eyes must see Him again."

In the crowded streets she had to listen to the cruel comments of hardhearted persons concerning the guilt and fate of the Redeemer. Yet she prayed for them all.

Then at a sharp turn in the street she came upon the procession. At last she saw Jesus again. But now He was staggering along, bound and chained, covered with bruises and saliva, constantly being jerked forward by the ropes which His merciless guards held. Through it all He remained a meek and silent victim, humbly submitting to a storm of inhuman mockery, curses and insults. For a second Mary was so shocked that she gasped:

"Is this my Son? O Jesus, my Jesus!"

Then she quickly prostrated herself on the ground and worshipped her Lord with special fervor as a reparation to His desecrated divinity. And when He passed close by her, Mother and Son exchanged a brief look charged with mutual love and compassion.

Following bravely after Jesus, Mary came to the palace of Pilate, and from a corner of the forum she witnessed the first Roman trial. As she saw with what furious hatred the enemies of Christ attacked Him and mercilessly sought His death, she held her mantle before her face and quietly wept tears of blood. Now she prayed that as far as possible she might accompany her Son until the end. And she also prayed that Pilate should clearly see the truth of Jesus' innocence. God granted both of her requests.

While the Saviour was being dragged to and from the palace of Herod, the Blessed Virgin obtained by her prayers that her angels might prevent their Lord from being tripped and thrown to the ground and trampled upon by the crowd.

When He was again brought before Pilate, the holy women heard a rumor that the Roman Governor was trying to release Jesus. Trembling and shuddering with all the hopes and fears of a mother, Mary's heart was cruelly torn between her natural desire for her Son's safety and her supernatural submission to the Will of God.

But soon Pilate weakly yielded to the fury of the enemies of Jesus by freeing Barabbas and condemning the Galilean to be scourged.

As the innocent Victim was being stripped and attached to a pillar, for an instant He turned His head toward His Mother, who was standing with the holy women not far from the scourging place, and it seemed as though He were saying to her: "O My Mother, turn your eyes from Me!" At this point Mary fainted in the arms of her companions.

Nevertheless, for forty-five minutes she witnessed in vision the scourging of her divine Son by three successive pairs of cursing Egyptian slaves armed with hard cords, thorny branches and chains equipped with sharp iron

hooks. The compassionate Mother of God felt in her body
all the torture of the blows with the same intensity as did
Jesus in His. Frequently low moans burst forth from her
lips. With Christ, she offered up all this suffering to atone
for mankind's sins of sensuality.

When Jesus was driven into the praetorium after the
scourging, to submit to the crowning with thorns, He wiped
the blood from His eyes in order to see His afflicted Mother.
As He passed, she lifted her hands toward Him in agony
and gazed after Him at His bloodstained footsteps. Then
she and Magdalen knelt down before the pillar to which
He had been attached, and with some cloth they reverently soaked up every drop of the Precious Blood of the
Saviour.

The Blessed Virgin was dressed in a long robe, almost
sky blue, and over it she wore a long, white, woolen mantle and veil. Her cheeks had become pale and haggard,
her nose pinched and long, and her eyes quite bloodshot
from weeping. Yet she still maintained her indescribably
plain and simple appearance and beauty.

Everything about Mary was so pure and innocent and
dignified that her unique sanctity was immediately evident
to all who saw her. Even under the stress of her intense
suffering, all her actions were restrained and gentle and
humble. As she gazed around, her look was filled with
quiet nobility. When she turned her head, her veil fell in
soft and graceful folds. Her clothes remained spotless and
in perfect order. More than ever there was something
supernatural about her purity and simplicity and holiness.
Not for one moment did she stop praying for the enemies and torturers of her Son.

When, after the crowning with thorns, which the Blessed
Virgin saw in vision, Jesus was again brought before the
people and Pilate exclaimed: "Behold the Man!" Mary fell
onto her knees and worshipped the Lord, while His enemies shouted: "Crucify Him! Crucify Him!"

But when Mary heard her Son formally condemned to
die on the Cross, though her heart was pierced with grief,

she did not faint, but calmly comforted John and three of her companions who had swooned away. She prayed to God to strengthen them, in order that they might stay with her until the end of the Passion.

During the carrying of the Cross, the Blessed Virgin begged John to take her to someplace where her Son would pass. They therefore waited at the entrance of a certain large house on the way.

As the tragic procession approached, Mary threw herself on her knees, and after praying fervently she turned to John and said:

"Shall I stay here? Oh, how can I bear it?"

John answered:

"If you do not stay, you will always bitterly regret it."

Soon some men carrying the instruments for the execution passed by. Looking at Mary in a triumphant and insolent way, one of them said:

"Who is that woman weeping so much over there?"

Another replied:

"She's the Galilean's Mother!"

When the brutes heard this, they made fun of Mary, pointing their fingers at her. One of the coarse youths threateningly shook the nails for the Cross in her face. But the Blessed Virgin, though she was deathly pale, only leaned against the door and watched intently for her Son.

At last, she caught sight of Him: He was almost sinking under the Cross, and His head was drooping in agony on His shoulder.

With His bloody, deep-sunken eyes He cast a look of intense compassion at His suffering Mother. Then, utterly exhausted, He fell onto His hands and knees under the Cross.

In her anguish and love Mary forgot the soldiers and executioners. She saw nothing but her afflicted Son. From the doorway she rushed through the procession to Him, and throwing herself onto her knees beside Jesus, she embraced Him lovingly and tenderly.

Confusion followed. The officers shouted orders to the

guards, while John and the holy women tried to draw Mary back.

One of the executioners said to Mary insultingly:

"If you had brought Him up better, He would not be here now!"

Several of the Roman soldiers, however, were deeply touched, and they conducted the Mother of Jesus to one side.

As the Saviour staggered on toward Calvary, Mary fell half fainting against a stone near the doorway, and two disciples carried her inside the house. By the redoubled fervor of her prayers, she obtained from God that a few minutes later her Son might be given someone to help Him carry His Cross.

After the procession had passed, Mary and John and their friends followed it along the sorrowful way to Calvary.

THE BLESSED VIRGIN SAID TO
ST. BRIDGET OF SWEDEN:

"At the first blow (of the scourging), I fell as if dead, and on recovering my senses, I beheld His Body bruised and beaten to the very ribs, so that His ribs could be seen.

"As my Son was going to the place of His Passion, some men struck Him on the back and others hit Him in the face. And He was struck so violently and so brutally that although I did not see the person striking Him, I distinctly heard the sound of the blows."

CHAPTER THIRTY-ONE

THE CRUCIFIXION
As Described by the Mother of Sorrows
to St. Bridget of Sweden

WHEN I CAME *with Him to the place of the Passion, I saw there all the instruments prepared for His death.*

He was ordered to take off His robe, and He immediately did so. And after He had undressed Himself, the soldiers said to one another: "These clothes belong to us, because He who is condemned to death will not use them again."

Now upon being ordered to do so, He lay down on His back on the Cross and stretched out first His right arm. Then His cruel executioners seized Him. First they attached His right hand to the beam, in which a nail hole had been prepared, and they drove the nail through His hand in the part where the bone was firmest.

Then they pulled His other hand in the opposite direction with a rope, as it did not reach the other nail hole, and they nailed it down in the same way.

Next they nailed His right foot, and over it the left, so that all the nerves and veins were torn apart and broken.

Then they replaced on His holy head the crown of thorns which

213

caused such deep wounds that His blood streamed down, filling His eyes and His ears and matting His whole beard.

When the first nail was driven into Him, through the shock of that first blow I lost consciousness and fell down as though dead. Everything turned black before my eyes. My hands began to tremble. And my anguish was so bitter that I could not look up again until He was completely attached to the Cross.

When I came to myself and arose again, I saw my Son hanging crucified in misery. And I, His deeply grieving Mother, felt such a shock through and through my whole being that I could hardly stand.

I also heard men saying to one another that my Son was a robber, others that He was a liar, and others that no one deserved death more than my Son, and when I heard such words my grief was renewed.

Now the crown of thorns, which covered half of His forehead, was pressing down onto His head so strongly that His blood was running down over His face and filling His eyes, hair, and beard. His whole head seemed to be nothing but one stream of blood, and in order to see me, as I stood by the Cross, He had to press the blood away from His eyes by contracting His lids and brows.

Because I was very close to Him during His Passion and did not allow myself to be separated from Him, for I stood right next to His Cross, and because the nearer something is to the heart the keener is its stab, so His suffering was more painful to me than to others. And when He looked down at me from the Cross, and I looked up at Him, tears streamed from my eyes like blood from veins. And when He saw me so overwhelmed with grief, my sorrow made Him suffer so much that all the pains which He felt from His wounds were surpassed by the sight of the grief in which He beheld me. Therefore I boldly assert that His suffering became my suffering because His Heart was mine. And just as Adam and Eve sold the world for an apple, so in a certain sense my Son and I redeemed the world with one Heart.

While He was hanging there, bleeding and pierced with nails, He had compassion for my suffering as I stood near Him, sobbing. With His blood-filled eyes He looked down at John and commended me to his care.

Then after He had entrusted me to the care of His Beloved Disciple, He saw me and His friends weeping inconsolably, and from the depths of His Heart He cried out in an overpowering voice, raising His head and His tear-filled eyes toward Heaven:

"My God, My God, why hast Thou abandoned Me?"

I was never able to forget that cry until my Assumption into Heaven. And yet He uttered it more out of compassion for me than because of His own suffering.

Then His eyes appeared half-dead, His cheeks sunken in, and His features grief-stricken. His mouth was open and His tongue was covered with blood. His abdomen had fallen in toward His spine and seemed to have collapsed. His whole body was pale and weakened from continuous loss of blood. His hands and feet were stretched out in the cruelest way, drawn and forced by the nails into the shape of the Cross. His beard and hair were all clotted with blood.

While He was hanging there so torn and livid, only His Heart was still vigorous, for it was of the best and strongest quality. At His birth He had acquired from my flesh an extraordinarily pure body and an excellent constitution. His skin was so fine and delicate that the slightest blow caused the blood to flow at once. And His blood was so red that it could be seen coursing under His clear skin.

And because His constitution was so very excellent, now death struggled fiercely with life in His pierced body. Alternately the pain rose from His torn limbs and nerves toward His Heart, which was still strong and undamaged, causing Him indescribable torture, and then the pains would flow back from His Heart into His limbs and thus prolong the agony of His death.

And yet, though He was in the midst of such suffering, when He looked down at His weeping friends, who, rather than see Him suffer thus, would have wished to undergo the same pains themselves, the sorrow which the suffering of His friends caused Him was far greater than all the bitter pain which He had to endure in His body and His Heart, for He loved them tenderly.

Then in the excessive anguish of His humanity He cried to His Father:

"Father, into Thy hands I commend My spirit!"

When I, His Most Sorrowful Mother, heard these words, in my keen grief of heart all my limbs trembled—and indeed as often as I later thought of that cry, I could hear it again in my ears.

Then the color of death came over those parts of His body that were not covered with blood. His cheeks hung down over His teeth. His ribs were extended and could be counted. His nose became pointed and thin.

Now as death was near and His Heart was breaking from the intensity of His suffering, His whole body quivered. His head rose slightly and then sank down again. His half-closed eyes opened partly. His mouth fell open, and we could see His tongue all covered with blood.

Then His hands shrank back a little from the nail holes, and His feet bore most of the weight of His body. His fingers and arms, which had been convulsively contracted, straightened out, and His back pressed against the Cross: Finally His head dropped, and His beard rested on His chest.

Then my hands became numb. Darkness appeared before my eyes. My face turned as white as a corpse. My ears could no longer hear, and I could not utter a word. My feet gave way. And I sank to the ground.

But when I arose again and saw my Son more despised than a person afflicted with leprosy, I directed my will completely toward Him. Then I fully understood that everything had happened in accordance with His Will and that it could not have happened unless He had permitted it. And I thanked Him for everything. A certain joy was even mingled with my grief, for I perceived how He, who had never sinned, had willed to suffer so much for sinners, out of His great love.

Now His half-closed eyes were turned downward, and His already dead body hung down. His knees had bent in one direction, and His feet had twisted around the nails in the other direction as on a hinge.

Then some persons who were present said in a mocking way: "Mary, your Son is dead now."

Others, who were more considerate, said:

"Woman, now the agony of your Son has come to an end in eternal glory."

And still others said:

"Though He is dead, He will rise again!"

And while they were saying this, a man came up and drove a spear so forcefully into His side that it almost came out on the other side. And as soon as he drew it out, its point was all red with blood. The Heart of my beloved Son was so violently and mercilessly pierced that the spear split His Heart in two.

When I saw that my Son's Heart had been stabbed through, I felt that my own heart was likewise pierced, and it was a wonder that it did not break.

While the others left the scene, I did not want to go away.

Later my Son was taken down from the Cross. Two men set up three ladders. One reached to His feet, the second came to His arms under the shoulders, and the third reached the middle of His body. Then one of the men climbed up the second ladder and drove the nail out of the one arm. Then he moved the ladder and drove the nail out of the other hand, for the nails extended far beyond the beam of the Cross. Then, while he held the body up and slowly came down a bit, the other man went up the ladder that reached to the feet and drove out the nails. When they lowered the body near the ground, one supported it at the head and the other at the feet. But I, who was His Mother, held Him in the middle. Thus we three carried Him to a stone which I had covered with clean linens.

All my Son's limbs had become stiff and cold in death, and the blood which had flowed over them during His Passion adhered to them. But I was indeed consoled that I could touch His body and take Him onto my lap, examine His wounds and dry up the blood.

I took His white body onto my knees. It was like the body of a man suffering from leprosy. His eyes were lifeless and filled with blood. His mouth was as cold as snow. His beard was twisted together like a rope. His face was contracted. He lay on my knees as He had hung on the Cross, like a human body that has been twisted apart in all its limbs.

I did not want to bend His arms, which had grown so stiff that in trying to fold them on His chest, I was only able to place them over His abdomen. His knees too could not be altogether stretched out, but remained up, as they had stiffened on the Cross.

Then they laid Him out on some clean linen, and with my cloth I washed His wounds and His limbs. And with my fingers I closed His eyes and His mouth, which were open when He died.

But I did not sew up the cloth, for I knew for sure that He would not decay in the tomb.

Then Magdalen and other holy women came up, and also there were many holy angels present, like bright sunbeams, to render honor to their Creator.

It would be impossible for anyone to describe how sad I was then. I was like a woman who gives birth to a child: after the birth her whole body is quivering, and although her pain is such that she can hardly breathe, yet in her heart she feels the greatest possible joy, because she knows that her son which she has borne will never again have to go through that suffering which he has just experienced. Thus, though I felt a grief over the death of my Son that could not be compared to any other, I also rejoiced in my soul, because I knew that my Son would not die again, but would live forever. And thus some joy was mingled with my sorrow.

Then they placed Him in the tomb.

Oh, how gladly would I have allowed them to entomb me alive with my Son, if it had been His Will! I can truly say that when my Son was entombed, there were two Hearts in one sepulcher. Is there not the saying: where your treasure is, there is also your heart? Therefore my thoughts and my heart were always in the Tomb of my Son.

After all these things had been accomplished, the good John came and led me to his house.

So you see, my daughter, what my Son suffered for you.

Consider therefore how great was my suffering at the Death of my Son, and it will not be hard for you to give up the world.

CHAPTER THIRTY-TWO

THE RESURRECTION

THE SUN had already set when the Blessed Virgin, St. John and the holy women returned to the Cenacle in Jerusalem late on the afternoon of Good Friday.

Going into the hall in which they had attended the Last Supper on the previous evening, the Mother of God thanked John and her companions for having remained with her throughout the Passion of her Son, and in His Name she promised them a special reward for having been so faithful. She also offered herself as a lifelong servant and friend to all the women.

They acknowledged this favor by kissing her hands and asking for her blessing, which she gave them. Then they begged her to take some rest and food, but Mary replied:

"My rest and consolation shall be to see my Son and Lord arisen from the dead. Yet you, my dear friends, must satisfy your needs, while I retire alone with my son John."

When she was alone in her room with St. John, she fell on her knees and said:

"Do not forget the words which my Son spoke to us on the Cross. You are my master and a priest of God. Henceforth all my joy shall be to serve you until my death, and my consolation shall be to obey you as my superior."

John humbly yielded to her wishes, and at her request went to provide some refreshment for the holy women, while Mary spent several hours alone in her room, meditating sadly on the Passion of her divine Son.

The other women—all except the three Marys—took some food and discussed the terrible events of that unforgettable day. They were filled with profound grief as they withdrew to their rooms for the night.

At midnight the Blessed Virgin and the holy women arose and prayed together for a while under a lamp.

At about four o'clock in the morning of the Sabbath, St. John came to console Mary, and she asked him to find Peter, speaking to him kindly, and bring him to see her. John was also to offer friendly greetings to the other Apostles and to give them hope of pardon for having left their Master during His Passion.

John met Peter coming to the Cenacle after having spent the night weeping and repenting in a cave near the Holy City. They found some of the Apostles and went to the Cenacle.

Peter alone went in to see Mary first. Falling at her feet, he said with sobs of intense sorrow:

"I have sinned, Lady. I have sinned before my God, and I have offended my Master and you!"

The Blessed Virgin knelt beside him and said:

"Let us ask pardon for your guilt from my Son and your Master."

Then she prayed for Peter and reminded him of the Lord's many acts of mercy toward great sinners and of his own obligation as head of the Apostles to give an example of strength in the Faith.

Next the other Apostles, weeping bitterly, presented themselves before Mary and asked her pardon for having forsaken her Son during His sufferings. The very sight of her caused them to feel perfect contrition for their sins and renewed love for their Master. The Mother of God encouraged them by promising her intercession in obtaining the pardon which they sought, and when they left her, they were inflamed with new fervor and strengthened by new grace.

They felt an inward reverence for St. John and a feeling of confusion in his presence, as he had been the only Apostle who accompanied his Lord to Calvary. But John showed only love and kindness to them all, and with the simplicity of an unspoiled child he gave place to everyone.

Throughout the Sabbath Day the holy women either prayed or mourned with the Blessed Virgin in the large hall of the Cenacle. The weak ones among them took a little nourishment, but the rest fasted all day.

The Mother of God continued to witness in vision the actions of her divine Son after His death. She saw Him visit the patriarchs and souls of the Blessed in Limbo. And now she saw the Saviour, in the company of the Patriarchs, hovering above the city, while He showed them the various places where He had suffered during the Passion. As they passed near the Cenacle, Jesus directed their attention to the Blessed Virgin and said to them:

"There is Mary, My Mother."

Early on Easter morning, at the very instant when the holy soul of Christ re-entered and revived His sacred body in the sepulcher, Mary experienced a mystical ecstasy in which her grief and sorrow were transmuted into ineffable joy and bliss. Just at that moment, after knocking, St. John stepped into her oratory, and finding her in the midst of a heavenly splendor and utterly transfigured with supernatural exultation, he understood that his Lord had just then arisen from the tomb.

Meanwhile the glorious body and soul of the Redeemer came forth from the holy sepulcher shining with all the brilliance of His divinity, and the risen Lord immediately showed Himself to His Blessed Mother, together with all the Saints and Patriarchs of the Old Testament. He was clothed in a long, white robe with a mantle that waved gently in the breeze as He advanced, reflecting all the colors of the rainbow, while His large wounds sparkled brightly.

Mary prostrated herself on the ground and humbly worshipped her resurrected Son until He took her hand, raised
her, and drew her to Himself in a marvelous mystical
embrace. Then in an ecstasy of fervent joy and love she
heard a Voice saying to her: "My beloved, ascend higher!"
And at the same time she was given a more profound and
intimate vision of the Divinity than she had ever had before.

Next she turned to the holy Patriarchs and the souls of
the Blessed, and as they bowed before her, she recognized
and spoke to her beloved parents, St. Ann and St. Joachim,
her good husband St. Joseph, and her friend St. John the
Baptist. All of them honored her as the Mother of the
Redeemer of the world. And together they praised the
Lord with hymns for His glorious victory over death, until
He left them in order to show Himself to Mary Magdalen.

Later when Mary Magdalen and the others came to
Mary and told her about Jesus' appearing to them, she
listened quietly and kindly and strengthened their faith
by quoting some of the scriptural prophecies concerning
the Resurrection of the Messias.

During the week that followed, when Thomas arrived
and hesitated to believe that the Master had indeed risen
from the dead, the other Apostles went to Mary and complained about his obstinacy. Seeing that they were becoming angry with him, she calmed them by assuring them
that Thomas' disbelief would in the end bring great benefit to others and glory to God, and she urged them to
wait and hope and not to be so easily disturbed. Meanwhile she prayed fervently for Thomas, and therefore the
Saviour soon enlightened him by allowing him to touch
His sacred wounds.

CHAPTER THIRTY-THREE

THE ASCENSION

M OST of the time during the forty days between the Resurrection and the Ascension, the Blessed Virgin remained in seclusion in the Cenacle, where the Risen Lord appeared to her and spoke with her frequently. She spent more and more time in prayer and contemplation, praising and adoring God by singing verses of hymns alternately with choirs of angels and saints. But most of all, she prayed and fasted for the Apostles and disciples and for the spread of the new Church. She prayed particularly for Peter as head of the Church and for John as her adopted son.

A few days before the Ascension, the Holy Trinity said to her as she was meditating in a corner of her room:

"Beloved, ascend higher!"

Then the Eternal Father declared:

"My Daughter, I entrust and consign to you the Church founded by My only-begotten Son, the new Law of Grace which He has established in the world, and the people which He has redeemed."

And the Holy Spirit announced:

"My Spouse, I communicate to you My Wisdom, and in your heart shall be deposited the mysteries and teachings and all that the Incarnate Word has accomplished in the world."

And the Son said to her:

"My beloved Mother, I go to My Father, and I leave you in My stead. I charge you with the care of My Church. I commend its children and My brethren to you, as the Father has consigned them to Me."

Then the Holy Trinity declared to the throng of adoring angels and saints:

"This is the Protectress of the Church and the Intercessor of the faithful. In her are contained all the mysteries of Our Omnipotence for the salvation of mankind. Whoever shall call upon her from his heart and obtain her intercession, shall secure for himself eternal life. What she asks of Us shall be granted."

Hearing herself thus exalted, Mary only humbled herself the more, adoring the Most Holy Trinity and offering herself with ardent love to work in the Church as a faithful and obedient servant of the divine will. And from that day she was endowed with the spiritual care of the Church, the Mystical Body of her divine Son, and became the loving Mother of all its children, until the end of the world.

On the evening before the Ascension, the Blessed Virgin and the Apostles and disciples assembled in the Cenacle, where the holy women had prepared a festival meal, with Mary's help. Although everyone realized that the Master would soon leave them, only His Mother knew that this was to be their last evening together on earth.

Mary stood modestly at the entrance of the large hall while Jesus blessed the bread, fish and vegetables which were distributed to the guests.

After the meal, the Saviour said to His followers:

"It is now time that as true and faithful disciples you become teachers of the Faith to all men. I am about to ascend to My Father. But I leave with you in My stead My own Mother as your Protectress, Consoler and Advocate, and as your Mother whom you are to hear and obey in all things. He who knows My Mother knows Me. He who hears her hears Me. And who honors her honors Me.

"As supreme head of the Church you will have Peter, for I leave him as My Vicar, and you shall obey him as the chief High Priest."

All present were deeply moved, and many were weeping.

Early on the morning of the Saviour's last day on earth, He left the Cenacle with His eleven Apostles. Mary, the holy women, and about a hundred disciples followed them as they slowly ascended the Mount of Olives.

When all had gathered on the top of the hill, Jesus stood on a large, flat stone and spoke to them with calm affection.

Then He said a few words to His Mother. She humbly knelt at His feet and asked Him to give them all His last blessing. As they knelt, Jesus raised His right arm, and turning toward the four points of the compass, He slowly and solemnly gave His blessing to the whole world.

Then the Saviour spread out His hands and directed His gaze toward Heaven. His whole body became increasingly luminous. The wounds of His hands glistened, and those of His feet shone brightly. A dazzling multicolored circle of light descended from the sky and completely enveloped Him.

Lowering His eyes, He looked a last time at His Mother and His friends, who were all deeply moved in this solemn moment. It was a look that they would never forget. It was filled with the utmost kindness and tender love.

Then He slowly began to ascend into the air, leaving on the stone a distinct impression of His sacred feet. As He rose higher and higher at a somewhat slanting angle, His wounds glowed brightly and His long, white garment shimmered. While the stupefied disciples gazed after Him with intense amazement and awe, His figure with its still gleaming wounds became so small and distant that it could scarcely be distinguished, until finally a cloud took Him out of their sight. During His ascension, a mysterious shower of luminous dewdrops appeared to fall on the crowd.

After a few moments, as the light became more nor-
mal, the dazed and shaken disciples were still staring at
the sky in complete silence, when suddenly they heard a
strong, clear voice. Looking down at the ground again,
they perceived two white-clad angels resembling young
men with long hair, standing on a nearby rocky ledge,
each holding a staff in his hand, like the Prophets of old.
Remaining absolutely motionless, the two angels said with
one voice to the crowd:

"Men of Galilee, why do you stand looking up to Heaven?
This Jesus, who has been taken up from you to Heaven,
will come in the same way as you have seen Him going up
to Heaven."

The angels then vanished as rapidly as they had come,
while all who were present bowed their heads and remained
thus for some moments. For now, with a profound shock,
they fully realized what had just happened to them: their
beloved Saviour had returned to His Father in Heaven,
leaving them to themselves on earth! Some of them were
so grieved and heartbroken that they fell to the ground
and wept disconsolately, like children. Others began to
talk excitedly to one another. Often they looked up into
the sky again, as if hoping to catch another glimpse of
Jesus. Some were rapt in silent thought and meditation,
while others became skeptical and acted as if they did not
believe what they had seen.

Only Mary, Peter and John were calm and serene, though
deeply moved. Mary spoke to John and pointed to the
stone, and they saw the footprints of the Saviour in it.
Many others came up and knelt there, bowing their faces
down to this spot.

Then gradually their first sorrow over the sudden sep-
aration changed into profound happiness as they understood that their Redeemer was watching over them from
the throne of His Father in Heaven, and as they also
recalled His promise to be with them always. Therefore
with great joy they quietly dispersed and returned to the

city in small groups.

Later that day the disciples assembled in the Cenacle for prayer. But they could not help feeling troubled again, because they missed Jesus so keenly. They looked at one another helplessly, like lost children, until they saw how perfectly calm and confident Mary was, and they turned to her for encouragement and inspiration, remembering that Jesus had told them always to go to her when they were troubled, for she would ever be for all of them a mother and a protectress.

CHAPTER THIRTY-FOUR

PENTECOST AND THE EARLY CHURCH

DURING the Ascension of Christ, the Blessed Virgin underwent a marvelous mystical experience: by the will and power of Almighty God her soul was raised with her divine Son, and she was told to choose between remaining henceforth in the glory of Heaven or returning to the world to guide and assist the new Church. But when she looked down and saw the pitiful condition of the bewildered followers of Christ just after His Ascension, she was stirred by compassion for them and for all mankind, and prostrating herself before the Holy Trinity, she said:

"Eternal God, I accept this task, and for the time being I renounce the peace and the joy of Thy presence. I sacrifice it to further the love which Thou hast for men. Accept this sacrifice, my Lord, and let faith in Thee be spread, and let Thy holy Church be enlarged!"

Thus, by her own free choice and with the blessing of God, Mary returned to help in founding the Church Militant on earth.

During the next nine days before Pentecost she made

an intensive retreat in the Cenacle with the Apostles, during which she prepared them for the coming of the Holy
Spirit. Every day, at the request of either St. Peter or St.
John, she spoke to the Twelve informally for one hour,
explaining to them the great Mysteries of the Christian
religion as her divine Son had taught them to her. She
also prayed regularly with the Apostles and disciples, and
gave them helpful instruction on mental prayer. Gradually they all realized that their departed Master had left
them an ideal guide in His modest and holy Mother, and
more and more they came to look upon Mary as their
Mediatrix with Him and as the Consoler and Mother of
His spiritual family, the Church. Now they knelt before
her whenever she gave them her blessing as they left or
entered the Cenacle.

Every day during this "novena" to the Holy Spirit, the
Apostles were all united in heart and soul and mind, and
while they prayed together their fervor and charity
increased.

Early on Pentecost morning in the Cenacle, Mary urged
the Apostles, disciples and holy women, who numbered
about one hundred and twenty, to pray and to renew their
ardor, as the hour was at hand when they were to be visited by the Spirit of God. They had often wondered anxiously just how this would occur, but now as they took
their places they had complete peace of mind. St. Peter
stood near one end of the hall in which the Last Supper
had been celebrated, while Mary and the rest of the Apostles stood around him. Thus they remained for some time,
quietly engaged in fervent prayer, with their arms crossed
on their chests and their eyes closed or looking down at
the ground. The disciples and holy women were praying
in various other rooms in the building, which soon became
filled with perfect silence.

Toward dawn, yet before sunrise, a luminous silvery cloud
descended from Heaven and covered the entire city of
Jerusalem, particularly Mount Sion and the Cenacle, over
which an enormous mass of light seemed to condense and

become transparent, like a sun throwing out its flames in all directions. Suddenly the sound of a violent wind arose, as though a cyclone were approaching from above, and the air resounded with a tremendous roaring that filled the whole house. Then this disturbance gave way to a display of light, a soft murmur, and a warm, healing breeze. From out of the cloud appeared rays which intercrossed seven times in a fiery rainbow and fell like burning drops onto the Cenacle.

At this moment the building and everything in it was flooded with a dazzling light. The Apostles and especially the Blessed Virgin seemed to be blazing with a mystical transparent luminosity. In the rapture of their ecstasy, they simultaneously raised their heads and opened their mouths, as though thirsting for heavenly grace. Then into each mouth there fell a jet of fire, a small parted tongue of live flame of varying degrees of intensity and color, in which the Holy Spirit came to them, filling each person with divine inspiration and grace and wisdom.

In the holy Mother of God these effects were altogether supernatural. She was utterly transformed and exalted in God.

The Apostles were also filled with a marvelous increase of grace, which they were never to lose. Into all of them, according to each individual's condition, were infused the Seven Gifts of the Holy Ghost: Wisdom, Understanding, Knowledge, Piety, Counsel, Fortitude and Fear. By this wonderful blessing the Twelve were transformed into truly apostolic founders and missionaries of the Church of Christ.

Similar graces were communicated proportionally to the rest of the disciples and the faithful in general. All those who had felt some compassion for the Saviour in His sufferings and death were interiorly enlightened and purified, so that they were later disposed to become Christians.

When all had received this mystical infusion from above, a holy inspiration filled the group in the Cenacle. They were stirred to the depths of their souls, and they seemed almost intoxicated with happiness and confidence. As they gathered around the Blessed Virgin, who as ever remained perfectly calm and recollected, the Apostles embraced one another, and throughout the little flock there flowed a new life and a new spirit of holy joy, faith and courage.

Then, while St. Peter and the other Apostles went out into the city and openly preached the Message of Christ with extraordinary fervor and inspiration, Mary remained in the Cenacle, prostrate on the floor, praying for the conversion of all who heard the Word of God. "And there were added that day about three thousand souls."

When the Apostles returned to the Cenacle, she welcomed them with great joy, and Peter introduced a group of the new converts to her, saying:

"My brethren, this is the Mother of our Redeemer Jesus Christ, whose Faith you have received. She bore Him, remaining a Virgin before, during, and after His birth. Receive her as your Mother and Intercessor, for through her you and we shall receive light, guidance, and release from our sins and miseries."

And at Peter's request the Mother of God gave them all her blessing and urged them to persevere strongly in the Faith.

During the days after Pentecost, Mary talked with many of the new converts in private interviews, and as all the secrets of their hearts were revealed to her, she gave each individual precisely the kind of practical advice which he or she most needed. And besides instructing groups of new Christians, she prayed fervently for them during many hours each day and night. Some wealthy converts offered her rich presents, but she always refused such gifts or inspired the givers to present them to the Apostles for distribution among the poor. The Blessed Virgin gave the women an unforgettable example by nursing the sick personally with touching kindness. Often she prepared the Apostles' meals and served them with impressive reverence.

On the seventh day after Pentecost, when about five thousand converts had been instructed, Mary prayed to her divine Son that they might receive the purifying Sacrament

of Baptism and that the Apostles might soon celebrate their
first Holy Sacrifice of the Mass, in order that the Bread
of Life might then be distributed to the new children of
the Church.

And the Lord said to her:

"My beloved Dove, let what thou wishest be done."

Then the Holy Spirit inspired St. Peter and St. John to
consult the Mother of God while planning these two ceremonies. And at a meeting of the seventy-two Apostles
and disciples who were priests, Mary explained the significance of the Holy Eucharist and the Mass. At this meeting also when the subject of money was being discussed,
Peter and John asked the Blessed Virgin to describe to
them the attitude that would be most pleasing to her Son,
and she said:

"My masters and brethren, many times during His life
our true Teacher, my divine Son, told me that one of the
important purposes of His coming into the world was to
uplift poverty and to teach it to mortals who have a hor-
ror of it. In His conversations, His teachings and His holy
life, He made me understand that the holiness and perfection which He had come to teach were to be based on
the most perfect voluntary poverty and contempt of money.
I am therefore of the opinion that we should all detach
our hearts from the love of money and of wealth."

In preparation for the Solemn Baptism and Mass, the
Mother of God helped the holy women in getting ready
the linens, white cloaks, and other objects which the Apostles would need; she provided the basins and bread and
wine, and she also cleaned and scrubbed the great hall
of the Cenacle.

While the Apostles were baptizing the converts, Mary
was present, but she modestly stood at one side of the
hall, praying for each of the reborn Christians, as a clear
light, which was visible to everyone, descended on each
person who was being baptized. Everybody present was
deeply moved.

Afterward St. Peter recited with the assembled Apostles

and disciples the same prayers and psalms that the Saviour had used at the Last Supper. Taking the unleavened
bread in his hands, he pronounced over it the words of
the Consecration, and he did likewise with the chalice.
After he had received the Blessed Sacrament, the Mother
of God humbly approached the altar, making three profound prostrations and touching the ground with her face,
and then from St. Peter's hands she received the Body of
her divine Son. When she returned to her place, for a long
time she remained in an ecstatic trance, wholly absorbed
and somewhat elevated from the floor, although her angels
prevented this fact from being observed. Thereafter she
very strictly limited the use of her five senses, and she ate
still more seldom and more sparingly than ever.

Some time later, when St. Peter and St. John were
arrested by the Pharisees, they prayed to Mary for help,
and in answer to her prayers for them, their divine Master allowed her to send one of her angels to effect the
acquittal of the two Apostles. Similarly she often sent some
of her angels to help, guide and encourage the other
Apostles when they were traveling and preaching the Message of Christ throughout the Holy Land.

The Blessed Virgin was especially kind to the saintly
young disciple named Stephen, and she forewarned him
that he was destined to be the first martyr of the Church.
Several times she was able to save him from being murdered by his enemies, and when he was finally arrested
and brought to trial, the Lord permitted Mary's angels to
carry her into the courtroom, where she appeared only
to Stephen and inspired him to make the splendid dis-
course which is recorded in the seventh chapter of the
Book of Acts. It was due to this first apparition of the
Mother of God that St. Stephen's face seemed to all who
saw him "as though it were the face of an angel." At the
end of his talk, through Mary's intercession, he was given
a vision of Christ at the right hand of God. And as the
brave disciple was being condemned to death by stoning,
the Blessed Virgin lovingly gave him her blessing and

encouraged him. During his martyrdom she prayed fervently for him, and then she witnessed and rejoiced over his reception by his Lord into the glory of Heaven.

Knowing that the Apostles were soon going to leave Jerusalem in order to preach the Message of Christ throughout the world, the Mother of God realized that they needed one short formula or creed in which the whole Christian religion would be summed up. She therefore prayed and fasted for this intention during thirty days, until the Lord inspired St. Peter and the other Apostles to consult her on this matter. After another ten days of prayer together, St. Peter met with the Apostles and the Blessed Virgin, celebrated Mass, and distributed Holy Communion to them. And while they were all praying to the Holy Spirit, they heard the rumbling of thunder and saw the Cenacle become filled with a supernatural light. Then Mary asked each of the Apostles to define one of the mysteries of the religion of Christ as the Spirit of God would inspire them. And so beginning with St. Peter, each of them in turn uttered one phrase after another of the Apostles' Creed exactly as we have it today. Very appropriately, St. John contributed the words: "Suffered under Pontius Pilate, was crucified, died and was buried"; while St. Thomas continued: "Descended into Hell, arose from the dead on the third day . . ."

Then the Blessed Virgin with her own hands wrote out many copies of this Creed for the various disciples preaching in different parts of Palestine, and her angels delivered the precious documents to some of the more distant followers of Christ.

Before the twelve Apostles left Jerusalem, Mary wove for each of them a brownish-gray robe similar to that of their Master, and she gave to each a large, wooden cross and a small, metal case containing some sacred relics of her divine Son: some of the thorns and pieces of the swaddling clothes and linens used at His Circumcision and Passion.

The Mother of God knew that Saul, the most fanatical persecutor of the new Church, would eventually be converted, and for a long time she prayed very fervently for him, offering to suffer and to die, if necessary, for his conversion. And as a direct result of her prayers and sacrifices, as well as those of St. Stephen the Martyr, Jesus appeared to Saul on the road to Damascus and transformed him into a sincerely penitent Christian, revealing to him among other things how much he owed to Mary's intercession. On the day after his Baptism, she sent one of her angels to give him her blessing and an assurance of her forgiveness and future assistance in his apostolate.

Soon after the conversion of St. Paul, the Blessed Virgin, while praying for the Church, was shown in a vision the coming sufferings of its early saints and martyrs. The Lord then explained to her that despite her intense desire to take upon herself all that the first Christians would suffer, in the plan of Divine Providence it was necessary that those holy martyrs should have such opportunities to earn their eternal reward and to advance the cause of the Church by their example. Later she described to Peter and John the conversion of Saul, their greatest enemy, and at the same time she warned them that all the followers of Jesus Christ would soon have to suffer cruel persecution at the hands of the enemies of His Church.

SPEAKING OF PENTECOST, THE BLESSED VIRGIN SAID TO VENERABLE MOTHER MARY OF AGREDA:

"My daughter, the children of the Church hold this blessing of Almighty God in small esteem and thankfulness. The Divine Spirit, in coming for the first time upon the Apostles, intended it as a pledge and proof that He would confer the same favor on the rest of the children of the Church, and that He was ready to communicate His Gifts to all who would dispose themselves to receive them. In our times, too, He comes to many just souls, although not so openly. Blessed is the soul who longs for this grace which enkindles, enlightens, and consumes all that is earthly and carnal and raises it up to a new union with God Himself.

As your true and loving Mother, I want you to have this happiness, and therefore I again urge you to prepare your heart by trying to maintain an unshatterable inner peace and calm, no matter what happens to you."

CHAPTER THIRTY-FIVE

MARY'S LAST YEARS

THE BLESSED VIRGIN lived about fifteen years after Our Lord's Ascension. Yet there were never any wrinkles or signs of age in her lovely features, which always remained just as they were when she was in her thirty-third year. As time passed, Mary became more and more serious and recollected. No one ever saw her laugh, but she did occasionally smile with a very touching expression. She became quite thin and pale, for she slept very little, often only a half hour, and she ate only very light meals consisting usually of nothing but plain bread and sometimes a little fish.

When she appeared among the Apostles on important occasions, she wore a large, white mantle and veil and a long, sky-blue scarf ornamented with embroidery. Usually she wore a simple, white robe. But she put on a black veil whenever she went along the sorrowful Way of the Cross in Jerusalem, for she regularly made devout pilgrimages to all the places which her divine Son had made holy by His sufferings during His Passion.

The Mother of God loved St. James, the brother of

St. John, with special tenderness because of his extraordinary generosity and fervor, which made him the first of the twelve Apostles to set out on an extended missionary journey and the first to suffer martyrdom. Consequently, after James left to preach the Gospel in Spain, the Blessed Virgin often sent him help and consolations through her angels. Once in Granada she appeared to him and saved his life just as he was about to be executed, and later in another apparition in Saragossa she informed him that God wanted him to found a shrine there in her honor and then return to Jerusalem and die a martyr's death.

At this time St. John, when Mary told him that Herod was about to persecute the Christians in the Holy City, urged her to seek a temporary refuge in Asia Minor. Although both of them would gladly have died as martyrs for Christ at any time, the Lord revealed to His Mother that she should now accompany John to the city of Ephesus.

Therefore, after again visiting all the holy places and after bidding a sad farewell to their friends, Mary and her adopted son John traveled to a port and embarked on a ship which sailed northward across the Mediterranean Sea. During her first trip on the water, the Mother of God prayed that the Lord might protect all ocean travelers who would ask for her intercession, and she gave her blessing to the fishes in the sea.

In Ephesus John and Mary settled in an isolated home of some poor women, where the Mother of God spent many hours praying fervently for the Christians who were suffering the cruel persecution of Herod in the Holy Land.

On his way back from Spain, St. James visited the Blessed Virgin. She encouraged him to face bravely his approaching death in Jerusalem and asked him to intercede for the Church as soon as he reached Heaven. After requesting her always to give Spain her special protection and to be with him at the end, James sorrowfully said a last farewell in this world to the Mother of his Lord and to his brother John. Then he left for Jerusalem, where he preached fearlessly until he was arrested and condemned to be beheaded. As he was being led to the place of execution, he prayed fervently for Mary's help, and just before he died, he was consoled by seeing a vision of the glorious Mother of God surrounded by her angels. And he silently said to her:

"Mother of my Lord, I beg you to offer the sacrifice of my life to your Son!"

Then Mary welcomed the soul of the first martyred Apostle of Christ and accompanied him to his triumphant reception in the glory of Heaven, where Almighty God said to her:

"My Daughter, for the exaltation of My Holy Name, for thy glory, and for the benefit of mortals, I now give thee My royal word that if men, at the hour of their death, call upon thee with affection, like my servant James, I will look upon them with fatherly mercy."

Meanwhile St. Peter had also been arrested by order of Herod. As the Blessed Virgin in her retreat in Ephesus saw in visions all that was happening to the Christians in Jerusalem, she prayed more fervently than ever that this severe persecution might soon come to an end. Thereupon the Lord instructed her to send back into Hell the demons who were stimulating the hatred of the Church's enemies, and to order one of her angels to free St. Peter from prison, and to consent to the decree of God's justice that Herod, since his hard heart was beyond redemption, be stricken dead, although Mary wept over the loss of that cruel ruler's soul.

During their brief stay in Ephesus, the Blessed Virgin converted a number of persons to faith in Christ by the example of her charity among the poor and the sick, whom she regularly assisted with her own hands, particularly when they were dying. She prayed especially for the deluded young pagan priestesses of the famous Temple of Diana and succeeded in bringing nine of them to belief in the true God.

One day the Blessed Virgin received a letter from St. Peter which, out of humility, she asked St. John to

open and read to her. Peter requested them to meet him
and the other Apostles in Jerusalem in order to decide
whether the practices of the Law of Moses should be retained
among the Gentile converts. Mary and John therefore took
the next ship to Palestine. During the journey the devils
tried desperately to make the boat sink in a series of terrible storms which lasted for fourteen days, until finally,
due to Mary's unwavering faith and prayers, her divine Son
appeared to her above the sea and calmed it.

As soon as she arrived in Jerusalem, although she wished
first of all to visit the Way of the Cross, the Blessed Virgin went right to the Cenacle to greet St. Peter. Then,
accompanied by her angels, she visited the holy places,
and when she came to Mount Olivet, Jesus showed Himself again to His Mother as a reward for having obeyed
St. Peter's summons before attending to her devotions.

When St. Paul and St. Barnabas came to Jerusalem for
the council, they went first of all to thank the Mother of
their Saviour for their conversion. And as Mary knelt and
kissed St. Paul's hands, he was favored with a mystical
insight into the unique role of the Blessed Virgin in the
Church of Christ.

St. Peter insisted that Mary should attend the first meeting of the assembled Apostles and disciples, at which he
announced that they would pray together to the Holy
Spirit for ten days before deciding the difficult question
that confronted them. On the first and last day he celebrated Mass and distributed Holy Communion. The Blessed
Virgin personally cleaned and decorated the hall of the
Cenacle for the first of these ceremonies. But during the
ten days she retired to her room, where she remained
without eating or speaking to anyone.

At this time she had a mystical experience in which she
was shown Lucifer and all his companions being obliged
to hear Almighty God announce to them that the Mother
of the Saviour would always defend His Church from their
attacks. Then the Lord told her to exercise her authority
and drive the demons back into the abyss, while the Holy

Trinity assured her that the Church would ever be assisted by the omnipotence of the Father, the wisdom of the Son and the love of the Holy Ghost.

On the tenth day the council met and wisely decided not to impose the ancient Jewish practices on the Gentile converts.

Later, when Matthew, Mark, Luke and John in turn began to write the Gospels, the Blessed Virgin not only prayed for them, but also appeared to each and requested him not to mention her except when absolutely necessary. Only St. Luke received her permission to write somewhat more freely about her, and he drew much of his information from her direct inspiration. Even when St. John wrote his Gospel some years after Mary's death, she appeared to him and told him that it was still not opportune for him to reveal the mysteries which he knew concerning her part in the plan of the Redemption, in order that many of the new Christians who had been idolaters should not make a goddess of the Holy Mother of their God.

When the Apostles and disciples left Jerusalem after the historic Council, the Blessed Virgin gave to St. Paul and Barnabas some relics of Christ's clothes and objects used in the Passion. She continued to take a close personal interest in the travels and labors of all the principal missionaries of the new Church, and therefore she commanded her angels to watch over them and report to her everything that happened to them.

Very often, at her command, her angels appeared visibly to the Apostles and encouraged them with messages from the Mother of their Master. At other times the angels invisibly accompanied and protected them, or warned them of dangers and indicated what they should do in special circumstances.

Besides frequently writing letters to the Apostles, Mary was allowed to appear to them on several occasions when they prayed for her help in some emergency. Thus she appeared to St. Peter when he was in Antioch and again in Rome.

With her own hands, she prepared all that was needed by the Apostles for the service of the altar.

Frequently, and especially on great religious feast days, she visited the poor and the sick in Jerusalem, consoling and assisting them by washing the women and children and by giving them nourishing food which she had cooked for them or some clothing which she had accepted for distribution among the needy.

The holy Mother of God had now attained a degree of radiant sanctity in which the mere sight of her was at times sufficient to convert even bitter opponents of the Church. A prominent and cultured Jew for whom she had been praying was one day inspired by his guardian angel with the desire of seeing, merely out of idle curiosity, the Mother of the now-famous crucified Jesus of Nazareth. Yet as soon as Mary quietly and prudently spoke to this distinguished man, he fell to the ground at her feet, confessing Christ as the Saviour of the world and begging for Baptism.

When Satan perceived all the good that the Blessed Virgin was accomplishing for the young Church, he resolved to destroy her in one concerted attack by all his demons, which they launched against her one day while she was praying alone in her room. During this intense spiritual conflict, Mary prayed for all souls who are afflicted by the devil, and the Lord granted her the power of protecting all who turn to her when they are tempted. Then the Saviour appeared to her as her loving Son, accompanied by St. Joachim and St. Ann and many Patriarchs, Prophets, and angels. And Almighty God gave Lucifer a vision of the Blessed Mother as "a woman clothed with the sun, and the moon was under her feet, and upon her head was a crown of twelve stars." And the demons realized with anguish that they were defeated and bound by the God-given power of this holy Virgin whom they had planned to destroy. Then the Lord said to His Mother:

"My Beloved, thou hast given Me human form. Thou hast followed and imitated Me above all My creatures. Be thou therefore the protectress of My Church. Command the infernal dragon that as long as thou shalt live in the Church, he shall not sow the seed of error and heresy, for during the days of thy life I desire that the Church derive this advantage from thy presence."

And as soon as Mary uttered the command, "that great dragon was cast down to the earth, and with him his angels . . ."

More and more as the years passed, the Blessed Virgin felt torn between her ever-increasing longing for union with God in Heaven and her compassionate love for the Church and for mankind. She therefore had to strive to achieve the right adjustment between the active and the contemplative life. However, as she prayed for divine guidance in this difficult problem, God raised her to a unique mystical state of continuous abstractive vision which became more intense every day and which filled her soul with infused wisdom. Thus by a special privilege she enjoyed without interruption, whether working or resting, a profound and intimate spiritual union of heart, mind, and soul with her beloved Son and God. Consequently, while remaining actively attentive to the needs and welfare of all the children of the Church, she was also able to be continually absorbed in prayerful contemplation.

Every day of her life after the death of her divine Son, and especially every Friday, the Blessed Virgin relived and commemorated the Passion of Jesus in all its harrowing details. In order to make reparation for the insults and tortures which He had suffered, she recited appropriate prayers and performed various acts of mortification for each of the hate-filled words and blows that sinful men had heaped on their God on Good Friday. Many times during these devotions she wept tears of blood which covered her face, and she was bathed in a bloody sweat, so intense was her identification with her Son's sufferings. She obtained St. John's permission to remain alone in her room each week from five o'clock on Thursday afternoon until Sunday morning. Then, beginning with the Washing of the Feet, she beheld in vision and compassionately re-experienced in her soul and body all that Jesus had endured for men during those hours in Holy Week.

Nearly every day she heard Mass, usually celebrated by St. John, and received Holy Communion, after which she would withdraw and remain alone in her room for three hours. So fervent were her preparation before and thanksgiving after Communion that often her divine Son responded by a personal visit to His Mother. During these hours of ecstatic contemplation, St. John sometimes saw rays of bright light darting forth from Mary as she prayed.

Toward the end of her life, through the intensity of her burning charity, the Blessed Virgin's soul had approached so closely to union with God that only the Lord's reluctance to deprive His Church of such an invaluable guide restrained Him from welcoming her forever into the glory of Heaven. She then began to suffer a ceaseless spiritual martyrdom, for she could no longer hold back the overflowing force of her yearning for Heaven and the Beatific Vision of God; yet she was too humble ever to ask for the privilege of liberation from mortal life. At this time, therefore, Almighty God rewarded her with the special grace of celebrating the joys of the Resurrection in a mystical way every Sunday and of enjoying a still more intimate union with Him in daily Communion. And He said to her:

"My most loving Mother, I shall be with thee in a wonderful new manner, as long as thy mortal life lasts. And soon thou shalt be free from the fetters of thy mortal body."

Henceforth, at the command of the Lord through an angel, St. John gave the Blessed Virgin Holy Communion every day until the end of her life. And at the moment when she received the Holy Eucharist, the Saviour manifested Himself to her in His sacred humanity in the form which He had when He instituted the Blessed Sacrament, but His appearance was more glorious and more resplendent than at the Transfiguration.

The Mother of God also commemorated every year with profound joy and gratitude the anniversaries of the Annunciation and the Nativity and many of the feasts honoring the Mysteries of the Incarnation and the Redemption which the Church has since instituted.

Every year on the feast of the Ascension, the Lord asked His Mother whether she would prefer to remain hence-forth forever in the joy of Heaven or whether she wished to return to the world to help the Church. Each year she humbly answered that if it was the Will of God, she would gladly return to labor for mankind, for whom He had suffered and died.

THE BLESSED VIRGIN SAID TO ST. BRIDGET OF SWEDEN:

"After the Ascension of my Son, I still lived a long time in the world. Such was the Will of God, in order that by seeing my patience and my conduct many more souls might be converted to Him, and in order that the Apostles and other elect souls of God might be strengthened. Also the natural constitution of my being required that I should live longer and that thereby my crown might be increased.

"During all the time that I lived after my Son's Ascension, I visited the places where He had suffered and where He had performed His miracles. Thus the memory of His Passion became so imprinted on my heart that it ever remained quite fresh in my mind, whether I happened to be eating or working.

"My senses were so completely withdrawn from worldly things that I constantly alternated between new supernatural yearnings and sorrows. Yet I controlled my grief and my joy in such a way that I did not neglect any of my duties toward God. My way of life among people was such that apart from my scanty meals I paid no attention to what human beings thought of me or expected me to do."

CHAPTER THIRTY-SIX

THE DORMITION

AFTER the Blessed Virgin had passed her sixtieth birth-day, the Holy Trinity, wishing to reward her perfect generosity in doing the Will of God throughout her life, sent the Archangel Gabriel to reveal to her when she was destined to die.

Upon entering her oratory, the archangel found her prostrated on the ground in the form of a cross, praying for sinners. The Mother of God respectfully rose to her knees as soon as she perceived Gabriel, who was accompanied by many angels bearing crowns and palms as symbols of various rewards for their Queen.

Gabriel greeted Mary with these words:

"The Lord sends us to announce to thee in His name the happy end of thy pilgrimage upon earth. Exactly three years from today thou shalt be taken up and received into the everlasting joy of Heaven."

The Blessed Virgin bowed to the ground and replied gratefully:

"Behold the handmaid of the Lord. Be it done unto me according to thy word."

Then for two hours she alternated with the angels in hymns of thanksgiving to God for this welcome news, and she asked the Lord and all the Saints and angels to help her prepare for death.

From that moment Mary intensified all her devotions as if she wished to make up for any past relaxation in her fervor. She immediately wrote to the Apostles and disciples to encourage them in their missionary work, and she exercised still greater zeal in strengthening the faith of all the converts whom she met. Although she kept her secret, her conduct was that of a person who is preparing to depart and who wishes to leave all her friends rich in heavenly blessings.

A few days later, however, she said to St. John:

"My son and master, in His condescending mercy the Lord has revealed to me that there remain only three more years until my passage into eternal life. I beseech you, my son, to help me during this short space of time to give the Almighty some return for the immense blessings which I have received from His generous love. And from the bottom of my heart I beseech you to pray for me."

Unable to restrain his tears, John answered:

"My Mother and my Lady, help your poor child who is going to be left an orphan . . ."

Seeing that his tender heart was stricken with intense pain, Mary gently consoled him and assured him that she would ever remain his Mother and Advocate in Heaven.

Although John was at first permitted to reveal the secret of their approaching loss only to St. James the Less, by a divine inspiration the other Apostles and disciples, wherever they happened to be, began to realize that the beloved Mother of their Saviour would not be with them on earth much longer. In fact Almighty God filled the whole of creation with a mysterious sorrow over the prospective death of its Queen. The light of the sun and stars and planets lost some of its brightness during the last days of her life. The birds of the air seemed to be especially affected, for often in the presence of St. John they surrounded Mary's oratory in great numbers and sang sorrowful notes until she ordered them to praise their Creator with joy as usual. And once while she was visiting the holy places, some wild animals from the hills around Jerusalem came up to her, bowed their heads, and uttered mournful sounds.

St. John became so grief-stricken that often he was unable to hide his sorrow. Several times some of the holy women saw him weeping, and in the end—for the Lord did not wish to take His Mother from them without warning—they persuaded John to disclose to them the cause of his grief. Thus the tragic impending loss of the Church eventually became known to Mary's closest friends, who henceforth begged her to take them with her or not to forget them in Heaven.

During the last two years of her life, the Blessed Virgin greatly increased her charity work. She healed in body and soul all the sick who came to her. She drew innumerable persons from sin to grace and made many new converts to the Church. She relieved the misery of the poor by giving them whatever possessions or gifts she had and often by performing miracles for them. In every way she generously strove to help the faithful personally before her death. And above all she consoled and encouraged them by promising that she would continue to help all Christians until the end of time.

During the last days of her life, the Saviour visited His Mother more often than before, comforting her affectionately and assuring her that He would soon place her on a royal throne in Heaven. On these occasions Mary fervently interceded for all living and future servants of the Church. Whenever she received Holy Communion, those who saw her noticed that her lovely features shone for several hours afterward with a marvelous radiance that filled her friends with mystical joy.

When the three years were nearly over, the Blessed Virgin asked John's permission to visit all the holy places for the last time. Accompanied by the Saint and by her many angels, she sadly went along the sorrowful Way of the

Cross, weeping as she recalled her Son's sufferings at each spot, and praying fervently that the faithful would venerate these holy places in future ages. She remained on Calvary for a long time, and such was the ardor of her charity as she prayed for mankind that she would have died then and there if she had not been sustained by divine power. The Saviour appeared to her on Calvary and said:

"My Mother and Helper in the work of human Redemption, I promise thee that I shall be most liberal with men. In Heaven thou shalt be their Mediatrix and Advocate. And I shall bestow My mercy on all those who obtain thy intercession."

Then, prostrate at His feet, Mary thanked her Son and begged Him to give her His last blessing, which He did before returning to Heaven. When John led her back to the Cenacle, she was so weak that he decided it was time to prepare a tomb for her. Mary herself selected a grotto in the valley near the Garden of Gethsemani.

Later, in the solitude of her oratory, the Mother of God sadly yet gratefully bade a last farewell in prayer to the holy Church Militant which she had so dearly loved and served as the Mystical Body of Christ.

Then she conscientiously made her last will and testament in the presence of the Blessed Trinity, to whom she humbly declared:

"Highest Lord, Father, Son, and Holy Ghost, of the goods of mortal life and of the world, I possess none that I can leave, for I have never possessed or loved anything besides Thee. Two tunics and a cloak I leave to John for disposal. My body I ask the earth to receive again. My soul I resign into Thy hands, O my God. My merits I leave to the Holy Church. I offer these merits for the Apostles and priests of the present and future ages and for all those who turn to me in order to obtain Thy protection. From this hour I desire to continue my prayers for all the sinning children of Adam as long as the world shall last."

The Saviour ratified His Mother's last will with these words:

"Let it be done as thou wishest and ordainest."

After thanking Him, Mary added a last request that the Apostles might be present at her death, so that they might bless her and pray for her. In reply Jesus assured her that the Apostles were already on their way to Jerusalem. In fact, Almighty God had dispatched a number of angels to notify all the Apostles in distant lands that the Blessed Virgin was soon to die and that they should hasten to her. Consequently they now began to assemble in the Holy City. When St. Peter arrived from Rome, Mary met him at the entrance to her oratory, and kneeling at his feet she asked for his blessing.

On the morning of her last day, the Blessed Virgin summoned the Apostles and disciples and holy women to the Cenacle. They were all deeply moved as they quietly gathered around her. With sad hearts they gazed for the last time at the holy Mother of their God: she was as poor and humble and lovely as ever. They noticed an extraordinary celestial light that seemed to enfold her.

Mary rose from her couch, and after kneeling and kissing St. Peter's feet she went to each of the eleven other Apostles for his blessing, and with each she exchanged a touching farewell. She thanked St. John with special affection for all his kindness. She also asked him to distribute her few clothes to a servant woman and to a poor girl who often helped her.

Then, after a moment's recollection, the Blessed Virgin said to all who were present:

"Dearest children, I have loved you with that tender love and charity which was given to me by my divine Son, whom I have seen in you, His chosen friends. My children, love the Church and love one another."

And turning reverently to St. Peter, she continued:

"I commend my son John and all the rest to thee, Peter."

Then she added, for all of them:

"I promise you that in Heaven I will ever look upon you as a Mother."

As she ceased speaking, everyone was weeping. Mary's

eyes too had filled with tears.

Then, glowing with a heavenly radiance, she sat on her couch. And as each of the Apostles, disciples, and holy women in turn knelt before her, she blessed them by touching their foreheads with her crossed hands.

Next Mary asked all her grieving friends to pray with her and for her in silence while St. Peter celebrated Mass at a small altar in an adjoining room.

Becoming absorbed in contemplation, she saw her divine Son coming down from Heaven in glory, accompanied by many saints and angels. Thereupon she prostrated herself before Him and kissed His feet, making the last and most intense act of faith, love, and humility in all her life.

The Lord gave her His blessing and said to her:

"My dearest Mother, the hour has come in which thou art to pass into the glory of My Father. And since, by My power and as My Mother, I have caused thee to enter the world exempt from sin, therefore also death shall have no right to touch thee at thy exit from this world. If thou wishest not to pass through it, come with Me now to partake of My glory, which thou hast merited."

But Mary joyfully replied:

"My Son and my Lord, Thou didst suffer death without being obliged to do so. It is proper therefore that as I have tried to follow Thee in life, so I follow Thee also in death."

The Saviour approved her last, generous sacrifice.

While the angels began softly to sing verses of the *Canticle of Canticles,* and the Apostles sadly recited prayers for the dying, St. Peter entered the room and gave Mary her last Holy Communion, after which he anointed her with the oils of Extreme Unction.

At this solemn moment the Cenacle was filled with a marvelous light and fragrance which everyone perceived. The presence of the Lord was revealed to several of the Apostles, and the chanting of the angels was heard by many.

Now the Mother of God had reclined on her couch.

Her plain mantle and tunic were neatly folded about her. Joining her hands in prayer, she kept her eyes fixed on her divine and glorious Son. The intensity of her love for Him and the fervor of her longing to be with Him completely transfigured her radiant features. She seemed to become utterly inflamed with the fire of her seraphic charity. On her beautiful face appeared an expression of heavenly joy, and her lips parted in the sweet, gentle smile of her youth.

Then, while a number of cherubic little angels hovered about her, and the choir of angels and archangels was singing the verses of the Canticle: "Behold, my beloved speaketh to me: 'Arise, make haste, my love, my dove, my beautiful one, and come, the winter has passed. . . .'" Mary whispered:

"Into Thy hands, O Lord, I commend my spirit."

Then the eyes of the Mother of God gently closed. And her soul, without effort, left her body.

She died of love.

THE BLESSED VIRGIN SAID TO VENERABLE MOTHER MARY OF AGREDA:

"My daughter, I wish to inform thee of another privilege which was conceded to me in the hour of my glorious Transition. It was this: that all those devoted to me who shall call upon me at the hour of death, making me their Advocate in memory of my happy Transition and of my desiring to imitate my divine Son in death, shall be under my special protection in that hour and shall experience my intercession.

"And since death follows upon life and ordinarily corresponds with it, the surest pledge of a good death is a good life, a life in which the heart is freed and detached from earthly love."

CHAPTER THIRTY-SEVEN

THE ASSUMPTION AND CROWNING

WHEN Mary's soul left her body, the soft chanting of the angels seemed to withdraw slowly from the Cenacle. Peter and John must have perceived the glory of her soul in this moment of its liberation, for they both looked up, while the other Apostles remained absorbed in prayer, with their heads bowed to the ground.

The Blessed Virgin's body lay radiant with light, surrounded by her thousand invisible guardian angels. Her eyes were closed, and her hands were folded on her breast.

When at last all the Apostles, disciples, and holy women present realized that their beloved spiritual Mother had indeed left them, their sorrow was so intense that only a special dispensation of divine power prevented some of them from dying of grief.

For some time they prayed and wept silently. Then they arose and sang a number of hymns in honor of their departed Queen.

Later Mary's two devoted servant girls were told to anoint and wrap her body in a shroud with the greatest reverence and modesty. But when they entered her room, they were so blinded by the dazzling mystical light surrounding her couch that they could not even see her body. Highly excited, they hastened to notify the Apostles. Peter and John then went into the room, perceived the bright light, and heard angels singing: "A Virgin before the Nativity, during the Nativity, and after the Nativity. . ." Kneeling down and praying for guidance, the two saints heard a Voice say: "Let not this virginal body be touched!"

They therefore brought in a plain wooden bier. And with their own hands they reverently took Mary's robe at both ends and carefully lifted her light body onto the bier. Numerous candles were then lit and set around it, and although they burned for many hours they were not at all consumed. During all this time great numbers of the faithful quietly entered the room, prayed for a moment, and left, weeping and mourning.

On the day of the funeral, the Apostles took up the bier and bore it in a solemn procession from the Cenacle to the tomb in the Valley of Josaphat, near the Garden of Gethsemani. All the Christians of Jerusalem, as well as an invisible multitude of angels, patriarchs, prophets and saints, accompanied the funeral, during which numerous miraculous cures and conversions of compassionate Jewish and Gentile spectators took place. Everyone was amazed at the delicious fragrance and heavenly music that followed the passage of Mary's remains.

When the procession reached the prepared tomb, St. Peter and St. John reverently carried the bier into the sepulcher, which was then filled with aromatic flowers and closed with a large stone, while everyone present wept and prayed in profound sorrow. The heavenly chanting of the angels continued, and many persons noticed an extraordinary light shining around the tomb. Gradually most of the mourners returned to the city, but some of the Apostles and holy women remained watching and praying before the sepulcher.

Meanwhile, immediately after Mary's death, Our Lord had entered Heaven, conducting the pure soul of His

Mother at His right hand. And presenting her before the throne of the Divinity, He said:

"Eternal Father, it is right that to My Mother be given the reward of a Mother. And since during all her life and in all her works she was as like to Me as it is possible for a creature to be, let her also be like to Me in glory and on the throne of Our Majesty."

This decree was approved by the Father and the Holy Ghost. And Mary's soul was immediately raised to the right hand of her divine Son and placed beside the throne of the Holy Trinity.

Later, after the funeral, the Lord descended in a dazzling beam of light to the tomb of the Blessed Virgin, accompanied by Mary's soul and by innumerable angels. Then the holy soul of the Mother of God penetrated into her body in the sepulcher, reanimated it, and rose up again united to it, utterly radiant, gloriously attired, and indescribably beautiful.

Now amid celestial music a magnificent triumphant procession ascended from the tomb to Heaven. First came the rejoicing angels and saints, and then Christ the King with His Immaculate Mother at His side, while the souls of all the Blessed in Heaven gladly welcomed and praised their new Queen and the whole universe seemed to be chanting exultantly:

"Who is this that cometh up from the desert, flowing with delights, leaning upon her Beloved?"

At the throne of the Holy Trinity the three Divine Persons received and welcomed Mary in a mystical embrace of eternal love, after she had bowed before Them in deep humility and reverence. She was attired in a marvelous sparkling robe that trailed behind her and scintillated with multicolored iridescence.

Then the Eternal Father announced to all the angels and saints:

"Our Daughter Mary has been chosen by Our Will from among all creatures as the first in Our favor, and she has never fallen from the position of a true Daughter.

Therefore she has a claim to Our Kingdom, of which she is to be acknowledged and crowned the lawful Sovereign and Queen."

The Incarnate Word declared:

"To My true and natural Mother belong all the creatures that I have created and redeemed. And of all things over which I am King, she too shall be the rightful Queen."

And the Holy Ghost said:

"By the title of My only chosen Spouse, to which she has faithfully corresponded, the crown of Queen is also due to her for all eternity."

Then the three divine Persons solemnly placed on Mary's bowed head a splendid gleaming crown of glory which far exceeds in beauty any crown that ever has been or ever will be awarded to a creature by God.

At the same time a Voice sounded from the throne, saying:

"Our Beloved and Chosen One among creatures, Our Kingdom is yours. You are the Queen and Sovereign of the Seraphim and of all Our ministering angels and of all the created universe. We give you power, majesty, and dominion over it. While filled with grace beyond all others, you humbled yourself to the lowest place in your own estimation. Receive now the supreme honor which you deserve, and participate in the sovereign power exercised by the Divinity over all that Our Omnipotence has created. From your royal throne you shall rule over Hell and earth and nature. Our own Will shall ever be ready to accomplish your will. You shall be the Protectress, Advocate and Mother of the Church Militant. Whenever any of the children of Adam call upon you from their hearts or serve you, you shall relieve them and help them in their labors and necessities. You shall be the Friend and Defender of the just and of Our friends. All of them you shall comfort, console, and fill with blessings according to their devotion to you. Therefore We make you the treasury of all Our graces. In your hands We place the distribution of Our grace and blessings. For We wish nothing to be given to the world that does not pass through your hands. And We will refuse nothing that you wish to grant. Whatever is Ours shall be yours, just as you have ever been Ours. And you shall reign with Us forever."

In execution of this divine decree, all the inhabitants of the Kingdom of Heaven, all the angels and saints and blessed, and especially St. Joachim, St. Ann, and St. Joseph, joyfully rendered homage and obedience to their glorious new Queen and Sovereign.

Meanwhile, on the morning of Mary's Assumption into Heaven, St. Peter and St. John had been watching and praying at her tomb with some of the faithful. Suddenly they noticed that the music of the angels had ceased. Looking up at the sky, the two Apostles were partly enlightened by the Holy Spirit and guessed that the Blessed Virgin's body might have been taken up to Heaven by God.

As they were debating whether to open the tomb, St. Thomas arrived from the Orient. When they told him that Mary was already dead, he burst into tears and earnestly begged them to allow him to have one last look at the Mother of his Lord. Peter and John consented and proceeded to open the tomb.

John and Thomas went in and reverently knelt down in prayer. Then John stood up, while Thomas held aloft a torch.

There was nothing on the bier but Mary's robe and mantle.

In wonder and awe the two saints gazed at the ceiling of the tomb. Then John ran to the entrance and cried to the others outside:

"Come and see—she is no longer here!"

St. Peter and the rest entered two by two in the narrow grotto. In mixed joy and sorrow they all wept as they slowly realized what an extraordinary honor and privilege God had accorded to Mary.

Peter carefully folded and took with him her mantle and robe. Then they all stood outside the tomb and sang hymns of praise to the Lord and to His holy Mother.

After they had replaced the large stone, they were standing gazing silently at the sepulcher when suddenly an angel appeared to them and said:

"Men of Galilee, why do you tarry here? Your Queen and ours is now living body and soul in Heaven and reigning in it forever with Christ. She has sent me to confirm you in this truth. And she recommends to you again the Church, the conversion of souls, and the spread of the Gospel. She wishes you now to return to your ministry. From her throne she will watch over you and protect you."

Then, celebrating this first feast of Our Lady's Assumption with deep joy and peace of heart, the Apostles and disciples went back to the Cenacle, praying together and singing hymns of thanksgiving to God.

THE BLESSED VIRGIN SAID TO
ST. BRIDGET OF SWEDEN:

"One day while I was admiring the Love of God in a spiritual ecstasy, my soul was filled with such joy that it could hardly contain itself. And during that contemplation my soul departed from my body. You cannot imagine what splendor my soul perceived then, and with what honor the Father, the Son, and the Holy Ghost welcomed it, and with what a multitude of angels it was carried upward.

"But those persons who were in my house with me when I gave up my spirit fully understood what divine mysteries I was then experiencing, because of the unusual light which they saw.

"Thereafter those friends of my Son who had been brought together by God buried my body in the Valley of Josaphat. Countless angels accompanied them.

"My body lay entombed in the ground. Then it was taken up to Heaven with infinite honor and rejoicing. There is no other human body in Heaven except the glorious Body of my Son and my body.

"That my Assumption was not known to many persons was

the Will of God, my Son, in order that faith in His Ascension might first of all be firmly established in the hearts of men, for they were not prepared to believe in His Ascension, especially if my Assumption had been announced in the beginning."

BIBLIOGRAPHY

NOTE: *An asterisk (*) indicates an edition used in this compilation.*

I. GENERAL

Gabriel of St. Mary Magdalen, O.D.C. *Visions and Revelations in the Spiritual Life.* Westminster, Md.: The Newman Press, 1951.

Garrigou-Lagrange, Reginald, O.P. *The Three Ages of the Interior Life, Prelude to Eternal Life.* St. Louis: B. Herder Book Co., 1947–1948, 2 vols. Reprinted by TAN Books and Publishers, Inc. in 1989.

Parente, Pascal P. *The Ascetical Life.* St. Louis: B. Herder Book Co., 1944.

—*The Mystical Life.* St. Louis: B. Herder Book Co., 1946.

Smith, Msgr. Matthew. *The Unspotted Mirror of God, a Compilation of Scriptural, Patristic, and Theological Doctrine about the Virgin Mary.* Denver, Colo.: The Register, College of Journalism, 1943.

II. ST. ELIZABETH OF SCHOENAU

A. WRITINGS

*Oliger, P. Livarius, O.F.M. *Revelationes B. Elisabeth, Disquisitio Critica Una Cum Textibus Latino et Cata-*

launensi. In *Antonianum,* Rome, Vol. I, 1926, pp. 24–83. (Before the publication of Fr. Oliger's research, these revelations had been ascribed to St. Elizabeth of Hungary.)

B. BIOGRAPHY

Butler-Thurston. *The Lives of the Saints.* London: Burns, Oates & Washbourne, 1937, Vol. VI, pp. 233–235.

III. ST. BRIDGET OF SWEDEN

A. WRITINGS

Leben and Offenbarungen der Heiligen Brigitta. Ludwig Clarus, ed. and tr. Zweite Auflage. Regensburg: G.I. Manz, 1888, 2 vols.

Revelationes Selectae. Colonia: J. M. Heberle, 1851. *(Bibliotheca Mystica et Ascetica,* Vol. VI).

The Revelations of St. Bridget, on the Life and Passion of Our Lord, and the Life of His Blessed Mother. Translated from the Latin. New York: Henry H. Richardson, 1862. Small book of excerpts published under this same title by TAN Books and Publishers, Inc. in 1984.

The Revelations of St. Bridget, Princess of Sweden. London: Theodore Richardson & Son, and New York: Henry H. Richardson & Co., 1874. (Introductory Note by Cardinal Manning).

B. BIOGRAPHY

Flavigny, Catherine Moitessier, Comtesse de. *Sainte Brigitte de Suède, Sa Vie, Ses Révélations et Son Oeuvre.* Paris: J. Leday & Cie., 1892.

Partridge, F.J.M.A. *The Life of St. Bridget of Sweden.* London: Burns & Oates, Ltd., 1888.

Redpath, Helen M., Bridgettine of Syon Abbey. *God's Ambassadress, St. Bridget of Sweden.* Milwaukee: The Bruce Publishing Company, 1947.

(Johannes Joergensen's definitive biography, which appeared in Denmark in 1941-1943, was published in England and America by Longmans, Green & Co.).

IV. VENERABLE MOTHER MARY OF AGREDA

A. WRITINGS

The Life of the Blessed Virgin Mary, Being an Abridgement of the Mystical City of God by Mary of Jesus of Agreda. Translated from the French of the Abbé Joseph Boullan. New York: P.J. Kenedy & Sons, 1872.

Mystical City of God . . . translated from the original authorized Spanish edition by Fiscar Marison (Rev. George J. Blatter). South Chicago: The Theopolitan, 1914, 4 vols. Reprinted by Ave Maria Institute, Washington, N.J. in 1972. (One-volume abridged edition published by TAN Books and Publishers, Inc. in 1978.)

B. BIOGRAPHY

Draugelis, Rev. S. J. *Madonna of Nazareth.* Eden Hill, Stockbridge, Mass.: The Marian Fathers, 1949. (See pp. 14-44).

Jeiler, Ign., O.S.F. *Herders Kirchenlexikon.* Freiburg-im-Br.: Herder, 1893, Vol. VIII, pp. 740-751.

Lais, H. *Eusebius Amort und Seine Lehre ueber die Privatoffenbarung.* Freiburg: Herder, 1941.

Lexikon fuer Kirche und Theologie, 2 ed. Freiburg: Herder, 1930, Vol. I, p. 147.

Pandolfi, Very Rev. Ubaldus de. *Life of Venerable Sister Mary of Jesus.* Evansville, Ind.: Keller-Crescent Printing & Engraving Co. (for the Monastery of St. Clare), 1910.

Royo Campos, Z. *Agredistas y Antiagredistas, Estudio historico-apologético.* Totana, Murcia, Spain, 1929.

Van den Gheyn, J., S.J. *Dictionnaire de Théologie Catholique.* Paris: A. Vacant & E. Mangenot, ed., 1903, Vol. I, cols. 627-631.

V. SISTER ANNE CATHERINE EMMERICH

A. WRITINGS

The Dolorous Passion of Our Lord Jesus Christ. London: Burns, Oates & Washbourne, 1942. Republished by TAN Books and Publishers, Inc. in 1983.

*The Lowly Life and Bitter Passion of Our Lord Jesus Christ and His Blessed Mother, Together with the Mysteries of the Old Testament. Edited by the Very Rev. C. E. Schmöger, C.SS.R.; translated from the fourth German edition. Paris: Desclée, De Brouwer & Co., and New York: The Sentinel Press, 1914-1915. 4 vols. Republished by TAN Books and Publishers, Inc. in 1979 and 1986 as The Life of Jesus Christ and Biblical Revelations, 4 vols.

The Passion of Our Lord Jesus Christ. Clyde, Mo.: Benedictine Convent of Perpetual Adoration, 1914.

*Vie de N.S. Jesus-Christ; La Douloureuse Passion; Vie de la Très Sainte Vierge. Tournai: Vve. H. Casterman, 1878-1881. 8 vols.

B. BIOGRAPHY

Anonymous, "The Case of Ann Katherine Emmerick," in The Fortnightly Review. St. Louis, Nov., 1930, pp. 254-255.

Danemarie, Jeanne (pseudonym of Mme. Marthe Ponet). The Mystery of the Stigmata. London: Burns, Oates & Washbourne, 1934.

Lexikon fuer Kirche and Theologie. W. Huempfner, O.S.A., Vice-Postulator. Freiburg: Herder, 1930, Vol. III, cols. 660-661.

Schmöger, Very Rev. Carl E., C.SS.R. The Life of Anne Catherine Emmerich. New York: Pustet, 1885, 2 vols. Republished by TAN Books and Publishers, Inc. in 1976.

Seiler, H. Im Banne des Kreuzes; Lebensbild der Stigmatisierten Augustinerin Anna Katharina Emmerich. Wurzburg: Rita Verlag, 1940.

Thurston, Rev. Herbert, S.J. "The Problem of Anne Catherine Emmerich" and "The Authenticity of the Emmerich Visions," in The Month. London, Sept.-Dec., 1921, and Jan., 1924.

Wegener, Rev. Thomas, O.S.A. Sister Anne Katherine Emmerich, translated from the French edition. New York: Benziger Brothers, 1898.

SUPPLEMENT TO
THE BIBLIOGRAPHY
(As of 1975)

Since 1950, important articles with updated bibliographies concerning the revelations attributed to the four mystics treated in this book have appeared in the following standard reference works: *Bibliotheca Sanctorum, Dictionnaire d'Histoire et de Géographie Ecclésiastiques, Dictionnaire de Spiritualité Ascétique et Mystique, Lexikon fuer Theologie and Kirche,* and the *New Catholic Encyclopedia.*

The two-volume biography, *St. Bridget of Sweden,* by Johannes Joergensen (d. 1950) was published in English by Longmans, Green in 1954. Dr. Anthony Butkovich is the author-editor of *Anima Eroica, Saint Brigitte of Sweden* (1966); *Iconography: St. Birgitta of Sweden* (1969); and *Revelations, Saint Birgitta of Sweden* (1972, excerpts), published by the Ecumenical Foundation of America in Los Angeles.

Mary of Agreda has been the subject of articles in the Servite magazine, *The Age of Mary,* Chicago, Jan.-Feb. 1958; and of two biographies: James A. Carrico, *Life of Venerable Mary of Agreda* (San Bernardino, CA: Crestline Book Co.,

1962; reprinted by The Marian Apostolate, Marian Fathers, Stockbridge, Mass.); and Thomas D. Kendrick, *Mary of Agreda* (London: Routledge & K. Paul, 1967).

To make Anne Catherine Emmerich better known, in 1973 Bishop H. Tenhumberg of Muenster (Westphalia, Germany) published two articles in his diocesan weekly in which he stated that she "is profoundly timely today because she enables us to make contact with the reality of the world of faith in an almost scientific way." The distinguished French Academician and Catholic author Jean Guitton wrote in 1974 that in connection with the current wave of interest in mysticism, a new, thorough, objective and "true" study of Catherine Emmerich is needed, as it would make possible our "considering in all its purity that inexplicable diamond which is the genius of Catherine Emmerich."

*   *   *   *   *

EDITOR'S NOTES (1991): In 1974 the Cause for Anne Catherine Emmerich was reactivated in Rome. Since her recorded revelations were not written by her, they have been eliminated from the Process as evidence. The Cause is said to be progressing.

It is reported that Kohlhammer of Stuttgart, Germany is in the process of publishing a definitive 6-volume edition of Anne Catherine Emmerich's description of the life of Christ as taken down by Clemens Brentano.

⚜ SAINT BENEDICT ✝ PRESS

Saint Benedict Press, founded in 2006, is the parent company for a variety of imprints including TAN Books, Catholic Courses, Benedict Bibles, Benedict Books, and Labora Books. The company's name pays homage to the guiding influence of the Rule of Saint Benedict and the Benedictine monks of Belmont Abbey, North Carolina, just a short distance from the company's headquarters in Charlotte, NC.

Saint Benedict Press is now a multi-media company. Its mission is to publish and distribute products reflective of the Catholic intellectual tradition and to present these products in an attractive and accessible manner.

TAN·BOOKS

TAN Books was founded in 1967, in response to the rapid decline of faith and morals in society and the Church. Since its founding, TAN Books has been committed to the preservation and promotion of the spiritual, theological and liturgical traditions of the Catholic Church. In 2008, TAN Books was acquired by Saint Benedict Press. Since then, TAN has experienced positive growth and diversification while fulfilling its mission to a new generation of readers.

TAN Books publishes over 500 titles on Thomistic theology, traditional devotions, Church doctrine, history, lives of the saints, educational resources, and booklets.

For a free catalog from Saint Benedict Press
or TAN Books, visit us online at
saintbenedictpress.com • tanbooks.com
or call us toll-free at
(800) 437-5876